Policing Immigrants

The Chicago Series in Law and Society

EDITED BY JOHN M. CONLEY AND LYNN MATHER

Also in the series:

Additional series titles follow index

Policing Immigrants

Local Law Enforcement on the Front Lines

DORIS MARIE PROVINE,
MONICA W. VARSANYI,
PAUL G. LEWIS, AND
SCOTT H. DECKER

THE UNIVERSITY OF CHICAGO PRESS   CHICAGO AND LONDON

Doris Marie Provine is professor emerita in the School of Social Transformation at Arizona State University. **Monica W. Varsanyi** is associate professor of political science at John Jay College of Criminal Justice, CUNY, and on the doctoral faculties of geography and criminal justice at the CUNY Graduate Center. **Paul G. Lewis** is associate professor in the School of Politics and Global Studies at Arizona State University. **Scott H. Decker** is the Foundation Professor of Criminology and Criminal Justice at Arizona State University.

The University of Chicago Press, Chicago 60637
The University of Chicago Press, Ltd., London
© 2016 by The University of Chicago
All rights reserved. Published 2016.
Printed in the United States of America

25 24 23 22 21 20 19 18 17 16   1 2 3 4 5

ISBN-13: 978-0-226-36304-2 (cloth)
ISBN-13: 978-0-226-36318-9 (paper)
ISBN-13: 978-0-226-36321-9 (e-book)
DOI: 10.7208/chicago/9780226363219.001.0001

Library of Congress Cataloging-in-Publication Data

Names: Provine, Doris Marie, author. | Varsanyi, Monica, 1971– author. | Lewis, Paul George, 1966– author. | Decker, Scott H., author.
Title: Policing immigrants : local law enforcement on the front lines / Doris Marie Provine, Monica W. Varsanyi, Paul G. Lewis, and Scott H. Decker.
Other titles: Chicago series in law and society.
Description: Chicago : The University of Chicago Press, 2016. | Series: Chicago series in law and society | Includes bibliographical references and index.
Identifiers: LCCN 2015041262 | ISBN 9780226363042 (cloth : alk. paper) | ISBN 9780226363189 (pbk. : alk. paper) | ISBN 9780226363219 (e-book)
Subjects: LCSH: Immigration enforcement—United States. | United States—Emigration and immigration—Government policy. | Central-local government relations—United States. | Immigrants—Legal status, laws, etc.—United States.
Classification: LCC JV6483 .P77 2016 | DDC 364.3086/9120973—dc23 LC record available at http://lccn.loc.gov/2015041262

♾ This paper meets the requirements of ANSI/NISO Z39.48-1992 (Permanence of Paper).

Contents

Acknowledgments

Writing a book about how local communities are responding to the call to become more involved in enforcing federal immigration law is a little like trying to photograph a flock of birds flying in all directions. Everything is in motion, including the federal government's own policies and practices. However, the issue is too important to bypass. We basically took a series of still photos from different methodological angles and examined them in light of our mix of expertise in geography, law, political science, and criminology. Our hope is that we have captured the variations in basic flight patterns that communities are taking and that we have offered a reasonably definitive picture of the multijurisdictional patchwork that is contemporary immigration enforcement at the local level.

Fortunately, we had a lot of help in conducting our research and putting this book together. Early on we were lucky to gain a very useful interview with Merrick Bobb, executive director of the Police Assessment Resource Center based in Los Angeles. During the various stages of the project, we benefited greatly from the assistance of a series of top-notch graduate and undergraduate students, many since graduated, who entered massive amounts of data into spread sheets, conducted research on various topics connected with our case studies, transcribed interviews, tracked down previous studies, organized our citations, and even accompanied one of the senior researchers in part of the interviewing phase of our work. We are very grateful to Jana Benson, Robert Davis, Michael Einstein, Chantal Fahmy, Sam Frank, Gabriel Ferreyra-Orozco, Mily Kao, Meghan Mc-Dowell, Richard K. Moule Jr., Jeffrey Ober, Eryn O'Neal, Lorraine Phillips, Denisse Roca Servat, Melanie Taylor, Stephanie Wakefield, Michael Walker, Amanda Wintersieck, and Briana Wright. As the project neared completion, Cindy Gorn, our cartographer, produced the various maps that appear in this volume.

We received essential financial help from several sources. The project got underway with a small seed grant from the North American Center for Transborder Studies (NACTS) at Arizona State University (ASU). The Office for the Advancement of Research at John Jay College of Criminal Justice provided funding for the cartography. The ASU Foundation provided support for the coding of data, editing, and collection of secondary data. ASU's College of Liberal Arts and Sciences funded a summer research assistant. We received valuable staff assistance at ASU from Melissa Weimer and Candace Matheus. We received major funding for the project as a whole from the Law and Social Science and Sociology Programs of the National Science Foundation (NSF), under grants SES-0819082 and SES-0921202. As always, any opinions, findings, and conclusions or recommendations expressed are those of the authors and do not necessarily reflect the views of the National Science Foundation.

We also wish to thank the journal *Law & Policy*, the University of Denver/Colorado Seminary, and Blackwell Publishing for the permission to publish, as chapter 3, a greatly revised version of Monica Varsanyi, Paul Lewis, Doris Marie Provine, and Scott Decker, "A Multilayered Jurisdictional Patchwork: Immigration Federalism in the United States," *Law & Policy* 34: 2 (2012): 138–58.

Drafting a book with four coauthors posed its own special challenges. Suggestions of two anonymous readers at the University of Chicago Press and from the observations of series editor Dr. Lynn Mather provided excellent guidance and ideas. We are also grateful to Executive Editor John Tryneski for his insightful comments and encouragement. As so many previous University of Chicago Press authors have observed, John Tryneski is an ideal editor—encouraging, but critically engaged and alert to basic themes and weak spots, and always conscious of the need to move a book toward publication at a reasonable price. John teams up with a wonderful assistant editor, Rodney Powell, who very capably and cheerfully does a lot of the heavy lifting involved in producing a book.

Family members, colleagues, and friends also assisted in important ways in the production of this book. Marie wishes to thank her husband Michael Shelton, who proved himself a careful and thoughtful editor of several chapters and a source of regular meals and much moral support. Friends Juliet Stumpf, Kitty Calavita, and Marjorie Zatz provided helpful ideas and constant support for this project. Monica wants to thank Joshua Muldavin, as always, for providing unwavering support during the research and writing, as well as her friends and colleagues Samantha

Majic, Joseph Nevins, and Jennifer Rutledge for their helpful feedback as the project progressed. Paul is grateful to Sarah Randolph for her patience and generosity, and to the leadership and staff of ASU's School of Politics and Global Studies for their assistance. Scott thanks both his wife JoAnn and his former dean, Debra Friedman, for their support. Collectively, Monica, Paul, and Scott wish to thank Marie for her extremely capable leadership as the project's principal investigator.

Finally, we are most appreciative of those busy people who shared their experiences and thoughts with us through the three national surveys we conducted of police chiefs and sheriffs, and through our interviews with individuals in our seven case-study communities. We met with mayors and city council members, law-enforcement executives, immigrant advocates, educators, religious leaders, social-services providers, and community leaders. All were generous with their time and ready to help us think through important questions. Any errors or omissions in our account of this material are our own.

CHAPTER ONE

Introducing the Conflicted Politics of Localized Immigration Control

On April 23, 2010, after signing SB 1070, Arizona's precedent set-ting "show me your papers law," Governor Jan Brewer immediately shook hands with Mark Spencer, president of the Phoenix Law Enforce-ment Association and a vocal supporter of the new law. Spencer's boss, Phoenix Police Chief Jack Harris, had taken the opposite position on SB 1070, which includes a variety of sanctions to achieve "attrition through enforcement."[1] Giving local police power to routinely inquire about the immigration status of people they encounter, he argued, would threaten the core crime-fighting mission of policing by promoting racial profiling, undermine community policing in neighborhoods with large numbers of immigrants, and dilute police resources at a time when budgets had been slashed and the number of officers had been reduced. Although many lead-ers in policing agreed with Harris, his opposition to SB 1070 may have cost him his job.[2] He was dismissed by the Phoenix city council a few months later, ending a thirty-nine-year career of service with the department.

This local scenario surrounding a controversial Arizona law contains many of the elements of a broader drama playing out in communities across the United States. This shift represents a sharp deviation from the past. During most of the twentieth century, US immigration enforcement oc-curred nearly exclusively in the borderlands. Now, as Angela Stuesse and Mathew Coleman observe, initiatives focused on local police and interior enforcement "have transformed immigration enforcement from a federally managed and outward-looking power, located at the territorial margins of the U.S. into an operationally diffuse and inward-looking power focused on resident immigrant populations deep within the country's heartlands."[3]

The contemporary context includes federal efforts to enlist local police and sheriffs as junior partners in the effort to detect and remove resident immigrants who lack, or have lost, the legal right to remain in the country. Federal authorities have sought to cast local law-enforcement officers as "force multipliers" to bring suspected unauthorized immigrants to their attention, while maintaining control of resource allocations, timing, and deportation decisions at the federal level. SB 1070 represented a challenge to this framing, demonstrating a new assertiveness by a few states determined to prioritize their own enforcement goals, essentially turning the tables on the federal government. Not surprisingly federal lawsuits were successful in blocking implementation of crucial provisions of Arizona's and similar "copycat" state laws in Alabama, Georgia, Indiana, and elsewhere.

What does immigration enforcement look like from the local level? Why, for example, do municipalities and police departments run the gamut, from eagerness to enforce federal law to active resistance, with most falling quietly in between? What are the implications of the federal executive's frequently changing initiatives—from loose supervision of local participation in immigration enforcement to near-mandatory participation and, most recently, to attempting a more nuanced approach? How are police departments and sheriffs' offices dealing with the complex political environment in which they find themselves? Is community activism having an effect on local law-enforcement policies? Can local law enforcement ever reasonably become the unproblematic "force multipliers" the federal government desires? Should it be? These questions suggest a link to more fundamental concerns about the role of law enforcement in a democratic society.

We respond to these questions with much-needed empirical data and analysis. Our research is based on three national surveys of local law-enforcement executives and in-depth case studies of seven carefully selected cities. The surveys of chiefs and sheriffs give us a basis from which to speak broadly about immigration enforcement at the local level, while the case studies add depth and richness to our analysis and allow us to hear from those who feel the impact of policies as well as those responsible for creating them.

We locate this study within the broader context of justice policy in a federal system. The division of powers between the national level and the states has always been a source of tension in the United States and a space where contradictions and controversy play out. Disagreements over the *substance* of American public policy often quickly turn into battles over *jurisdiction* between the national government, the states, and sometimes, local governments.[4] This is inevitable because the interests, resources, and vision at each level are not necessarily aligned, as generations of scholars have pointed out.[5] While the bloody Civil War is an extreme example of cross-level conflict, contemporary examples are plentiful and include major controversies over civil rights, education, labor, and crime policy. The potential for conflict among levels of government is clear in immigration policy, which, though claimed by the national level as its own exclusive domain, nevertheless has profound local and state-level effects. It should not be surprising that the federal government's failure to enforce its own law against people who have bypassed its requirements has opened this issue to hot political debate and to a variety of responses among states, municipalities, and law-enforcement organizations.

Complicating this situation is the narrow and somewhat ambiguous basis for the federal government's claim of exclusive power to make and enforce immigration policy. Although the courts have consistently upheld the national government's claim of sole or plenary power, immigration enforcement has always involved power sharing with locals and sensitivity to regional differences.[6] This is particularly true in recent years, as the federal government has reached out directly to law-enforcement agencies in cities and counties to assist in its enforcement mission. The national-to-local focus of our research distinguishes it from most of the available literature on immigration federalism, and federalism generally, which tends to focus on the state/federal relationship.[7] We have nevertheless benefited from scholarly discussion of the potential for conflict and cooperation that exists across levels of government in a robust federal system.

In highlighting the central role that city and county governments and their law-enforcement units are playing in this emerging landscape, we find it helpful to describe the overall pattern as a *multijurisdictional patchwork* of enforcement policies and practices. Localities play a key role in immigration enforcement, both through formal devolution of responsibilities, and, more generally, through their discretion and power to affect implementation. State-level policies give the appearance of uniformity, but the reality is submerged variety. In effect, despite claims to the contrary, the United States has no consistent, uniform ability to enforce its immigration laws within the nation's interior.

The patchwork that is immigration enforcement presents serious challenges to transparency and consistency in law enforcement. As we discuss in chapter 2, two cities that share a jurisdictional border can have diametrically opposed immigration-enforcement policies. The street dividing East

Haven and New Haven, Connecticut, became ground zero for enforcement by East Haven police (which locals refer to as "border patrol"), while on the other side of the street in New Haven immigrants were welcomed with a municipal identification card to facilitate their integration. In the city of Mesa, Arizona, the county sheriff thwarted the city's effort to focus its enforcement efforts on criminal activity rather than immigration enforcement. Not long after this standoff, the state legislature backed the sheriff with SB 1070, which preempted all local policy on immigration policing throughout the state.

Attempts to maintain welcoming approaches toward unauthorized immigrants tend to be threatened from every direction. Aggressive local law-enforcement efforts tend to "bleed" across jurisdictional lines, creating fear of police even where there are efforts to build or maintain trust. The result is an enforcement-oriented race to the bottom, with restrictive localities tending to undermine the approaches of more receptive localities, and thus frustrating the long-held right of communities to chart their own course on public safety and policing matters.

Helping to maintain a variety of approaches, however, is the tension between enforcement of immigration laws against law-abiding, but undocumented, residents and the principle of community policing based on trusting relationships with all residents in a community. Local perspectives, relatively insulated from federal controls, tend to resolve this tension in ways that suit local needs.[8] As Sally Falk Moore argued in a seminal article, groups develop their own norms, practices, and routines that filter policies from above, creating what are, in effect, "semi-sovereign fields" of law and policy that may not be consistent with prescriptions from outside authorities.[9]

We also suggest that in immigration enforcement there is a significant "gap" between the supposedly uniform federal law and local action. Such "gaps" have intrigued scholars since the legal realist movement began over a century ago.[10] Our study focuses on *how* local action has come to deviate so greatly from any single national mandate. We consider, in some detail, the law "in between," where local bureaucrats and professions make important decisions about how and when enforcement will take place.[11] Valerie Jenness and Ryken Grattet introduced this term in the context of a police department's implementation of a state hate-crime law, but its utility is much broader and applies helpfully to the informal and formal devolution of federal immigration enforcement authority to municipalities and counties and their law enforcement agencies.

The attempt to engage local police and sheriffs in immigration enforcement is part of a broader trend toward harsher policies regarding unauthorized immigrants and legal permanent residents who have committed crimes, and the "punitive turn" in American society.[12] Relevant changes include a growing number of grounds for deportation, lessened due-process protections, long terms of imprisonment for border crossers, fewer exceptions to removal decisions, and weakened judicial discretion to offer relief from removal.[13] More active involvement of federal immigration authorities with law-enforcement agencies, jails, and courts in the nation's interior is an important part of this trend, which legal scholars have dubbed "crimmigration." [14] Crimmigration appears to be a worldwide trend in immigrant-receiving nations, reflecting deeper changes in social and economic relationships at a global level.[15]

In the American context, the merging of traditional crime-fighting responsibilities with immigration enforcement has proven to be a game changer in the public mind. Being found in the country without authorization is not currently a crime, but it is increasingly regarded as such because of the merging of law-enforcement responsibilities with immigration enforcement. Policies beget attitudes, as Suzanne Mettler and Joe Soss have cogently observed.[16] In this case the result of current policies is greater fear of immigrants and a general hardening of attitudes toward them.[17]

Partnering with local law enforcement cedes most control over enforcement to the local level and in a nontransparent way. While public debate has focused on the failure of federal lawmakers to reform immigration law, life-changing decisions are occurring daily at the local level at the hands of local law-enforcement officers. The majority of encounters between the government and potentially deportable individuals begin on the street in these exchanges. In immigration law, as law professor Hiroshi Motomura observes, "the discretion to arrest has been the discretion that matters."[18] Post arrest, a case can easily move toward deportation. Yet the federal level has little to say about when such arrests will occur and under what conditions.

Individual discretion is a basic characteristic of law-enforcement work, making it difficult to establish realistic, transparent policies for local-level immigration enforcement. The emphasis that has been placed on detecting unauthorized immigrants has led observers to note the inevitability of racial bias based on vague, potentially ad hoc standards. The impact of this law-enforcement approach falls particularly on Latinos, for in the United States the face of an illegal immigrant is, in many minds, poor and

Mexican or Central American.[19] Frequent changes in policy and emphasis at the federal level also complicate the situation.[20]

Every day, police and sheriffs face challenges created by this shifting terrain. The uncertainty and lack of controls in this highly dispersed system place immigrants with problematic or nonexistent legal status in a permanent condition of deportability, attempting to avoid any contact with legal authorities. The economic impact of a population consigned to living largely outside the legal system is significant, with its consequence of exploitation by employers, unscrupulous businesses, and individuals.[21] Also significant is the impact on public security of a policy that puts part of its resident population at risk of deportation for any contact, voluntary or not, with law-enforcement authorities.[22]

The stakes are high. Nearly 41 million immigrants reside in the United States, about 13 percent of the total population, and that number is rising.[23] About 11.3 million of those immigrants lack legal status. In addition there are unknown numbers of legal permanent residents who may be subject to deportation because of past or pending criminal convictions.[24] When a police officer or sheriff encounters a person that the officer suspects might be unauthorized, there is a range of options. Will the officer look for opportunities to stop and question individuals who "look" undocumented? What form of identification will be accepted as sufficient, once an officer's suspicions have been aroused? Will an officer ignore legal status in minor cases, either to avoid the burdensome paperwork or for more principled reasons? Such street-level decisions, with their potentially disastrous consequences for the immigrants involved, must be made by officers in the field with limited guidance from law-enforcement agencies. Written policies and training programs for officers regarding encounters with immigrants are relatively rare, perhaps because such explicit direction could go viral in the tense political atmosphere over unauthorized immigration.

The federal government has avoided critically examining how local law-enforcement agencies identify and process the suspected unauthorized immigrants they turn over to federal immigration agents. Generally, only the most extreme and notorious cases draw their attention. By its passivity, federal authorities have insulated themselves from charges of racial profiling and other forms of overzealous enforcement at the intake point in the process. Federal concern has focused, not on the means by which suspected unauthorized immigrants are brought into the system, but on the deportation outcomes the government achieves. Since the mid-1990s the goal appears to have been to increase, by any means possible, the number of deportations that the Department of Homeland Security and Immigration and Customs Enforcement (ICE) can report. Initiatives during President Obama's second term in office appeared to change that trajectory in small ways, but even these changes provoked loud complaints, lawsuits, and a series of bills in Congress designed to reduce executive discretion to prevent deportations.

How We Investigate Local Immigration Policing

We surveyed police chiefs from large and medium-sized cities in 2007–8, and in 2009–10 we completed two similar surveys of county sheriffs and of police chiefs in smaller municipalities. The large-city survey was sent to 452 police chiefs in cities that were listed in the American Community Survey of 2005 as falling into the category of municipalities that had sixty-five thousand or more residents. These 452 represented the universe of chiefs in cities of this size that employ their own police departments. We received 237 survey responses, a response rate of 52 percent.

For our sample of county sheriffs, considerations of cost and relevance meant we needed to narrow our sample well below the roughly three thousand counties in the United States. Many counties have tiny populations and few immigrants. Rather than trying to survey them all, we chose to limit our contact to sheriffs in counties that met two criteria: (a) a foreign-born percentage of the population of at least 6 percent, as of the 2000 census; and (b) at least twenty thousand total residents. To this set we added seven additional counties that were slightly below the 6 percent threshold but that had at least twenty-five thousand foreign-born residents as of 2000. Of the 449 counties thus selected (roughly the same number as of big-city chiefs), 252 provided usable responses, a response rate of 56 percent.

Finally, the survey of smaller municipalities—primarily suburbs, but with a smattering of rural towns and small central cities—was undertaken to learn about immigration policing practices in communities that are often outside the public eye on immigration issues, but that have witnessed a growing in-migration. The 450 municipalities we contacted all were below the sixty-five thousand–population threshold used in the first survey and were sampled from among the communities located in the counties that met our relevance criteria above. To ensure that the sample was nationally representative of this set of localities, we stratified the sample both by population size and by region of the country.[25]

    We selected seven cities for in-depth study based on their demograph-
ics, form of local government, location, and enforcement patterns, using
data from our surveys to help us cluster results into case types. A basic
requirement was the presence of an immigrant population sufficiently large
to produce some kind of local political and social response. Lacking the
resources to examine megacities like Chicago and Los Angeles, we focused
on medium-sized cities. We sought to maximize the diversity of the local
arrangements we encountered. The resulting mix, which took us from the
Southeast to the Northwest and points in between, represents a highly varied set of responses to the flow of immigrants into the community. The cities included in the case studies were Allentown (PA), Dodge City (KS), El
Paso (TX), Mesa (AZ), New Haven (CT), Raleigh (NC), and Salem (OR).

Plan of the Book

In the six chapters that follow we attempt to unpack the most salient issues that arise from the multijurisdictional patchwork of immigration enforcement in the interior of the United States. Together these chapters
offer a comprehensive analysis of the intergovernmental relationships that
have emerged and are evolving as the nation moves more aggressively
toward a comprehensive approach to enforcing federal immigration law.
Our concluding chapter discusses best policy options in the contemporary
context.
    In chapter 2 we lay the groundwork for the current multijurisdictional
patchwork with a brief historical account of the evolving role of local law
enforcement in immigration control. In the first hundred years of the nation's existence, states and localities were the active agents in immigration control. Only gradually and sometimes hesitatingly did the federal
government begin to assert authority to control entry and enforcement.
Favorable judicial decisions and the federal government's growing capacity to regulate helped consolidate its power. States and localities were increasingly consigned solely to the task of integrating immigrants into local communities, assisting in enforcement only when called on by federal
authorities. This division of labor was never entirely satisfactory. Daniel
Tichenor and Alexandra Filindra describe the federal government historically as "reluctant and lethargic" in addressing the challenges of immigration, noting that: "States have often been among the first to enter
the void—proposing, enacting, and implementing policy innovations and

controls amidst inertia at the national level."[26] The claim to plenary power at the national level has proven particularly unstable in recent decades. In 1996 Congress began to devolve enforcement responsibility downward through various partnering programs. Shortly thereafter, states and localities began to assert authority to assist, and sometimes to resist, federal enforcement initiatives. Often this has involved states and localities fashioning their own responses to unauthorized immigration, as evidenced by an explosion of state and local immigration-related legislation that began around 2005. [27]

Chapter 3 focuses in detail on the patchwork of approaches to immigration enforcement that subnational governments are taking, even within particular metropolitan areas. States and cities that seek to discourage unauthorized immigrants from settling within their boundaries are seizing opportunities provided by the federal government's devolution of immigration enforcement authority to police unauthorized migrants in their communities. In contrast, places where immigrants are valued as essential to the local economy are finding ways to accommodate and incorporate these immigrants into their communities. From a local perspective, federal intervention, necessarily spread thin in nonborder areas of the country, has become a resource that can to some extent be managed by local decision makers in the service of their own goals. As this chapter demonstrates, law-enforcement organizations and the political subdivisions they protect have a good deal of control over how actively they cooperate with federal enforcement efforts. The situation is more complex, of course, when states, counties, and municipalities disagree among themselves about the desirability of welcoming immigrants, especially those without authorization. The goal of this chapter is to explore the patchwork of immigration-enforcement policies, both nationally, drawing on our survey data, and locally, with accounts of several of our case studies.

In chapter 4 we seek to explain *why* the immigration-enforcement patchwork exists. What accounts for the sharp differences among municipalities in their response to the almost unprecedented flow of immigrants into the United States in recent decades? Prior research has come to somewhat varying conclusions about what motivates state and local legislators to enact restrictive or welcoming laws, or no laws at all. Our study takes this question to the street level: What makes some local police agencies more enforcement oriented than others? Some local governments have left this matter to the discretion of their law-enforcement leaders, whereas others have attempted to encourage more or less aggressive policing of unauthorized immigrants. We consider a number of "suspects" in the intensification of local immigration policing, such as rapid demographic change, crime rates, economic vulnerability, and the political leanings of local voters. Examining these contextual factors alongside our survey-based measures of local immigration-policing practices, we describe which of this panoply of influences are most likely to shape the response of local police.

Local engagement in immigration enforcement raises the question of how these agencies operate. What are their operational priorities and professional commitments, and how does their organizational culture and structure affect what they do? Chapter 5 steps inside local law-enforcement organizations to examine how they approach encounters with suspected unauthorized immigrants. This involves a careful look at the role of individual discretion in police work and the institutional structures that attempt to guide its exercise. Although police departments display a military-style organization and command structure, the reality is that it is difficult to effectively control the on-the-street-behavior of police officers and sheriff's deputies. Individual discretion cannot be expunged from law enforcement: it is fundamental to the work. We draw on findings from previous research on policing, as well as from our case studies and survey data, to examine the role of discretion in immigration policing and the steps that some law-enforcement organizations are taking to avoid excessively zealous enforcement. This exploration of discretion in immigration enforcement has only become more salient as the federal government has continued to extend its immigration enforcement reach to the local level through programs such as Secure Communities, and its more recent replacement, the Priority Enforcement Program. Both programs rely on local jails to inform the federal government about the immigration status of arrestees, which in turn, relies on the discretion and arrest powers of local law-enforcement agents.

The remaining piece of this puzzle is communities and the activists who seek to influence local policy toward immigration enforcement. Chapter 6 looks at the micropolitics of local immigration enforcement, finding wide variety in local responses. As the nation has shifted to an enforcement-oriented agenda, some localities are concluding that their interests are better served by rejecting that trend and fashioning a more welcoming approach to immigrants, including immigrants without documentation and those who have lost legal status because of past, sometimes minor, convictions. It has also become evident that it is impossible to single out immigrants for deportation without disrupting families, some of which include American citizens. Vulnerability to deportation also poses an obvious threat to public safety when fears of deportation reduce a witness or victim's willingness to come forward with information the police need. As political and law-enforcement leaders absorb the reality that local police and sheriffs are not, and cannot be, the simple "force multiplier" that the federal government and some state legislatures desire, communities find it beneficial to develop more nuanced policies. Many of these policies build on long-established professional commitments within law enforcement to community policing.[28] This chapter brings our study full circle, to the democratic principles that justify a multilevel system of government.

We conclude in chapter 7 by suggesting how we as a nation might move forward in designing and implementing a more just and effective approach to immigration enforcement. This must, at a minimum, involve separating the community-engaging function of local policing from assistance in enforcing federal immigration law, except in serious criminal cases where local police would necessarily be making an arrest and recommending confinement before trial. Our study shows that the context in which local police and sheriffs work, and the operational and professional goals to which they are committed, are incompatible with immigration enforcement. While federalism has much to recommend it as a method of managing conflict in controversial areas of law and policy, its application in the enforcement of immigration law involves hazards and pitfalls that compromise public safety and create a space where democratic controls do not and cannot exist. Policies also influence the way Americans regard each other, framing those targeted by a punitive policy as less deserving than others.[29] The merging of local policing and immigration control carries dangers for the inclusion of minorities who might look "foreign" as full members of American society. We hope this book will contribute to a needed conversation about this issue by providing evidence of what is happening at the local level of law enforcement, which is really where the action is on the immigration issue.

CHAPTER TWO

The Evolution of Devolution

Controlling immigration in a large, rich country with long land borders and a thirst for growth is no simple matter. Efforts to control immigration inevitably create tensions between groups at the local level who feel the positive and negative effects of migration and the national government that sets the overall standards and controls enforcement efforts. Managing immigration is, in the words of one observer, "an ongoing political negotiation."[1] The evolution of this relationship, particularly as it concerns immigration enforcement within the national interior, tells much about the American state and the robust federalism that defines its powers. This history also tells a complex and conflicted story about the meaning of membership in American society. Immigrants do not enjoy some of the legal protections available to citizens, which makes them particularly vulnerable to popular fears and anxieties. As Will Maslow reminds us: "Unrestrained for all practical purposes by the prohibitions of a constitution and undeterred by the fear that the voteless objects of its antipathy will resort to political reprisals, a legislative body is free to embody into law its fears, hostilities, and suspicions of the alien."[2]

The effort to control immigration spans the history of the nation, offering insight into how the American system of federalism works in practice. Certain tendencies will be obvious in this story. It becomes clear that this system is designed to tolerate, for a time, strong differences of opinion about the wisdom of welcoming or restricting immigrants. It is also obvious that the characteristics of immigration law have been determined not only by generalized thinking about the desirability of population growth but also by race-specific fears, anxieties, and beliefs predominant at the time. In this respect immigration law is not unlike domestic law.[3] Another similarity with domestic law is the tendency for immigration law on the books to be far afield from immigration law in action; much depends on administrative capacity. Growth in the size and power of the federal government that occurred toward the end of the nineteenth century, as will be shown, changed the character of immigration law and the balance of activity between the state and federal levels.

The nation's approach toward unauthorized immigrants, those "impossible subjects" who do much of the economy's hard labor, has waxed and waned over time.[4] For the first hundred years or so of its existence, the national government lacked the capacity to control, or even monitor, the flow of immigrants or their settlement patterns. To some extent, states and local communities stepped in to fill this void, enforcing their own controls over membership within their areas through direct action and legislation. As the national government grew in size and power, Congress and the president came under increasing pressure to assert more control. The trend toward increasing federal restraints on immigration began around the end of the nineteenth century. This arrangement remained in place until the 1990s, when for the first time the federal government ramped up its efforts to engage states and localities in immigration enforcement on a formal, on-going basis. The discussion that follows traces this evolution, beginning with the early landscape of local control.

The Era of State and Local Control (Pre-1880s)

Although Article I, Section 8 of the US Constitution gives the federal level sole power over the naturalization of immigrants, it does not mention control of immigrant entry, work, and residence as a function of government at any level. That was not a problem in the early years of the nation's history when the generally accepted goal in most parts of the country was to attract European settlers to populate and develop the country. Nor did the federal government have the capacity to restrict immigration from abroad. At the local level, however, there were incentives to impose some controls. A key concern was with economic dependency and pauperism. Local communities, by tradition and law, were responsible for supporting their indigent residents. Interpreting their policing powers broadly, they treated the regulation of immigrant entry as a public health and safety matter clearly within their local jurisdiction.[5]

For example, in New York City and Boston, a complex system of public inspection, taxation, and social relief evolved. In Castle Garden, New York's huge immigrant-receiving facility, a wide variety of relocation services was available, including luggage tagging for travel westward and arrangements for self-deportation in occasional problem cases.[6] In the South, the impetus for exerting local control was connected with the region's dependence on chattel slavery. The free movement of Blacks—principally foreign seamen on arriving merchant ships and freedmen from the North—was a real threat to maintaining the slavery-based economy.[7] Federal control of immigration would have challenged this closed system, and so the South strongly opposed all proposals to alter the status quo.

The federal government was unprepared at first to take on the South, particularly because its own capacity to enforce its laws in the region was weak. In this pre–Civil War period the federal government was underfunded and small. Federal inaction, of course, meant that states and localities were at liberty to regulate immigration as they saw fit.[8] As Gerald Neuman has written, "The nineteenth-century search for the mysterious line between the [state] exercise of police power and the [federal] regulation of commerce left indeterminate room for state control of immigration."[9]

Early state-level immigration restrictions generally targeted certain undesired classes of immigrants. State laws often prohibited the entry of convicts, both from abroad and across state borders. Most of the original states had this type of legislation in place by the early nineteenth century. In the Northeast, as noted above, port cities, in cooperation with their state governments, inspected arriving ships and imposed quarantines on immigrants with contagious diseases.

Locally imposed head taxes on arriving immigrants were more controversial. The obligation to support arriving immigrants unable or unwilling to work gave rise to a slew of local- and state-level head taxes payable either by shipping companies or by immigrants themselves. In the 1840s, for example, New York created a state board charged with both collecting and disbursing head taxes in support of its almshouses, workhouses, job placement services, and relocation. The New York Commission, which included the mayors of New York City and Brooklyn, among others, collected over $11 million in thirty years.[10] Officials felt justified in imposing these costs on immigrants and the ships that conveyed them because, as New York Commissioner of Emigration Friedrich Kapp observed: "Our State . . . acts in the interest of the whole Union, by efficiently protecting all the immigrants on their arrival and by preventing the spread of diseases imported by them over the country at large, and this while deriving far less advantage from immigration than the Western States."[11] In the less settled Midwest and western regions, the issue was how to attract desirable, that is, Northern and Western European, immigrants. A number of these states passed legislation to encourage immigrant settlement, some using their power over voting qualifications to extend the franchise to European immigrants, despite their lack of citizenship status.[12]

The federal government did not object to these assertions of state power. Not until 1891 did Congress enact legislation to discourage the arrival of immigrants with contagious diseases. It did so, not in defiance of states, but at their request. Northeastern states, fearful of the arrival of so many poor, potentially dependent residents, had been pushing hard for federal legislation after losing battles in the courts to preserve their power to collect revenue from immigrant arrivals and the shippers that brought them. By this point the federal government no longer had to convince the South to go along. The Union victory in the Civil War had, practically speaking, mooted the South's earlier opposition to federal controls.[13]

An early example of the Supreme Court's reasoning in voiding locally imposed taxes upon immigrant arrivals can be seen in a consolidated group of lawsuits known as the Passenger Cases.[14] Statutes in New York and Massachusetts had imposed head taxes on immigrant arrivals in their ports in order to defray the costs of their care and to raise revenues for port operations. The Court declared such state laws contrary to the Constitution on grounds that the federal government has sole authority to regulate foreign commerce and these ships (and their contents) were such commerce. As Justice Catron said in explaining his vote: "The ship rode in the harbor of New York, with all persons and property on board, as a unit belonging to foreign commerce. She stood as single as when on the open ocean, and was as exempt from the state taxing power."[15]

The time was thus ripe for the kind of federal laws for which the northeastern states had been advocating for some time. State representatives from the region had even drafted model legislation to help convince the federal government to act. This cooperative spirit is clear from the earliest federal legislation, which mirrored earlier state-level laws. The federal government simply assumed responsibilities that the states could no longer cover in light of the Court's rulings against state-level head taxes. The federal government nevertheless benefitted greatly from the expertise of state and local immigration workers. For a time in New York City, state inspectors worked alongside their new federal counterparts when inspecting ships and incoming migrants. Not until 1921 did New York fully hand over its quarantine operations to the federal government.[16]

Rise of Federal Plenary Power over Immigration: 1880s–1900s

By the 1870s and 1880s, despite persisting local-level controls, federal involvement in immigration policy and enforcement seemed imminent. The national government had grown stronger in the wake of the Civil War and the war's outcome had uncoupled debates over international migration and the movement of free Blacks. The arrival of foreigners on American shores was continuing apace. The increase was striking. In the 1830s, fewer than half a million immigrants had arrived from Europe, but the number of arrivals started to grow significantly in the 1840s. By the 1860s and 1870s, over two million were arriving from Europe each decade. Records show that around three hundred thousand Chinese immigrants had also arrived between 1850 and 1889.[17] The Supreme Court by then had entirely dismantled the system of state head taxes on incoming immigrants on the grounds that it interfered with the federal power to regulate foreign commerce. Constitutional challenges were bringing to a close the era of state and local control over immigration.

Justice Miller wrote for a unanimous Court in the case that put the nail in the coffin of state and local head taxes, *Henderson v. Mayor of New York* (1875):

> A regulation which imposes onerous, perhaps impossible, conditions on those engaged in active commerce with foreign nations, must of necessity be national in its character. . . . It is equally clear that the matter of these statutes may be, and ought to be, the subject of a uniform system or plan. The laws which govern the right to land passengers in the United States from other countries ought to be the same in New York, Boston, New Orleans, and San Francisco.[18]

With this decision, the federal government could have created a uniform, national head tax, but under pressure from industrialists and others desiring cheap, immigrant labor, government officials dropped this idea and instead adopted the practice then prevalent in the states of restricting undesired classes of immigrants. As of this time, there were no numerical quotas on the number of immigrants who could come to the United States.

The Supreme Court also played a significant role in expanding federal authority by strongly backing Congress in litigation over a series of laws first adopted in 1882 and amended in subsequent years. These laws, which became collectively known as the Chinese Exclusion Acts, emerged after a harsh political fight that initially split the Republican Party, which had been inclined to encourage Chinese labor for its value as a hard-working labor pool. On the other side was a solidly opposed Democratic Party and, according to Daniel Tichenor, "a formidable political alliance of classic exclusionists favoring racial cleansing and egalitarian nationalists of a nascent labor movement seeking protection from Chinese contract labor."[19] Complicating the situation was the fact that the federal government had concluded the Burlingame Treaty with China in 1868, an agreement that guaranteed the relatively free flow of low-wage labor from China to the United States. The executive branch and many commercial interests were anxious to maintain good diplomatic relations with China and Japan, which were emerging as valuable trading partners.

Yet California was a rising force in national politics and could not be ignored. There was intense pressure from that source to reduce the flow of Asian immigrants. Migration from China was at an all-time high, and the completion of the cross-national rail network and depletion of local gold mines had forced many already-settled rural Chinese immigrants into California cities. Racist anti-Chinese sentiment, which had begun to stir in the 1850s, soon morphed into harassment and discriminatory laws that laid special taxes on the Chinese and created regulations designed to inhibit Chinese entrepreneurs and discourage settlement.[20] Anti-Asian sentiment was growing around the country and eventually solidified in Congress, provoking enactments that became increasingly draconian.[21]

In the first version of what was to become the initial Chinese Exclusion Act, Congress imposed a twenty-year moratorium on further immigration of laborers from China and made it more difficult for resident Chinese to visit their native country and return. President Chester Arthur vetoed the bill, citing treaty obligations. A new bill was then introduced shortening the ban on Chinese labor immigration to ten years, but also providing for the deportation of Chinese, barring state governments or courts from naturalizing Chinese immigrants, and requiring current Chinese residents to obtain special certificates for re-entry if they left the United States. The revised bill sailed through Congress, and President Arthur signed it into law.[22]

Chinese residents in California and elsewhere did not quietly accept the growing body of restrictive legislation directed against them. Rejected visa applicants, confident of their rights, filed hundreds of lawsuits seeking relief. Their appeals gave the Supreme Court at least twenty opportunities to define the scope of federal power to exclude foreigners.[23] The Chinese community on the East Coast was large and wealthy enough to hire top lawyers, who believed that the law was on their side. The litigants were soon to be sorely disappointed, however.

In a series of decisions dubbed the Chinese Exclusion Act cases, the Supreme Court consistently interpreted federal power over immigration in expansive terms. The first major case of the era involved Chae Chan Ping, a US resident who had been denied re-entry after a visit to China. Congress had changed the law to his disadvantage when he was abroad. In an 1889 decision, *Chae Chan Ping v. United States*, the Court declared that the federal government enjoys "inherent sovereign powers" in the realm of immigration.[24] The Court articulated three fundamental principles that continue to guide federal immigration policy: (1) The exclusion of aliens is a fundamental sovereign right of any government; (2) Control over immigration is an element of foreign policy properly under political control, and therefore not subject in most cases to judicial review; and importantly (3) Local and state governments do not have power over immigration policy. As the Court stated, "For local interests the several States of the Union exist; but for national purposes, embracing our relations with foreign nations, we are but one people, one nation, one power."[25]

Within the next few years the Supreme Court held that Congress could enact laws that make even long-resident immigrants vulnerable to deportation and deny them basic rights like habeas corpus relief.[26] While noncitizens do enjoy a basic constitutional guarantee against arbitrary governmental procedures, the Court reasoned in *Fong Yue Ting v. United States*, they have no constitutional or other basis for seeking to remain in the United States. The striking breadth of the decision in *Fong Yue Ting v. United States* provoked three impassioned dissents, but the majority opinion has come to define the federal government's plenary power over immigration.

While earlier cases like *Henderson v. Mayor of New York* had grounded federal power over immigration law in the Commerce Clause, the Chinese Exclusion cases provided an even broader anchor in the inherent power of a national government to control its foreign affairs and maintain its sovereignty. The key reference in the Constitution, the Court ruled, was the naturalization clause, which located at the federal level the power "to establish a uniform Rule of Naturalization."[27] This took the Naturalization Clause much further than its authors could possibly have envisioned. The intent at the Founding had been to nullify provisions in the Articles of Confederation that had allowed individual states to set local standards for naturalization.[28] Daniel Tichenor and other scholars of the era consider the Chinese Exclusion Acts and the judicial decisions supporting them to be a watershed in US immigration law: according to Tichenor, "In just five years, a solid legal groundwork was laid for the exclusion, restriction, and expulsion of immigrants. Subsequent judicial rulings reaffirmed the broad, unencumbered power of Congress and its administrative agents to regulate immigration."[29]

The legislation and the case law associated with Chinese exclusion took for granted a racial hierarchy that endured in American law and public policy until the civil rights era. For example, in the 1860s, while the Chinese were suffering increasing levels of hostility in California and other west-coast states, the US Army began conducting a scorched earth campaign against Native Americans. Gilbert King reports that General William Tecumseh Sherman's top priority after the completion of the transatlantic railroad was to not let "thieving, ragged Indians check and stop [its] progress."[30] After one bloody Indian raid, Sherman recommended acting with "vindictive earnestness against the Sioux, even to their extermination, men, women, and children." Upon assuming the presidency, General Ulysses S. Grant took steps to implement this approach.[31] Another indication of the nation's racial hierarchy of the era was the federal government's 1877 decision to withdraw its troops from the Southern states, cutting short the early benefits of Reconstruction and setting the stage for a pervasive system of state-backed discrimination against African American citizens.[32]

One way to make sense of such policies against the backdrop of a democratic, egalitarian, rights-based system is to recognize that competing narratives inform American political development. As Desmond King and Rogers Smith insightfully argue: "American politics has historically been constituted in part by two evolving but linked 'racial institutional orders': a set of 'white-supremacist' orders and a competing set of 'transformative egalitarian' orders."[33] David FitzGerald and David Cook-Martin take this analysis a step further, drawing on historical documents from across the western hemisphere to show that democratic governments have been the first to select immigrants by race and among the last to outlaw discrimination.[34]

The importance of the Chinese Exclusion Acts lies, not just in their institutionalization of racist premises about human difference, but also in their clear-cut assertion of federal power over immigration. Before this period, governance at the federal level tended to be preoccupied with distribution of benefits on a regional level. It was, in political scientist Stephen Skowronek's words, "a state of courts and parties," except, of course, in its wartime efforts.[35] Stirrings of federal power were already occurring with the 1872 Post Office Act and Reconstruction. The Chinese Exclusion Acts marked a temporary high-water point in this trend, with federal agents controlling all key ports of entry and administering federal immigration law to achieve federal purposes.[36]

In the broader context of US immigration at the time, however, this was still a limited step toward federal control. Though the Supreme Court had given Congress virtually unlimited power to set and enforce whatever immigration policy it deemed appropriate, the long, sparsely populated land borders of the country were well beyond federal capacity to control. At the time the Supreme Court rejected Fong Yue Ting's and Chae Chan Ping's appeals, the southern border with Mexico and the long Canadian border were little more than lines on maps.[37] Active borderland economies in the Southwest reflected this fact, with agricultural and mining economies based on transient immigrant labor.[38] Because flows across the states along the southern border were easy, migrants often came to work on a seasonal basis, leaving their families based in Mexico. Their situation made them vulnerable to economic downturns and to the day-to-day exploitation from Anglo employers. William McDonald describes sometimes-violent conflict among groups in the region, with immigration playing a secondary role to banditry and labor disputes.[39]

An egregious example occurred in Bisbee, a border town in the then Arizona Territory, which in 1907 organized its own deportation initiative to end a strike by foreign miners. A particularly sore point was the sharply differing pay scale for foreign and Anglo workers. The so-called Mexican wage paid a fraction of the Anglo wage, despite the fact that Mexican and Chinese workers undertook the most hazardous jobs. Employers and local citizens were determined to break this strike, and so Bisbee's local law-enforcement officers, with the assistance of deputized citizens, loaded over a thousand foreign workers, most of them Mexicans, onto boxcars and shipped them east into the desolate southern desert of New Mexico. They escaped death only because US soldiers stationed in the area discovered and rescued them.[40]

Consolidation of Federal Immigration Powers throughout the Twentieth Century

In asserting the supreme power of the federal government regarding immigration policy in the Chinese Exclusion Act cases, it will be recalled, the Supreme Court consigned the states to the limited role of integrating these new residents into their communities. This assignment made the states subject to the Fourteenth Amendment's equal protection clause, which requires states to treat all its residents without discrimination. Not surprisingly, this mandate has not always been well received by state and local governments. State legislatures have repeatedly sought to diminish the rights of some of their foreign-born residents and their American progeny on the basis of discriminatory conceptions of racial and cultural identity.

The Supreme Court began to rule against such state laws, ironically, at the very time it was giving full force to the Chinese Exclusion Acts. In one famous example, *Yick Wo v. Hopkins* (1886), the Court ruled that city officials in San Francisco could not administer their fire safety rules in a way that singled out Chinese-owned laundries.[41] This logic played a key role in a much later case, *Graham v. Richardson* (1971), which invalidated the efforts of several states to impose alienage exclusions on state-funded welfare programs. To allow such laws, the Supreme Court ruled, would allow states to enact de facto immigration policies.[42]

The equal-protection standard that the Court articulated in cases invalidating state alienage laws, however, is not relevant if the federal government undertakes a mass deportation initiative. The federal umbrella of nearly unfettered discretion also covers state and local law-enforcement officers who assisted in these operations. As the twentieth century progressed, the federal government did initiate such cooperative efforts from time to time, creating a rough-hewn working relationship between federal immigration personnel and law-enforcement agencies at various levels. David Fellman describes a regime of mutual aid, which he labeled "cooperative federalism," by which federal authorities asked for help from local police to implement large-scale projects like a 1919–20 roundup under the aegis of the Palmer Raids to deport foreign "radicals." Local police benefited from these relationships when they sought to deport foreign criminals.[43]

Efforts to detect and deport immigrants who had entered or remained in the country illegally were rare, but when they occurred, they were massive and their scale required local law-enforcement assistance to be effective. Hiroshi Motomura observes that the persistent demand for workers has helped to create an immigration system marked by "selective admissions combined with selective underenforcement. . . . [W]hat has mattered has not been the line between the legal and the illegal, but rather the exercise of enforcement discretion. It can often turn harsh, but it can also be lenient."[44]

The first extensive deportation operation occurred in the throes of the Great Depression. In a series of raids across the western states, federal immigration agents worked with local law enforcement to deport tens of thousands of people. The total number of deportees, Daniel Kanstroom reports, increased from 2,762 in 1920 to 38,796 in 1929. During this period more than 92,000 people were deported and more than 36,000 were found to have entered without proper documents or by fraud or deception. The number of legal entrants also dropped from an annual average of 62,000 in 1923–29 to 2,500 in 1930.[45]

These summary deportations were indiscriminate as well as harsh. Some of those forced to leave were American citizens of Mexican origin and American citizen children of Mexican immigrants. Operation Wetback, initiated in 1954 under President Eisenhower's authorization and with co-operation from the Mexican government, was even broader in its range and effect. There were over a million apprehensions in the first year of Operation Wetback, though the numbers declined precipitously in subsequent years.[46] The operation lasted a decade and resulted in over eleven thousand formal complaints from legal workers claiming that they were improperly detained or deported.[47]

Throughout the twentieth century, another area in which federal immigration agents have necessarily depended on local police and sheriffs has been the apprehension of "criminal aliens," immigrants suspected or convicted of violating domestic penal laws and some specified immigration laws.[48] There are significant limits to local powers, however. One's presence in the United States without legal authorization is not a crime; it is a *civil* law violation. A long line of legal precedent holds that local law enforcement lacks the legal power to arrest in this situation.[49] Another practical limitation is the lack of local expertise in the complex realm of immigration law, which has made it more difficult for local and federal agents to work together to make solid stops and arrests. Peter Schuck and John Williams note what was until recently a lack of coordinated databases allowing police to check on immigration violations, a tendency for federal authorities to miss some cases eligible for removal, and increasing local frustration with the criminal alien removal program.[50]

States have long played their own role in taking direct action to discourage immigrant settlement, an issue that is now, of course, salient in political debates over immigration control. The first wave of these laws tended to arise mainly in the Southwest, a geographical connection that can be explained in part by timing, a strong tradition of states' rights in the West, and the location of large numbers of unauthorized immigrants arriving from Mexico and further south. Once these states were well established enough to pass laws attempting to regulate alien settlement, they became embroiled in lawsuits over the legal dividing line between local authority to address the welfare of their communities and federal power to set and enforce immigration law. Soon after it achieved statehood in 1912, for example, Arizona adopted legislation giving preference to citizen workers over immigrants, only to be reversed by the Supreme Court in *Truax v. Raich*. In his 1915 opinion for the Court, Chief Justice Hughes reminded the state that:

> An alien admitted to the United States under the Federal law has not only the privilege of entering and abiding in the United States, but also of entering and abiding in any State, and being an inhabitant of any State entitles him, under the Fourteenth Amendment, to the equal protection of its laws.[51]

This interpretation of the law remains in effect. In 1982 the Supreme Court rejected a Texas law that withheld funds for the education of children lacking legal status in *Plyler v. Doe*.[52] In both the Arizona and the Texas cases, however, members of the Court were sharply divided over the power of states to enact the legislation at issue. Such cases and the division within the Supreme Court itself reveal tensions inherent in a system of immigration control that locates most power to admit and remove immigrants at the federal level, while doing little to mitigate the effects of immigration at the local level.

That division reappeared again when the Supreme Court decided another Arizona case, this one brought by the Department of Justice to challenge SB 1070, a law designed to "mirror" certain federal enforcement requirements at the state level so as to facilitate arrests of suspected unauthorized immigrants. In 2010, shortly after SB 1070 was signed into law, legislatures in twenty-four states considered proposals for "show me your papers" legislation like Arizona's. But the trend quickly stalled, with ten states killing these bills in 2011 and most others ending their sessions without taking action, as they waited for the outcome of the federal suit against SB 1070. The five exceptions were Alabama, Georgia, Indiana, South Carolina, and Utah. All these laws were attacked by civil rights organizations, including the American Civil Liberties Union, which made their defeat a priority in its national program.

In *Arizona v. United States* (2012), Justice Anthony Kennedy, writing for the majority, rejected most of SB 1070's provisions challenged by the Department of Justice: "The federal power to determine immigration policy is well settled. Immigration policy can affect trade, investment, tourism, and diplomatic relations for the entire Nation, as well as the perceptions and expectations of aliens in this country who seek the full protection of its laws."[53] The Court's decision, despite spirited dissents from three justices, seems to have settled this matter. Indiana ceased enforcing its law soon after the Supreme Court's *Arizona* judgment, while Alabama and South Carolina reached settlements ending their state-level enforcement initiatives. Judges have blocked enforcement of Utah's law and parts of Georgia's legislation. No new state laws of this type have been adopted.

The issue of local efforts to enforce federal immigration law, however, was not settled by this case. The Court left standing a crucial part of SB 1070 allowing local police to question suspected unauthorized immigrants during their regular duties, provided the stop is not prolonged. For decades, even without statutory authority, police and sheriffs have done exactly that. The US Commission on Civil Rights noted this problem in its 1980 report on civil rights issues in immigration. The commission described several examples of unconstitutional activities by local law enforcement, including a case in Moline, Illinois, where the city police department's practice was to enter local neighborhood establishments and interrogate persons of Latino ancestry about their status in the United States. The commission also noted the frequency of "investigative" stops that ended in arrests of legal residents who could not prove their legal status on the spot: "Notwithstanding the policy statements of the Department of Justice," it concluded, "some local police have apparently continued to enforce Federal immigration laws."[54] The commission recommended "Congress should clarify the Immigration and Nationality Act to specify that immigration laws should only be enforced by INS."[55]

That said, local legislation is not always hostile to immigrants. Beginning in the 1980s, some local and state governments flexed their immigration muscle by passing sanctuary ordinances to protect individuals and families fleeing from violence from the civil wars raging in Central America at that time.[56] These laws and resolutions reflected sharp disagreement with the federal government's support for the military regimes in the area and its refusal to grant Central American migrants refugee status. By the mid-1980s, at least twenty cities, including Los Angeles, San Francisco, Seattle, Chicago, Cambridge, Massachusetts, and Ithaca, New York had passed sanctuary ordinances. New York and New Mexico adopted statewide legislation. These laws generally prevented local government officials (including police) from communicating the immigration status of local residents to federal immigration authorities.[57] A few churches have revived this tradition in protest of the current deportation policies of the United States as they bear on immigrant families and individuals perceived as valued members of their communities.[58]

These important examples aside, however, during most of the twentieth century, the federal government was overwhelmingly in charge of immigration policy making and enforcement. The line of demarcation between levels of government held fairly constant in this period, despite significant growth in the immigrant population, particularly in the number of unauthorized immigrants who crossed the southwest border into Texas and California.

From the perspective of the political leadership and many citizens in the affected states, the federal government was guilty of not exercising its enforcement power to limit the flow of unauthorized immigrants. The porous border has remained a favorite object of complaint about federal inaction. But the underlying problem for states concerned about unauthorized immigration arises at least in part from federal action, not inaction. When Congress adopted the 1965 Immigration and Nationality Act, it limited, for the first time, the amount of legal immigration that could occur from Mexico and other nations within the western hemisphere. The quota on western hemisphere immigration took no account of the proximity of Mexico to the United States or the historic pattern of labor flows across the southern border, resulting in a massive bottleneck on legal immigration and the "illegalization" of millions of border crossers attracted to US jobs.[59]

A solution was finally hammered out, the 1986 Immigration Reform and Control Act (IRCA), which was a compromise that promised greater attention to workplace enforcement at the same time that it provided legal status for an estimated three million unauthorized resident immigrants, over half of whom were agricultural workers. This legalization program, still the largest in the world, did not, however, provide a permanent fix for unauthorized immigration. Although IRCA drastically reduced the number of illegal immigrants, its promise of more vigorous workplace enforcement turned out to be a mirage. Employers could avoid the consequences of IRCA by claiming not to know that the hiring papers (I-9 forms) they accepted were forged or contained false information. The upshot was that the "magnet" of jobs—that is, employers willing and eager to hire immigrant labor—continued to attract legal and unauthorized immigrants to the United States, as it always has. At the same time, newly legalized immigrants provided a kind of familial magnet that also encouraged immigration. By the early 1990s, with the undocumented population estimated to be around three million, pressure was once again building for a more forceful approach to unauthorized immigration, particularly immigration from Mexico.

The Balance of Power Shifts: The 1990s and Beyond

In 1994, California, long a top destination for both legal and illegal migrants from Mexico, once again set the stage for increased enforcement. This time, in a move designed to send a message to Congress, the political leadership backed a ballot initiative designed to discourage immigrants without legal status from settling in the state. Proposition 187, which was approved by 59 percent of the California electorate in the November election, sought to deny unauthorized immigrants in the state access to public schools and to almost all public services. Additionally, in an early attempt by the state to harness its police powers in the name of immigration enforcement, it called for police officers throughout the state to investigate and report the immigration status of arrestees. Only emergency medical care was exempt from the new requirements. Although a federal judge ruled Proposition 187 unconstitutional before it could take effect,[60] the political message was clear: Californians were dissatisfied with federal inaction and the presence of so many unauthorized immigrants in their state.[61]

Federal legislators treated Proposition 187 as a wake-up call and soon began crafting national-level legislation to tighten immigration enforcement. For the first time, local police and sheriffs would be brought into the enforcement process via a federal statute. In 1996, Congress adopted two laws that still remain in force and continue to shape immigration enforcement. The Antiterrorism and Effective Death Penalty Act (AEDPA) gives local police the authority to arrest previously deported noncitizen felons and deputizes local police to assist federal immigration agents in urgent cases. The Illegal Immigration Reform and Immigrant Responsibility Act (IIRIRA) is a complex law with border-enforcement provisions, increased penalties for transporting immigrants, deportation procedures, and rules on government support for immigrants. Most significantly for this discussion, IIRIRA authorizes the training of local and state police to enforce federal immigration laws. Congressional committee discussions prior to the adoption of IIRIRA suggest that legislators were seeking to enlist local police as a "force multiplier" in the effort to strengthen federal immigration enforcement in the nation's interior. Concerns about competing priorities at the local level were raised by a few members of Congress, but were brushed aside by sponsors of the legislation.[62]

The outcome of these deliberations was the approval of two types of federal-local policing partnerships: one to assist in the identification of arrested unauthorized immigrants during the period in which they are booked into jail, and the other to enforce federal immigration law on the street as part of patrol duties. Both required federal training and a formal memorandum of understanding between the federal government and the local law-enforcement agency that has applied to the program. These memoranda became known as "287(g) agreements" after the location of the authorizing statute in the Immigration and Nationality Act, as amended by IIRIRA.[63] Devolution of federal power to the local level, it appeared, had finally come of age in immigration policy.

In providing for an expanded, ongoing, and formal relationship between federal immigration agents and local police, these laws marked a sea change in federal attitudes.[64] For the first time, the possibility existed for local police and sheriffs' departments to be enlisted, through signed memoranda of understanding, into the process of immigration enforcement within their own jurisdictions. Despite Congress' evident enthusiasm for partnerships with local law enforcement, however, federal legislation had to be framed in terms of a request, rather than a command that local law enforcement officials would be obliged to obey.[65] The constitutional arrangement that the Founders put in place envisions state and local control over most matters of crime, punishment, and public safety. The arrangement is in keeping with the overall tendency in American political arrangements to disperse power and retain significant functions at the local level. Indeed, local responsibility for the protection of public welfare had been the principal rationale in the eighteenth and nineteenth centuries for state and local efforts to control what types of immigrants were welcome within their jurisdictions.

Local control of crime and justice has meant the establishment of more than 12,500 police departments in the cities and towns that dot the United States, each operating independently from the others, and also independently of federal control as long as they remain within constitutional bounds. As of 2008 there were over a million full-time state and local law-enforcement officers, including 765,000 sworn personnel, with about half of all agencies employing fewer than ten full-time officers.[66] Coordination across police departments is rare. Police departments are under the political control of municipal governments, which seldom engage in detailed oversight. The nation's over 3,000 county sheriffs operate even more independently because they are, with few exceptions, popularly elected and are therefore only loosely bound to any political authority except to the courts for alleged law violations.

In this context it is perhaps not surprising that the 287(g) program got off to a slow start. For five years, state and local law-enforcement organizations ignored the federal government's initial offer of training and formal partnerships to enforce immigration law. The September 11, 2001, terrorist attacks on the World Trade Center and the Pentagon encouraged the newly formed Department of Homeland Security (DHS) to issue more urgent invitations to participate, and a few law-enforcement organizations responded. The first memoranda of understanding were signed by the states of Alabama and Florida in 2002. At its peak, however, only about seventy agencies participated, the majority of them county sheriffs who chose the less-extensive jail identification option over street patrols to identify undocumented immigrants.

The Department of Justice also took part in the effort to achieve greater participation by local police and sheriffs in immigration enforcement. The tactic was a classified memo from Attorney General John Ashcroft to local police and sheriffs re-interpreting longstanding policy and practice that had strictly forbidden local participation in enforcement of federal immigration law, except under the direct and constant supervision of federal agents. This 2002 memo, which has never been withdrawn, contradicts the former hands-off approach, claiming that local police and sheriffs have inherent authority to act on their own in enforcing federal immigration law.

The context for this 180-degree turnaround by the attorney general and for the unrolling of the 287(g) program was growing public dissatisfaction with the pace of federal immigration enforcement and a sense at the federal level that its own resources and personnel were insufficient to the task of enforcing immigration law in the nation's interior. Only about eighteen thousand federal employees do immigration and customs work, counting all federal agencies involved.[67] The inclusion of local police in immigration enforcement offered a way for the federal government to greatly increase enforcement capacity without paying for it and without

losing ultimate control over who would be deported. Local law enforcement would only be involved in bringing suspected unauthorized immigrants to federal attention and would have no say in subsequent decision
making. From a federal perspective, this administrative response to the
increasing calls for enforcement seemed much simpler and more feasi-
ble than comprehensive immigration reform. The feeling was that, while
comprehensive reform might alleviate the need for local "force multipliers," the necessary legislative action would be difficult to achieve. Time
has proven that assessment correct.

The federal government's push for increasing involvement of local
law enforcement in immigration enforcement generated significant controversy. The major national law-enforcement groups, which include the
Major Cities Chiefs and International Association of Chiefs of Police, and
many research foundations associated with policing, including the Police
Foundation, Police Executive Research Foundation, and the Vera Institute of Justice, expressed concerns about the 287(g) program as it was implemented. Even the US Government Accountability Office was critical of
the program's implementation. A key issue was the potential for immigration duties to undermine trust in local law enforcement. The biggest fear
was that members of immigrant communities would become afraid to call
the police when they were witnesses to or victims of crimes.[68] The Major
Cities Chiefs' "Statement on Immigration" from 2006, for example, states:

- Local enforcement of federal immigration law undermines the trust and cooperation with immigrant communities that are essential elements of community
  oriented policing.
- Local agencies do not possess adequate resources to enforce these laws in addition to the added responsibility of homeland security.
- Immigration laws are very complex and the training required to understand
  them would significantly detract from the core mission of the local police to
  create safe communities.
- Local police do not possess clear authority to enforce the civil aspects of these
  laws. If given the authority, the federal government does not have the capacity
  to handle the volume of immigration violations that currently exist.
- The lack of clear authority increases the risk of civil liability for local police and
  government.[69]

The failure of the 287(g) program to attract many local law-enforcement
agencies and persistent criticism that it lacked essential controls eventually

led to the DHS's decision to phase it out.[70] Criticism focused especially on street-level "task force" agreements, which essentially deputized local law-enforcement officers to act in the role of immigration agents, arresting suspected unauthorized immigrants for violations of federal immigration law. The most egregious example of over-aggressive enforcement practice that came to light was among the Maricopa County (Arizona) sheriff deputies. The county sheriff, Joe Arpaio, had embraced the 287(g) program with gusto, engaging the maximum 160 deputies in the effort—far more than in any jurisdiction nationwide. Deputies conducted traffic stops focused on Latino-looking drivers, raids of places that employ large numbers of immigrants, and crime-suppression sweeps in neighborhoods, many of which have large Latino populations. On television and at every opportunity, the sheriff made no secret of his enthusiasm for deporting unauthorized immigrants.

The sheriff office's well-publicized activities helped to reveal the potential for constitutional violations in the administration of the 287(g) program and to create momentum for corrective action. In 2008, the Department of Justice launched an investigation of claims of racial discrimination among Maricopa County sheriff's deputies. After three years of investigation, the Department of Justice concluded that the Maricopa County Sheriff's Office (MCSO) had "engage[d] in a pattern or practice of unconstitutional policing" and that it "engages in racial profiling of Latinos; [and] unlawfully stops, detains, and arrests Latinos."[71] These practices, some of which occurred under 287(g) authority, had created "a 'wall of distrust' between MCSO officers and Maricopa County's Latino residents."[72] The DHS then terminated the sheriff's 287(g) task force agreement, eliminating its right to act in the name of federal immigration authority. The sheriff's office, however, continued many of these same activities without federal authorization, using state laws against identity theft, human smuggling, and fraud in employment applications to arrest immigrants. The Arizona legislature signaled its support for this type of aggressive enforcement by passing SB 1070 in 2010.

In 2012, at about the same time the Supreme Court was mulling over the fate of SB 1070, DHS was phasing out the 287(g) program nationwide, not because it was dissatisfied with local involvement in immigration enforcement, but because it wanted greater oversight, lower costs, and considerably *more* local participation than the 287(g) program had generated. Near the end of 2012 DHS announced that no "task force" agreements would be renewed and that all "jail enforcement" agreements would be reviewed; early the next year it cut the operations budget by $17 million.[73]

Although the risk of unlawful profiling and unwarranted stops animated many of the program's critics, DHS remained relatively indifferent to this problem as it rolled out Operation Secure Communities to replace its failed program. Secure Communities *mandated* local participation in immigration enforcement. It built on the fact that when an arrestee is booked into a local jail, that person's fingerprints are checked against Federal Bureau of Investigation databases for outstanding warrants and other information. Operation Secure Communities added a pass of the booking information through immigration databases. A match or "hit" with any of these databases would come to the attention of the local jail or holding facility and federal authorities, who could ask for a "hold" of up to seventy-two hours to facilitate transport to an immigration facility where further investigation might lead to the individual's deportation. Secure Communities was piloted in fourteen communities in 2008 and then gradually rolled out across the United States.[74] The federal government argued that Secure Communities was a more cost-effective model than its 287(g) program because it did not require training of local law-enforcement officers.[75] The cost of training officers, however, could not have been a major motivator in the decision to move to a mandatory program. In 2012 the federal government spent nearly $18 billion on immigration enforcement, significantly more than the total for all other federal law-enforcement agencies combined.[76]

In this period the rate of apprehension and removal of unauthorized immigrants and legal immigrants with past criminal convictions was growing rapidly. Immigration prosecutions reached an all-time high in 2013, up 22.6 percent over the past five years. Prosecutions at the border for illegal re-entry rose 76 percent.[77] Under the Obama administration, the federal government also deported many more individuals than ever. Until 2014, when there was a slight drop in deportations, the number hovered at around four hundred thousand each year with roughly thirty-four thousand people awaiting their hearings on any given day.[78]

Secure Communities, despite its apparent success in increasing deportations, failed to offer a clear solution to the problems that had plagued the 287(g) program: racial profiling and pretextual stops designed to detect immigrants without legal status.[79] The mandatory nature of Secure Communities also rankled many law-enforcement organizations, particularly those in large cities anxious to nourish good relationships with immigrant communities. Both of these issues receive more detailed attention in later chapters.

Whether the federal government could impose detention responsibilities on local law enforcement became the subject of litigation in 2013 and

2014 when several courts held that an Immigration and Customs Enforcement (ICE) request to hold an arrestee suspected of being undocumented exposes the holding facility (and municipality) to civil liability.[80] In November 2014 DHS ended uncertainty about legal liability by terminating Secure Communities and replacing it with a much more limited initiative, the Priority Enforcement Program.[81] This new program takes aim at convicted criminals (rather than people arrested for any crime or infraction). It also replaces federal requests for detention (detainers) that had caused so much controversy with simple notification. These changes represent a significant movement toward greater federal sensitivity to the needs and aspirations of local law enforcement and a clear backing away from the resented mandatory approach to local engagement in immigration enforcement.

Presidential initiatives have also changed in the face of harsh criticism. In June 2012 President Obama announced that the federal government would henceforth defer enforcement action against young people who meet certain eligibility criteria.[82] Deferred Action for Childhood Arrivals quickly became known by its acronym, DACA. By mid-2014, over five hundred thousand young immigrants without legal authorization had received authorization under DACA to remain for an additional two years without fear of deportation and with the ability to work or go to school.[83]

In November 2014 President Obama attempted to use his executive powers again to extend temporary protection to unauthorized parents of US citizens who have lived in the country for at least five years, to larger groups of students, and to unauthorized spouses and children of persons with legal residence or citizenship. Deferred Action for Parents of Americans and Lawful Permanent Residents (DAPA) was executive action on a grander scale: up to five million unauthorized residents could receive a reprieve from their vulnerability to deportation as a result of the president's action. This reprieve was highly controversial among Republicans in Congress, who deemed it an example of presidential overreach. The future of deferred action via executive authority remains in doubt. The challenges include litigation being pursued by seventeen states that has resulted in a federal district court's temporary injunction blocking implementation of DAPA and an expanded form of DACA, bills in Congress to revoke executive discretion over categories of immigrants, and an increasingly conservative Congress that is riven into rival camps regarding immigration reform.[84]

The impact of President Obama's executive actions and other executive efforts to add nuance to the federal government's use of prosecutorial discretion has been mixed.[85] DHS reported a slight drop in deportation numbers in 2014 but also claimed an increase in illegal immigration.[86] President Obama signed a 2015 appropriations bill increasing immigration-enforcement funding to record levels; the bill added an additional $1 billion to the budget of federal enforcement agencies and reaffirmed a requirement that the agency employ a minimum of 21,370 agents, reflecting continued federal adherence to its enforcement-first approach.[87]

Crimmigration: The Most Recent Chapter in Immigration Federalism

The implications of stepped-up immigration enforcement for local police and sheriffs are the subject of the rest of this book. Here it is important to note that *how* the federal government handles cases of unauthorized immigrants has evolved over time in ways that make deportation more likely. Most striking is the melding of the criminal law and civil immigration procedures, a mixing that has tended to reduce immigrant rights and to increase the effectiveness of the administration's efforts to remove persons in the country illegally. Some elements of this trend, which scholars have dubbed "crimmigration," involve small changes in the law with big consequences for immigrants.[88] Other elements of crimmigration involve administrative decisions to bring criminal cases in situations where civil proceedings had been used in the past. Crimmigration also refers to the weakening of procedural protections that occurs in proceedings that mix civil and criminal elements.

Immigration violations still span a civil/criminal divide, with some falling on the civil side as offenses to be handled by bureaucratic means, and others being named as crimes and subject to adjudication by a criminal court. For example, being caught crossing the border "without inspection" has long been a crime, specifically a federal misdemeanor. A person who makes his or her way beyond the border, however, does not commit a crime by being in the country illegally. That is a civil violation subject to administrative, not criminal, proceedings. This arrangement works to the federal government's advantage because it allows for many enforcement actions—often ending in deportation—to occur without the constitutional protections afforded to all persons accused of crimes, such as the right to prompt arraignment, bail, and the assistance of a lawyer.

The artificiality of this civil-criminal split has spawned a variety of ad hoc solutions designed to help immigrants achieve representation, or at least sound legal advice before hearings.[89] Still, it is entirely possible for an immigrant child to appear without legal counsel at a deportation hearing because the constitutional right to a lawyer does not apply in a civil case. This became clear in hearings involving the Central American children who came unaccompanied across the border in large numbers in the spring and summer of 2014. Their lack of legal representation to assert claims as potential aslyees opened a new chapter in the federalization of immigration enforcement as bar associations and a few cities and states promised to supply lawyers, prompting the federal government to pledge aid as well. Despite the pledges of legal aid to these children, however, the Transactional Records Access Clearinghouse (TRAC) reports that, as of October 31, 2014, lawyers represented only 32 percent of the unaccompanied children appearing in immigration courts.[90]

Congress has also played a role in the evolution of crimmigration. Legislation adopted in 1996 drastically reduced the ability of judges to grant relief from deportation. Congress has also reclassified some civil violations as "aggravated felonies"—a label that applies only in the realm of immigration law. Activities typically associated with unauthorized immigration, such as using a false Social Security number, passport, or birth certificate, have become federal crimes. Even marriages undertaken to avoid deportation carry serious criminal penalties. The trend toward harsher treatment also extends to *legal* immigrants who commit crimes. The chance of getting deported for criminal activity was once reserved for the most serious offenses, but crimes triggering deportation have been vastly extended to include even misdemeanors like shoplifting and tax evasion.[91] The law can be applied retroactively for crimes committed even decades ago where the sentence imposed was probation or a warning.

Illegal re-entry after deportation has also become a major source of criminal prosecutions. In the past, most people caught crossing the border were allowed to return home voluntarily, but in 2005 the federal government instituted Operation Streamline in one Texas district, and other district courts along the southern border soon followed. The idea was to use prison time to create a potent disincentive to illegal re-entry. To handle the caseload that Operation Streamline creates, defendants are arraigned in groups, effectively batch processing their appearance before a federal judge. Border-crossing defendants appear in court in shackled groups of up to seventy, with a single defense lawyer representing them. The charge is illegal entry or re-entry, a crime punishable by up to ten years in prison. The heavy penalties encourage guilty pleas to a much lesser prison term, typically 180 days in a federal penitentiary. Largely as a consequence of this program, over half of all defendants prosecuted and facing incarceration in federal prisons are now immigration offenders.[92]

Many elements of this stepped-up approach to enforcement have been criticized for mixing elements of civil and criminal procedures in a way that leads to manifest injustice. Legal scholar Stephen Legomsky describes the risk of error in high-stakes proceedings where individual rights are circumscribed through an "asymmetric" incorporation of criminal-justice norms, priorities, and procedures into immigration law.[93] The high penalties and weight of adversarial adjudication apply in these civil cases, but not the protections routinely accorded individuals in criminal cases, including the right to representation, to discovery of incriminating evidence, or to a jury of one's peers. Legomsky condemns this as "a deportation regime so substantively harsh and inflexible that too often the penalties are cruelly disproportionate to the transgressions."[94] Many legal scholars agree with this characterization, including Juliet Stumpf, who coined the term "crimmigration" to critique the trend toward criminalization of immigration violations.[95] This is a trend with a parallel in other settings, including schools and welfare offices and city streets, where new forms of criminality have been developed and "zero tolerance" and harsh penalties have become the rule.[96] Together they mark an increasingly punitive direction in American society, a development Marie Gottschalk and others have described as a movement toward the "carceral" or "punitive" state.[97]

States and Localities and "Back-Door" Immigration Policy

At the state and local level, one can discern a vague resemblance to legislative strategies deployed two centuries ago to discourage undesired groups of people. This time the object is unauthorized immigrants, not convicted criminals or paupers. The trend began slowly, but by the mid-2000s, apparently spurred by rising controversy over unauthorized immigration, state and municipal legislatures were beginning to adopt immigration-related legislation.[98] Most of their activity was crafted to eliminate rights and privileges that unauthorized immigrants had formerly enjoyed without questions about legal status. The trend toward legislative activism

TABLE 2.1 **State Legislative Immigration-Related Activity, 2005–13**

	2005	2006	2007	2008	2009	2010	2011	2012	2013
Bills introduced	300	570	1,562	1,305	1,500	1,400	1,607	983	*
Resolutions adopted	0	12	50	64	131	138	109	111	253
Laws enacted	45	84	240	206	222	208	197	156	184
Vetoed	0	6	12	3	20	10	15	11	7

*National Conference of State Legislatures did not supply this information, though it notes that about 1,300 bills have been introduced on average since 2007.

occurred, not just in places long accustomed to immigration, like Texas and California, but in so-called new immigrant destinations, such as Pennsylvania and North Carolina.

In 2005 the National Conference of State Legislatures (NCSL), a center for sharing news and developments in state policy making, began to track immigration-related state laws and resolutions. Their data indicate growing numbers of proposals and resolutions each year, with a smaller number of laws adopted, some of which are vetoed by the governor.[99] Table 2.1 indicates a dramatic increase in the volume of state-level bills introduced after 2006 and the steadily increasing number of resolutions. On average since 2007, about 1,300 state bills related to immigration have been introduced each year. The vast majority of these bills are discarded in the legislative process and governors veto a few of them. Still, the recent volume of law-making activity remains impressive. Observing this awakened interest in state-level, immigration-related lawmaking, Peter Markowitz suggests that in the near future, immigration reform, both favorable and unfavorable, is more likely to emerge from the state level than the federal level.[100]

The top priority in these state bills has been the restriction of employment to persons with legal status, not immigration enforcement per se.[101] In general the bills fall into areas traditionally within the purview of state governments, such as setting standards for professional licenses.[102] The innovation is the requirement of legal status to receive benefits, effectively sending a signal that unauthorized immigrants are not welcome in the state. Some bills developed before SB 1070 direct local law enforcement to work more closely with federal immigration authorities.[103] Since the Supreme Court's 2012 decision in *Arizona v. United States*, however, omnibus law-enforcement bills have virtually disappeared from legislative agendas.[104]

There are also areas in which some state legislatures have shown themselves prepared to offer protection to unauthorized immigrants, primarily by providing health and welfare benefits, driver's licenses, and in-state tuition for applicants lacking legal status. Limiting the scope of E-Verify and encouraging police to prioritize community-oriented policing over immigration enforcement are other areas in which a few states have adopted laws that work to the benefit of persons without secure legal status. Nearly every state is involved; by midyear 2015, for example, all but four states had enacted some kind of immigration-related legislation during their legislative session.[105]

Nearly 150 cities have also developed or considered developing legislation to signal their antipathy toward unauthorized immigrants. The small city of Hazleton, Pennsylvania, became a well-known example of this kind of legislation, thanks to the efforts of its mayor, Lou Barletta, to publicize the city's 2006 Illegal Immigration Relief Act (IIRA).[106] Such laws were designed to avoid federal preemption by staying within the boundaries of municipal jurisdiction: business licenses and housing rental policy. This strategy, though successful in avoiding a lawsuit initiated by the federal government, nevertheless has embroiled these municipalities in litigation from groups supportive of immigrant rights. Thus far, the lower courts have ruled most of these city-level laws unconstitutional on the grounds that they tread, albeit by indirect means, into territory normally reserved by the federal government.[107] Congress probably accelerated the trend toward state and local attempts at regulating immigration by its failure to act on immigration bills before it in both 2006 and 2007 and by the continuing stalemate around comprehensive immigration reform.

Conclusion

Despite enormous growth in the size and capacity of the federal government to create and implement policy over the past 150 years, the local level appears to be reclaiming a measure of its earlier role in regulating whom it will welcome within its territorial limits. A few states have taken steps to welcome immigrants, including those without secure legal status. Ten states and the District of Columbia now provide limited-function driver's licenses to people without legal status. Some major cities have signaled their welcome by refusing to commit to cooperating with recent aggressive federal immigration-enforcement initiatives. Most states, however, have shown their disapproval of settlement by unauthorized immigrants by, for example, denying in-state tuition to residents who cannot prove legal status, even if they have lived in the state for many years. Courts have upheld such legislation.

At some point, however, laws that restrict on the basis of legal status run afoul of the plenary power doctrine that gives sole power over immigration policy to the federal government.[108] This did not stop Arizona and the five states that followed its example from attempting to craft a larger role for their states in immigration enforcement. The fact that such laws were likely to face a hostile reception in the courts was clearly not as important to their backers as the political message that these laws convey. These leaders have followed the example of California's Proposition 187, the 1994 law that quickly lost in the courts, but precipitated significant federal action to control the border. Federalism, as Anna Law noted, is indeed a constant negotiation, but it is also a political contest in which attitudes about who belongs in American society come more clearly into view.[109]

While there has been little inclination at the federal level to let go of its monopoly of power to determine and to enforce the boundaries of *legal* membership, this is not the only question up for debate. States and localities, while looking for more local control over immigration and immigrants, are making their own decisions about *substantive* membership in their communities. At one end of this spectrum are Arizona and other states and localities that favor tough enforcement measures against those who lack legal status, even if that means deporting long-settled immigrants and families with American children. They are essentially embracing the federal government's definition of membership as a matter of legal status. At the other end of the spectrum are states and municipalities that are pushing back and implicitly adopting a substantive approach toward membership that recognizes immigrant settlement as a commitment that should be honored in law. President Obama's recent exercises of discretion that redirect federal enforcement efforts to protect some settled immigrants from deportation reflect that perspective.

All the signs suggest that measures to enforce immigration law within the national interior will be a perennial source of controversy, whether or not the federal government adopts comprehensive immigration reform. No fix will be permanent, and any fix will be controversial. On the other hand, any enforcement measure that takes settled people from their homes and jobs will inevitably raise the question of whether legal status is as important as the ties of social membership that develop at a local level over time.[110] The chapter that follows takes this discussion in a contemporary direction, exploring how conflicting values and perspectives on immigrants at the local level and the federal government's own tolerance for variation have together created a confusing and contradictory patchwork of local policies affecting the enforcement of immigration law.

CHAPTER THREE

The Problematic Patchwork of Immigration Federalism

In October 2013, California Governor Jerry Brown signed the Trust Act,[1] which prohibits local law-enforcement agencies from detaining people for deportation if they are arrested for a minor crime and otherwise eligible for release. The passage of this act was widely understood as a reaction to the federal government's Secure Communities program, which relied on Immigration and Customs Enforcement (ICE) requests to local law enforcement to hold individuals believed to be in violation of immigration laws.[2] Not surprisingly, the signing of the Trust Act caused significant tensions between federal immigration enforcement priorities and state-level law-enforcement policy. Shortly after the implementation of the Trust Act on January 1, 2014, another jurisdictional layer was added to this already complex situation. California's Kern County Sheriff, Donny Youngblood, stated that he would continue to cooperate with ICE and the federal government, despite the Trust Act: "If I release someone during that 48-hour period, and they go out and commit this heinous crime, what the media is going to say is, 'Sheriff, federal law says you shall hold them, and you didn't, and look what happened.' So, the sheriff is in the cross hairs again, it's one of those state-federal laws that conflict."[3]

The jurisdictional patchwork has grown even more complex. An increasing number of cities, counties, and states have passed measures that resist compliance with Secure Communities.[4] In September 2011, the Cook County Board of Commissioners, following San Francisco and two counties in New Mexico, voted to ignore ICE requests for detainers in misdemeanor cases, justifying their move on the basis of the estimated $15 million they had been spending in yearly detention costs. The commissioners, whose jurisdiction includes Chicago and surrounding suburbs, had already established Chicago as a "sanctuary" city, forbidding local governments to engage directly with ICE and prohibiting refusals of services for undocumented immigrants.[5] Other large cities, various counties, and at least two states—Massachusetts and Connecticut—have also declared that they would refuse federal requests to detain people accused of minor crimes who are believed to be in the country illegally.[6] King County, the largest in the state of Washington, after a close vote, passed an ordinance to limit participation.[7] Upon discovering that half the Boston residents deported under Secure Communities had committed no crimes, the mayor-elect declared that he wanted to withdraw from the program entirely.

In this chapter we use our research on immigration policing to offer empirical evidence of the wide variation emerging from the devolution of enforcement responsibilities to the local level. Viewed through the lens of local law enforcement, immigration federalism looks more like a patchwork of overlapping and potentially conflicting authority than a systematic approach to a national enforcement agenda. Federal rules do not require coordination between the various and overlapping policy-making bodies, which creates significant potential for cross-jurisdictional conflict. We dub this outcome a "multijurisdictional policy patchwork" of enforcement authority: an emerging, confusing, and often contradictory geography of immigration enforcement in the United States.

The policy patchwork emerges in several ways, as chapter 2 noted. A significant source of variation arises out of the federal government's devolution of immigration policing powers via 287(g) agreements, Secure Communities, and most recently, the Priority Enforcement Program that replaced Secure Communities. Another potent source of variation is grassroots legislative efforts in jurisdictions across the United States. Cities, counties, and states were not compelled to sign 287(g) agreements, but some did. And jails across the country were at one point compelled to participate in Secure Communities, but some did not, though most did. Some cities, counties, and states have "sanctuary" policies and practices that prohibit their workers from participating in federal immigration enforcement efforts, whereas other cities, counties, and states have passed controversial immigration policing policies that harness the state's criminal justice system to arrest a broader range of noncitizens than federal enforcement priorities demand.[8] As our case studies below demonstrate, jurisdictions with diametrically opposed approaches to immigration enforcement may be located in the same urban region, be neighbors, or even have overlapping territories.

The federal government has not been consistent. Its devolutionary policies [particularly the 287(g) program] have promoted an enforcement patchwork. Yet the Department of Justice was unequivocal in its suit against SB 1070 that such local variation is both unconstitutional and illegal under federal law, stating, "The Constitution and the federal immigration laws do not permit the development of a patchwork of state and local immigration policies throughout the country."[9] The Department of Justice's strong claim is not even consistent with its own practices. Even federal agents enforce federal law in different ways across the country.[10]

In the chapters that follow, we explore reasons why localities take different approaches to immigration enforcement (chapter 4), and how police departments and sheriff offices add to that variation through their own policies and the exercise of individual discretion on the front lines of law enforcement (chapter 5). Our aim in this chapter, however, is to illustrate how the policy patchwork is developing across the country. We draw on our survey data and in-depth case studies in three communities: Mesa, Arizona; New Haven, Connecticut; and Raleigh, North Carolina. We start by considering the broader arguments regarding the promises and pitfalls of the patchwork and conclude by reflecting on how our evidence informs these discussions.

Promises and Pitfalls of the Patchwork

The pros and cons of the enforcement patchwork as an explicitly geographical phenomenon have not received much attention from scholars or other observers, though there have been vigorous debates and extensive discussion of the pros and cons of immigration federalism, broadly speaking. Scholars have, on the whole, divided into two camps: those making a case for immigration federalism and those arguing against its desirability.[11] An early proponent was Peter Spiro, who framed his support in terms of what he called "steam valve federalism" in immigration policy making.[12] Reflecting on California's Proposition 187 and the 1996 laws in Congress, and drawing a parallel to the passage of the Chinese Exclusion Acts in 1882 and 1888, Spiro argues in favor of state-level immigration policy activism. As he writes, devolution:

> presages new possibilities for state-level modulation in immigrant policy that
> will more efficiently represent wide state-to-state variations in voter prefer-

ences and that may ultimately benefit aliens as a group. First, state level authority will allow those states harboring intense anti-alien sentiment to act on those sentiments at the state level, thus diminishing any interest on their part to seek national legislation to similarly restrictionist ends.[13]

Under steam-valve federalism, "one state's preferences, frustrated at home, are not visited on the rest of us by way of Washington."[14]

Others have explored different positive impacts of immigration federalism. Peter Schuck suggests that immigration policy making at the state and local level will not necessarily be hostile to immigrants.[15] Still others view the devolution of immigration policing authority as a crucial "force multiplier" in the war on terror, with state and local law enforcement better able to act as the frontline officers for federal immigration enforcement initiatives.[16] From a slightly different angle, both Cristina Rodríguez and Clare Huntington argue for a more robust multilayered immigration regime.[17] Rodríguez makes the case that, despite de jure federal exclusivity in immigration policy making and enforcement, we actually have a "de facto multi-sovereign regime." She sees "a structural need for federal, state, and local participation in immigration regulation" and immigrant integration.[18] Similarly, a number of scholars argue that cities can be—and often are— important sites for the development of progressive policies and practices, in contrast to the enforcement orientation of the federal government.[19]

Other scholars take a much more skeptical and critical view of immigration federalism. For example, Pratheepan Gulasekaram and Karthick Ramakrishnan have recently argued that instances of state and local immigration policy actually build, rather than dissipate, energy for similar legislation in other states and localities.[20] In their view, the failure of federal immigration reform has left states and localities open to the opportunistic actions of "restrictionist issue entrepreneurs" who hitch their wagons to a cascade of similar legislation. Concerns have also been expressed that devolution and the rise of grassroots immigration policy activism have opened the door to discrimination by local authorities against noncitizens, including legal permanent residents.[21] These scholars see in the devolution of federal enforcement authority an erosion of the traditional barrier against state and local discrimination on the basis of national origin that was imposed by the equal protection clause of the Fourteenth Amendment. They argue that under immigration federalism, as it is currently evolving, immigrants are much more at the mercy of discrimination by the local state. In short, while much of the federalism literature refers to states in a positive way as "laboratories" for the development of social policy, Michael Wishnie notes their potential to be "laboratories of bigotry" under immigration federalism.[22] Muzaffar Chishti and Huyen Pham, among others, also express concern that the devolution of immigration policing will do serious harm to police-community relationships.[23]

The emergence of "policy-patchwork federalism" is not confined to immigration. It also characterizes federal management of other contentious policies. For example, in exploring state-level hydraulic fracturing ("fracking") policies, Cynthia Bowling and Mitchell Pickerill argue that "fragmented federalism" is problematic, given the increasingly complex landscape of intergovernmental relations that it engenders.[24] The patchwork of immigration federalism and immigration enforcement that we discuss in the remainder of this book, however, has much more dire—and in some cases, mortal—consequences. When immigrants get caught up in the enforcement patchwork, they can be deported from the country, removed permanently from their families and livelihoods, and, in some cases, placed in serious danger in the countries to which they are deported.[25]

With this chapter, we contribute to the scholarship exploring contradictory *geographies* of local immigration policy making and enforcement.[26] Our analysis of the policy patchwork, situated within the various literatures that bear on immigration enforcement and the broader issues of federalism, thus offers fresh insights into an emerging phenomenon, with implications, not only for the evolution of American federalism but also for communities across the United States. With this in mind, we turn to our empirical evidence.

State Legislation and the Patchwork

One facet of the immigration policy patchwork can be visualized easily at the state level. Drawing on data collected annually by the National Conference of State Legislatures (NCSL), we counted the number of years between 2005 and 2013 that any given state adopted one or more laws designed to restrict the opportunities of immigrants.[27] These include opportunities for people without secure legal status to rent apartments, find employment, and obtain driver's licenses or other permits. This also includes efforts to restrict movement through laws mandating aggressive enforcement by local police. Mapping these data graphically by state, it is clear that there is no uniform approach to immigration across the United

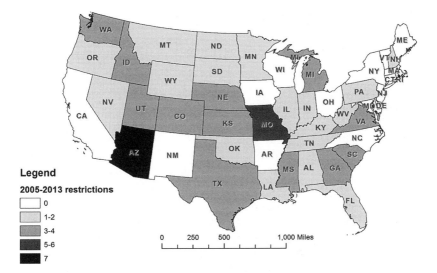

FIGURE 3.1. Number of years in which restrictive immigration legislation was passed, 2005–13

States (see fig. 3.1). Where some states, such as California, New York, New Mexico, and Wisconsin (in white on the map in fig. 3.1) did not pass any restrictive legislation between 2005 and 2013, others, including Nebraska, Missouri, Georgia, and (at the top of the list) Arizona (shaded more darkly to reflect greater legislative activity), have been very active in pursuing an anti-immigrant agenda.

This map reveals several curious patterns. Note the marked contrast in approaches between some neighboring states, for example, California, Arizona, and New Mexico. Where California and New Mexico passed no restrictive immigration legislation between 2005 and 2013, Arizona's state legislature passed restrictive legislation every year, more than any other state in the nation. A similar contrast is apparent between the neighboring states of Iowa, Missouri, and Arkansas. Where Missouri passed restrictive immigration laws in five out of seven years, Iowa and Arkansas passed none. Unlike California and New Mexico, however, which both adopted several immigrant friendly statutes, in Iowa and Arkansas there were strong, but failed, attempts to pass restrictive legislation throughout this period. One can also see a strong contrast between North Carolina and the nearby southern states of Georgia, South Carolina, and Virginia, all of which passed restrictive immigration laws in four out of seven years.

Though sandwiched between Virginia and South Carolina, North Carolina's legislature did not follow their example.

North Carolina offers a striking example of the policy patchwork in more ways than one, however. While there were no restrictive immigration laws passed at the *state* level, North Carolina (along with Pennsylvania) led the country during this period in *municipal* and *county*-level anti-immigration policy activity, including the signing of 287(g) memoranda to empower local police and sheriffs to assist in immigration enforcement. So in North Carolina, while the state did not act, cities and counties exploited available resources to enact anti-immigrant agendas.

In this rest of this chapter, we shift our focus from the state to the local level and draw on data from our three surveys of local law-enforcement executives—city police chiefs and county sheriffs—to further describe the patchwork of immigration practices and policies that has emerged in this era of crimmigration[28] and immigration federalism. Then, in chapter 4, we will explore possible explanations for the evolution of this patchwork.

Patchwork of Local Policies and Practices

In many cases, police agencies take cues from their local governments in developing their departmental policies and practices regarding immigrants. A pro-enforcement city manager or mayor and council are likely to hire a pro-enforcement police chief, for example. To gauge the political context in which law-enforcement executives are making decisions, we asked police chiefs and sheriffs about their local government's stance on immigration issues. Would they characterize it as supportive (pro-immigrant), enforcement oriented, or silent with no policy at all? As evidenced by table 3.1, there were significant differences in responses, revealing a high degree of local variation in immigration policies and practices across the United States. Nearly twenty percent of large-city governments noted supportive local policies, versus nearly 30 percent with enforcement-oriented policies, while 47 percent stated that they had no official policy at all. Among small cities, a much larger proportion, 63 percent, had no official policy toward immigrants. It is perhaps unsurprising that in small cities, with small budgets and few full-time staff, local policies were infrequent. Big cities, on the other hand, often engage by necessity with long-standing immigrant communities and so might be expected to have addressed the issue.

Also of note is the significantly smaller percentage (9 percent) of sher-

TABLE 3.1 **Local Government Policy toward Immigration Enforcement**

	Large cities, %	Small cities, %	Sheriff offices, %
Supportive ("sanctuary" or "don't ask, don't tell")	18.8	12.7	9.1
Enforcement oriented ("encourage/ expect enforcement")	29.1	16.5	24.4
No official policy	47.0	62.9	53.9

iffs reporting a pro-immigrant county government. With large cities twice as likely, and small cities forty percent more likely, to have pro-immigrant policies, a greater potential exists for neighboring or overlapping local governments and bureaucracies to be operating at cross-purposes. As our case studies below demonstrate, it is not unusual for a city that has a supportive policy to be embedded in a county with an enforcement orientation. Or a large city might have a pro-immigrant policy orientation, but be surrounded by small cities that have either an enforcement orientation or no official policy at all.

Our surveys revealed that the policies and practices of local law-enforcement agencies varied as much as those of local governments (see table 3.2). We asked police chiefs and sheriffs to report on their interactions and relationships with the federal government, either by way of signing 287(g) agreements or having ICE officers embedded in their departments (or both). The answers of police chiefs were significantly different from those of county sheriffs. Sheriffs were much more likely than city police departments to have signed 287(g) agreements with the federal government. These agreements provide for federal training of local law-enforcement personnel. The agreements are of two types. One is to cooperate in making investigations or arrests for civil immigration violations. The other trains jail personnel to report immigration data during the booking process after arrest. A sheriff's office might sign on to both programs. Fifteen percent of sheriffs, versus 3–4 percent of local police among our respondents, had signed at least one 287(g) agreement. Another sign of sheriffs' closer relationship with ICE is that 20 percent reported having ICE officers embedded in one or more of their units, compared with 8 percent in the large cities we surveyed, and less than 2 percent in the small cities.

A likely explanation for these differences is that county sheriffs hold a unique position, simultaneously serving as jailers, administrators of a county agency, and politicians. In contrast to police chiefs, who typically

TABLE 3.2 **Frequency of Immigration-Related Policies and Practices among Police Departments and Sheriff Offices**

	Large-city police departments, %	Small-city police departments, %	Sheriff offices, %
287(g) task force MOU	3.8	4.2	15.0
287(g) jail MOU	3.0	4.2	15.2
ICE officers embedded in department	7.6	1.7	19.7
No ICE participation/assistance	13.5	34.2	25.2
Has a written policy regarding interactions with immigrants	38.8	26.6	32.7
Offers training for officers on interactions with undocumented immigrants	45.1	31.6	34.6

Note: ICE, Immigration and Customs Enforcement; MOU, Memorandum of Understanding. Section 287(g) was a federal statutory provision enabling state or local police to be cross-trained for enforcing federal immigration law, on patrol and/or in the jails.

are appointed by their local governments, 97 percent of the sheriffs we surveyed were elected. The sheriffs' political independence and responsibilities for jails may make them more responsive to popular pressures regarding immigration enforcement, whether the sentiment is pro- or anti-enforcement in a particular county. Eighty-three percent of the sheriffs who responded to our survey also run their county jail system.

The costs involved in housing immigrants in detention also tend to bring sheriffs into cooperative relationships with federal immigration officials. These relationships sometimes cause controversy. Many counties (and state prison systems) complain that their expenses for detaining immigrants amount to a major unfunded mandate from the federal government. But for other counties, the arrangement appears to be mutually beneficial. For counties with excess capacity in their jails, housing federal immigration detainees may provide a significant revenue stream. Among our responding sheriffs who operate jails, 60 percent said they receive at least some reimbursement from the federal government to defray the costs of detaining unauthorized immigrants. For 21 percent, such reimbursements cover most or all of the county's costs. These factors help clarify why 41 percent of responding sheriffs deemed federal officials "influential" or "very influential" in shaping their offices' immigration-enforcement practices and policies. By contrast, only 21 percent of big-city police chiefs viewed federal officials as influential in this respect.

Variation and the patchwork are not only the result of conflicting official policies. When we asked respondents whether their department or office had an official policy instructing officers on what to do regarding immigration status, more than half the city chiefs (51 percent) and 44 percent of county sheriffs said they had no such policy. Others said that they did not know if they had a policy (1 percent of chiefs, and 5 percent of sheriffs) or that they had a policy that was unwritten (9 percent of chiefs, and 18 percent of sheriffs). Indeed, only approximately one-third of big-city chiefs and sheriffs, and one-quarter of small-city police departments had written policies on the topic. Similarly, just under half of big-city police departments offered training to their officers on how to handle interactions with presumed undocumented immigrants. Only a third of sheriffs and small-city police departments offered similar training. This dearth of written policies or explicit guidance and lack of training leaves the door wide open to the deployment of officer discretion, which inevitably has a wide range of outcomes. The discretion inherent to the policing of immigrants is the subject of chapter 5.

The Patchwork of Perceptions

Our survey also asked chiefs and sheriffs to respond to a series of questions gauging their attitudes on various immigration-related policing issues (see table 3.3). We found significant differences in these responses, which again points to the wide variation of approaches to immigration enforcement developing across the United States. Whereas just over half of city police chiefs "agree" or "strongly agree" that "gaining the trust of unauthorized immigrants is a priority in my department," only one-third of sheriffs and small-city police chiefs agree or strongly agree with this statement. This may reflect the fact that many big cities in the United States have long been immigration destinations, and that big-city police chiefs have come to understand that effective policing depends on the cooperation and trust of local immigrant communities. Similarly, more city police chiefs agree that "victimization of immigrants is considered a significant problem in my department" (30 percent) than do sheriffs (20 percent) or small-city police chiefs (16 percent). Of course, contextual factors unrelated to the immigrant-friendliness of a department, such as the local crime rate or the socioeconomic status of local immigrants, may be responsible for some of these differences. Finally, one question sparked a strong positive response from all groups. When asked to respond to the statement, "Immigration enforcement is considered the responsibility of the federal government," 70 percent

TABLE 3.3 **Police Chiefs and Sheriffs Who "Agree" or "Strongly Agree"**
with Given Statement

Statement	Large-city chiefs, %	Small-city chiefs, %	Sheriffs, %
Gaining the trust of unauthorized immigrants is a priority	52	36	30
Victimization of immigrants is considered a significant problem	31	16	20
Immigration enforcement is considered the responsibility of the federal government	71	61	60

of big-city chiefs agreed or strongly agreed, and so did 60 percent of small-city chiefs and sheriffs.

Overall, the survey findings suggest that individuals perceived to be undocumented immigrants may be treated disparately, depending on whether they happen to encounter law enforcement within a municipality or in a neighboring unincorporated area, and also depending on the degree to which ICE officials are involved with the law-enforcement unit. The confusion is particularly acute for newly arrived immigrants, who are unlikely to understand the nuances of the multijurisdictional character of US law enforcement. Unpleasant experiences or anxieties relating to police forces in one jurisdiction may affect their relationship or perception of local police in another jurisdiction, regardless of its policies. In that sense, fear of one particular police force acts as a sort of contagion affecting other communities in the area as well, as the case studies below illustrate. The authority of the county sheriff to check the immigration status of all suspects transferred to the local jail facility also can become the fulcrum for a heightened sense of threat among unauthorized immigrants throughout the county, as can be seen the case study of Raleigh, North Carolina below.[29]

Another source of disparate treatment depends on the appearance of the individual suspected of being in the country illegally. The perception that a person is in the country without authorization is not race or ethnicity neutral. The face of unauthorized immigration in the United States in the popular mind, and probably in the minds of most law-enforcement officers, is Latino.[30] Speaking Spanish, looking "Mexican," and listening to Spanish-language radio have all been cited as a basis for arrest in reported cases.[31] As other studies have shown, the apprehension and deportation of immigrants is also biased toward Mexicans and Central Americans.[32]

Case Studies: The Patchwork in Action

Although the survey data provide a valuable national perspective on the patchwork, evidence from particular communities can make more vivid and comprehensible the variegated geography of enforcement that many immigrants face. The case studies that follow offer an up-close perspective on the variations in law-enforcement approaches to immigration enforcement within particular cities and metropolitan areas. We draw on the cases in our research that most clearly illustrate the policy patchwork, as well as its troubling contradictions, particularly for immigrant communities.

Mesa, Arizona: Conflict between Overlapping Jurisdictions

Mesa is a city of more than 463,000 people within the Phoenix metropolitan area. Along with Phoenix and more than twenty other smaller nearby cities, Mesa lies within sprawling Maricopa County, one of the nation's most populous counties (see fig. 3.2). Mesa's demographics distinguish it from some of its neighbors. Twenty-six percent of the population was Latino and 15 percent were foreign born, at the time of the 2012 American Community Survey. Latinos, despite their numbers, have not had much political power in Mesa historically. Since its founding by Mormon pioneers in 1878, Anglo members of this religion have exerted influence disproportionate to their numbers, while the opposite has been true of Latino residents.[33] The diversity of the population has nevertheless, at least in recent years, encouraged city leaders to define a measured approach to immigration enforcement. Under the leadership of George Gascón, who served as chief of police from 2006 to 2009, the police department dramatically increased its investment in community policing, and crime rates fell significantly among all population groups.[34] Part of this effort involved the creation and implementation of a written policy determining when officers might inquire about immigration status and when to report suspected unauthorized immigrants to federal authorities. At about the same time, the city applied for a 287(g) agreement to manage its incarcerated population.

The city's interest in maintaining a workable balance between immigration enforcement and community policing enjoyed the support of city officials, as well as the two local fraternal police organizations. Maricopa County Sheriff Joe Arpaio, however, opposed it. The depth of this conflict

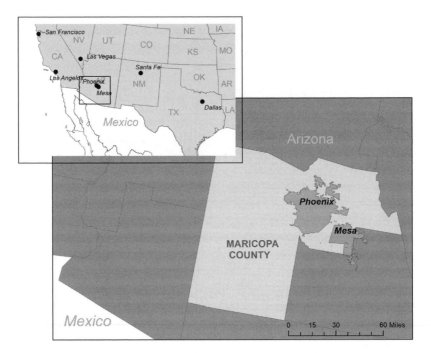

FIGURE 3.2. Mesa, Arizona, and surrounding jurisdictions

became clear in the wake of an October 2008 midnight raid of the Mesa
City Hall and library by heavily armed sheriff deputies searching for unauthorized custodial personnel employed by a contractor of the city government. With no prior notice of the raid to Mesa authorities, the deputies arrived at a city park to don riot gear and then entered city buildings
to hunt for undocumented immigrants, creating a potential for a lethal
misunderstanding between police agencies. The sheriff was acting under
federal authority. In February 2007 the county had signed a 287(g) agreement that included power to detain and arrest suspected unauthorized
immigrants; the sheriff authorized federal training for 160 deputies—the
most of any local law enforcement agency in the country.

Mesa city officials were outraged at the sheriff's action. Probably due
to this political heat, the sheriff promised that he would announce any
future raids beforehand. Nevertheless, for residents who lack legal status
or who have friends or family members with immigration status issues,
the situation remains perilous. Residents continue to complain of racial

profiling and pretextual arrests by the sheriff and some other police agencies in the area.

Formal complaints and litigation over the policies and practices of Sheriff Arpaio provoked the Department of Homeland Security in 2011 to end the sheriff's 287(g) authority to make immigration arrests, limiting his federal immigration-related authority to jail identification. That decision occurred shortly after SB 1070, Arizona's "show me your papers" law was due to take effect. The Department of Justice, however, was able to block implementation of four key provisions of Arizona's statute by challenging Arizona in the courts.[35] Sheriff Arpaio vowed to continue with his workplace raids and immigration sweeps even without 287(g) authority but continued to encounter legal roadblocks. In 2013, federal district judge Murray Snow found him guilty of racial profiling and exceeding his authority and permanently enjoined his office from further roadside sweeps.[36] The sheriff's deputies were required to undergo retraining and to make other changes to prevent further racial profiling. A pending suit also challenges the sheriff's authority to conduct workplace raids to find immigrants using false identification to secure work.[37] The sheriff, who has been elected five times, but by increasingly narrow margins, remains defiant, but subdued by the requirements Judge Snow has imposed on the department.

The situation in Mesa illustrates how federal devolution creates a multijurisdictional patchwork of immigration-enforcement authority. In this case, the conflict is between levels, with the county asserting its jurisdiction to patrol the entire county as it sees fit, regardless of the policies or wishes of cities within the county. In most areas of the nation, such conflicts are avoided through comity, a principal of reciprocity by which one jurisdiction extends certain courtesies to others by recognizing their laws and decisions. Federal devolution does not take into account the possibility that comity will be ignored and that policing agencies will come into conflict over enforcement policy.

The federal government's undifferentiated approach to devolution means that Mesa residents are unable, as a practical matter, to implement their own approach to community safety. It is not clear whether *any* political authority can control a sheriff's immigration-enforcement decisions. As popularly elected officials, sheriffs act relatively independently of their county governing board. Nor can the federal government be sure how its enforcement authority is being exercised under current policy. A study by the Migration Policy Institute questions the ability of ICE to ensure that

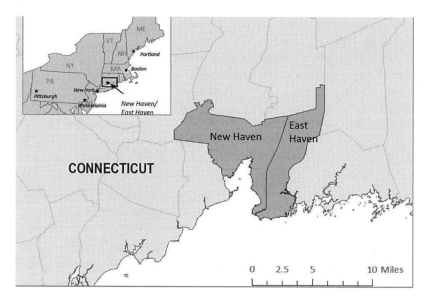

FIGURE 3.3. New Haven, Connecticut, and surrounding jurisdictions

its stated priority of targeting serious criminal offenses will be honored at the local level.[38]

New Haven, Connecticut: Conflict between Neighboring Jurisdictions

New Haven is a city of 130,000 people (26 percent Latino and 16 percent foreign born) in southern Connecticut and is perhaps best known as home to Yale University (see fig. 3.3). In recent years, the city has developed a reputation as an innovator concerning strategies for the integration of immigrants. The police department has a General Order that prevents police officers from inquiring about a person's immigration status or acting upon a National Crime Information Center (NCIC) "hit" for immigration violations, except when investigating criminal activity. Moreover, New Haven was first in the nation to adopt a municipal identification card, which can be obtained by any New Haven resident regardless of immigration status. The police, many local businesses, and city government accept it as valid identification.

Both initiatives emerged from the efforts of a diverse coalition of interests. Two local grassroots organizations, Unidad Latina en Acción (ULA) and JUNTA for Progressive Action, Inc. (JUNTA) joined with representatives of the New Haven police department, city government, Yale law-school faculty, members and leaders of the congregation of Saint Rose de Lima Catholic Church, and other community members to work out an immigrant-friendly approach to local policing. They acted out of growing awareness that immigrants in the community were being victimized, in large part because they did not have valid forms of identification. A state law prevented noncitizens from obtaining drivers' licenses.

The situation facing undocumented immigrants in New Haven at that time echoes stories in communities throughout the United States. Without valid identification, these immigrants could not open bank accounts, and thus kept their money at home or on their person in cash. As they walked home from work on payday, they were being robbed and assaulted by criminals who saw them as "walking ATMs." At that time distrust of the New Haven police in the immigrant community meant that such crimes often went unreported. The situation provoked ULA and JUNTA to commission a report, "A City to Model," for then-Mayor John DeStefano Jr. and City Hall to consider. The report presented six proposals to foster immigrant integration and public safety. What emerged was the General Order, adopted by the New Haven police department in December 2006, and a policy of providing municipal ID cards, which was approved by the New Haven Board of Aldermen in the summer of 2007.

Conflicts inherent to a multilayered jurisdictional patchwork are nevertheless manifest in New Haven. While there are no counties—and by extension, no sheriffs—in Connecticut, and no discernible tension between the city and state, there have been tensions between the federal government and the City of New Haven. Within thirty-six hours of the passage of the municipal ID legislation, ICE conducted an immigration raid in the city—the first ever, not only in New Haven but also in Connecticut. ICE agents banged on individuals' doors, yelling, "Police!" thus exploiting the carefully fostered trust between New Haven city police and immigrant communities. Thirty-two people were arrested. Most observers are convinced that the raid was in direct retaliation against the city's newly adopted municipal ID card. Shortly after the raid, the Worker and Immigrant Rights Advocacy Clinic at Yale Law School filed a federal lawsuit claiming that ICE agents violated the constitutional rights of those arrested and contesting the detention and deportation orders of those arrested. The suit was settled in 2012 in favor of the detained immigrants.[39]

The city government also found itself at odds with the neighboring municipality of East Haven, with which it shares a border. In stark contrast to

New Haven's policy, the East Haven police force, in accordance with the wishes of the mayor, pursued for many years a "tough on immigrants" stance. Its officers regularly called ICE when they were holding a suspected undocumented immigrant. Many Latino residents of New Haven complained that East Haven police regularly parked their patrol cars on the border of the two cities and pulled Latinos over on pretextual grounds, a policing strategy that many called "border patrol." In 2009 a Department of Justice inquiry found a pattern of racial profiling and racially biased policing, which led to a 2010 lawsuit citing repeated racially motivated abuses by East Haven police officers. The lawsuit was settled in 2014 in favor of the Latino defendants.

A third source of conflict is internal. Some members of the New Haven police force are opposed to the General Order, believing that it violates federal law. After the ICE raids, for example, one officer stopped an individual whose name came up on an NCIC search. According to the General Order, New Haven police officers are not permitted to respond to NCIC hits, but the officer disregarded departmental policy and called ICE, who came and arrested the individual in question.[40] Indeed, representatives of the union for officers in New Haven expressed their opposition to official city policy during interviews.

New Haven, in short, is constrained in its policing policies by pressure from federal authorities, from a neighboring jurisdiction, and from within the ranks of its own police force. This case suggests that the devolution of federal authority in the contemporary period of immigration federalism has created a legal resource to be exploited by persons favoring more extensive local partnerships to enforce immigration laws. The potential for conflict is evident in communities like New Haven that prioritize community trust and other community-policing goals over immigration enforcement. The policy patchwork created by devolution of federal authority to the local level thus limits local political authority without clarifying the role of the federal government.

Raleigh, North Carolina: Interagency Relations and "Dual Deniability"

Raleigh, with a population of 284,507, is located in Wake County, North Carolina (see fig. 3.4). The Latino population has grown dramatically over the past two decades, largely in response to the demand for labor in the construction and agricultural sectors of the Wake County economy. Latinos now comprise about 9.3 percent of the population. Neither the

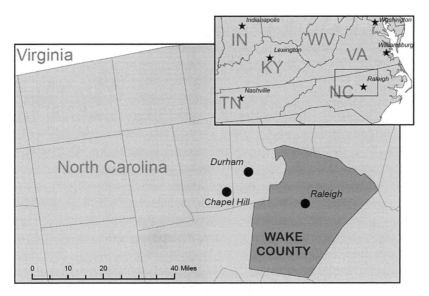

FIGURE 3.4. Raleigh, North Carolina, and surrounding jurisdictions

City of Raleigh nor its police department had a policy concerning immigration enforcement at the time of our study, but the Wake County Sheriff's Department did, having entered into a 287(g) agreement in 2008 in order to provide more authority for the identification (and potential deportation by ICE) of undocumented immigrants.

With no policy at the city level and a 287(g) agreement for jail identification at the county level, an individual law-enforcement officer has wide discretion in deciding how to respond to suspected undocumented immigrants. Any police officer in the county, including environmental conservation officers and state police, can arrest and bring in suspects, knowing that arrestees will have their immigration status checked when processed at the jail. The 287(g) agreement is thus a resource for any officer who desires to use arrest authority to deport undocumented residents. Yet the sheriff can correctly claim that his officers make only a small portion of the arrests, and therefore the sheriff is not responsible for determining whether pretextual arrests or racial profiling have occurred in most cases. Both city and county police agencies thus achieve "dual deniability" regarding enforcement policy.

Latino residents do not necessarily distinguish between enforcement agencies, nor does it necessarily matter in terms of one's likelihood of deportation. The situation has led many in the Latino community to become fearful of all law enforcement and government officials and to presume that racial profiling is widespread. A representative from the sheriff's office argued that there is no discriminatory intent involved. While establishing the identity of all persons brought into custody is admittedly an important custodial function performed by those who have responsibility for running local jails, the sheriff's policy effectively erodes Raleigh's effort to chart another course.

Community groups claim that Raleigh's policing practices, combined with the sheriff's 287(g) Memorandum of Understanding (MOU), have led immigrants to forego driving to their jobs, school, churches, or community activities because they are mistrustful of law enforcement. They claim that immigrants have become less willing to serve as witnesses or report instances of victimization because of the possibility of deportation. These groups see a sharp decline in the area's initial support for immigrants as low-cost labor in rapidly expanding enterprises. Our informants note that recent efforts by Raleigh community groups to reach out to law enforcement and to increase communication have not been successful. While the sheriff claims that officers are not racially profiling and that victims can freely come forth without the fear of deportation, undocumented immigrants remain fearful. A policy patchwork has developed in Raleigh because of the mixed message that the county's 287(g) agreement creates in a locality that was once more welcoming toward immigrants, regardless of their legal status.

Conclusion: The Problematic Patchwork

Devolution of governmental authority, whatever its specific focus, creates opportunities for more variation in local policy regimes than would ordinarily be the case under a national policy. Flexibility in policy administration is often celebrated as a way to better reflect the needs and preferences of local residents than a one-size-fits-all national policy, or as a way to experiment with new and different ways of carrying out public services. Those who argue for devolution of immigration-enforcement authority stress these qualities, suggesting that devolution should also be seen as a "steam valve," reducing pressure on the central government in a hotly contested policy area by allowing each locality to define its own approach to enforcement.[41]

The implications for local governments are more significant than the laissez-faire "steam valve" approach might suggest. Unlike many public services that are more routine or technical in nature, the devolution of immigration enforcement to the local level is not a practice that merely honors varying local "tastes" for a public good.[42] Rather, variation in approaches to unauthorized immigration reflects differences in judgments about whether some classes of residents should be treated differently based on national origin and legal status and whether those who lack legal status should be removed if that option is available.

Nor can immigration enforcement be easily grouped with policy domains like education, employment training, or "fracking."[43] In these areas, subnational variation in policy may be undertaken in the service of national goals and therefore be less problematic. Immigration policy, however, is an example of what Bayless Manning calls intermestic policy, an area of government activity that stands at the juncture of international affairs and domestic policy.[44] The implications of enforcement can be drastic at an individual level and significant at a community level, raising fundamental issues about who belongs in the community and who can remain.[45] At the same time, enforcement decisions can have international ramifications. This is also a complex area of law, one in which the expertise required to enforce standards is not easily acquired. The standards themselves are not even entirely clear to legal scholars, who remain sharply divided over whether local police can legitimately enforce civil immigration violations.[46]

Immigration federalism and local immigration enforcement also do not fit the usual model of "cooperative federalism." Immigration federalism tends to bypass the traditional role of the state government as the point of devolutionary contact in policy implementation. Instead, the relationship is federal to local, despite the fact that local governments in many other situations are regarded as subordinate "creatures of the state." Legal scholar Rick Su had dubbed this unusual convergence "immigration localism."[47] But even at the local level, coordination among neighboring jurisdictions is lacking. Cities appear to act in isolation as they decide (or decide not to decide) whether and how to participate in enforcement. Their actions are relatively independent of what other municipalities or counties in the region may be doing. Indeed, our survey results suggest that only a small handful of chiefs and sheriffs emulate immigration-policing practices from other localities in the area; instead, these practices are shaped much more by actors within their own agency or jurisdiction.[48] The decisions that localities make may well be more influenced by local political dynamics than by any objective "need" for enforcement.[49] Nor is there an effort to achieve any professional consensus among law-enforcement leaders in a particular metropolitan area regarding best practices.

The human implications of the current trend toward more frequent and formal local engagement in immigration enforcement are significant. Approximately 4 percent of the United States population, around eleven million people, lack legal status. Many of these individuals are members of families that also contain legal residents. Immigrant neighborhoods also tend to contain a mix of legal statuses. Enforcement efforts that target unauthorized immigrants also draw US citizens and legal permanent residents into intrusive contacts with the police. The enforcement effort may also be perceived as racist or haphazard because there is significant discretion at the individual level, and because police departments may operate in overlapping jurisdictions.[50] Supreme Court case law is unclear about the extent to which ethnic appearance can be used to guide law-enforcement decisions.[51] A 2007 survey conducted by the Pew Hispanic Center found that over half of all Latinos in the United States fear that they, or someone close to them, may be deported.[52] The policy patchwork means that no local government is in a position to allay that fear. Nor, under current devolutionary policy, can the federal government ensure that enforcement will protect the civil rights and liberties of American citizens and legal residents.

The federal government has remained largely silent regarding alleged abuses by its local law-enforcement partners in making immigration-related stops and arrests. Nor has the federal government responded forcefully when its local partners engage in "shadow immigration enforcement": using their regular policing powers to arrest suspected immigrants, with the knowledge that they will be screened for immigration violations once booked, as described in the Raleigh case study.[53] At the same time, the federal government has sometimes responded aggressively to local policies of nonenforcement, as in the New Haven case. This devolution of immigration enforcement to the local level, in combination with the federal government's own lack of consistent policy, has created a kind of nonpolicy policy in which there is no safe place for immigrants who lack secure legal status. The federal government has thus extended its reach, even as it has reduced its oversight.

In this chapter we have described the emerging immigration-enforcement policy patchwork and ruminated on its implications. In the following chapter, we draw on our survey data to consider what factors may influence local police agencies to take varying approaches to immigration enforcement. And while this chapter has addressed the *policy* patchwork, chapter 5 engages with yet another layer of complexity: the role of officer- and agency-level discretion in immigration enforcement, or in other words, the informal enforcement *practices* (as opposed to policies) that play a central role in law enforcement.

Going Their Own Way: Community Context and Its Influences on the Patchwork

Chapter 3 showed the wide variability in local policing practices and policies toward immigrants and immigration, and some of the consequences of interlocal differences. But *why* do these differences among counties and cities arise in the first place? Are they a function of variations in local conditions that are sometimes blamed on immigrants, such as high unemployment or crime rates? Are police practices toward unauthorized immigrants more lenient in communities where the local economy is heavily dependent on immigrant labor? Or perhaps, do local political sentiments, such as the relative share of liberals and conservatives in the electorate, shape how the police deal with immigrants?

A long vein of literature discusses the circumstances under which local governments are likely to be supportive of minorities or other marginalized local populations.[1] Until recently, however, there has been little research on what shapes local policy toward unauthorized immigrants. Unlike other minority groups, unauthorized immigrants are ineligible to vote, as are legal immigrants who have not yet naturalized. This lack of scholarly attention to the local politics of immigrants is beginning to change, although some of the recent studies focus on the state rather than local level. The emerging research tends to fall loosely into two camps. Some studies suggest that demographic change and tensions in "new immigrant destinations" are the most important determinants of the reception that unauthorized immigrants will receive.[2] Other research points to partisanship within the local electorate or to the opportunism of "restrictionist issue entrepreneurs."[3] At least one study indicates the importance of both demographic and partisan variables.[4] A handful of studies take a different approach, detailing the varied and often conflicting ways in which immigration politics and enforcement policies evolve at the state and local scale.[5]

Our research, with its focus on the practices of police toward immigrants, is more specific than some of the studies cited above, but, like many of them, we investigate the possible influence of both local demographics and local politics. Our surveys of police chiefs and sheriffs focused on decisions to detect and detain *unauthorized* immigrants. It should be noted, however, that legal permanent residents are also subject to potential deportation as a consequence of a variety of legal violations. Law-enforcement decisions involving immigrants cut a broad swath. These decisions may have life-altering implications, not just for immigrants, but also for citizens in households where there is a mixture of legal statuses.

Our surveys reveal wide variations in local immigration policing, as chapter 3 noted. We suspect that the patchwork of policing practices can be partly explained by the realities of law enforcement in a highly decentralized governmental system. With more than three thousand counties and nineteen thousand municipalities, local governance and local policing in the United States inevitably involves wide variation in local institutions, community demographics, and political cultures. The potential for variation, even within a single metropolitan area, was evident in the cities discussed in chapter 3 (Mesa, New Haven, and Raleigh). Those cases suggest why local governance is often described by scholars as "fragmented" or "polycentric," reflecting the dozens, even hundreds, of jurisdictions that claim authority over some piece of the metropolitan turf.[6] So, in one sense, it should be no surprise that when localities are given discretion over police interactions with immigrants, policing patterns will differ considerably from community to community, even within a particular state or metropolitan area.

State governments, of course, provide guidance and direction for—and sometimes serious constraints on—what local governments and local police can do.[7] Nevertheless, localities are not merely "creatures of the state" in responding to federal devolution of authority for immigration enforcement. Cities and counties are vital and active political units, with local election campaigns and, in larger jurisdictions, local media coverage that helps to create distinctive political dialogue, and sometimes controversy, about issues like immigration. Some communities lean liberal and some conservative, with potentially significant consequences for the messages that police receive about what types of enforcement approaches are expected. Local decision makers are influenced, too, by mixed signals from the legal system, professional organizations of police, and key interest groups, such as the business community and civil rights organizations.

The potential for significant variation *within* states suggests that the fifty states are in many respects the wrong level of analysis for understanding local immigrant policy making. This is particularly true with respect to decisions regarding the policing of unauthorized immigrants. States typically are only peripherally involved in funding police and sheriffs and in setting many of the policies that have the effect of welcoming or discouraging immigrants. Nor can state-level research tell us about the actual level of variation that is occurring within the state. In the patchwork phenomenon we are describing, much of the key variation occurs at the substate level.[8]

This chapter considers a basic, foundational set of factors arguably influential in determining local policing practices toward immigrants. Our focus here is on the local context, but on factors *outside* the police department (or sheriff's office) itself. (We will consider some of the internal organizational dynamics of police agencies in chaps. 5 and 6.) To preview, our findings suggest that some of the factors often assumed to increase the pressure for local immigration enforcement—factors such as rapid immigration into a community, high crime rates, or high unemployment—are *not* major influences on police practices.

The potential contextual influences that we consider include the following:

Legislative *policies* on immigrant-related topics promulgated by states and localities.

Two *community conditions* often thought to inflame attitudes toward immigration: unemployment and crime rates.

The local *economic base*, namely the relative importance to the community of industries that tend to employ immigrant workers.

Demographic factors, including the size of the community, its percentage of foreign-born residents, and the rapidity of ethnic change in the area.

The *political or electoral setting*, namely the relative strength of liberal and conservative leanings or Republican and Democratic voter sentiment in the area.

The locality's *proximity to the Mexican border.*

We address these potential influences one at a time, first describing why they might be important in shaping the activities of local police. Drawing on our survey results, we then assess whether there appears to be a connection with local immigration policing. We do not attempt a comprehensive "explanation" of interlocal variations in immigration policing here. Too many of these potential explanatory factors are themselves interconnected in causally complex ways to make such a project very useful. For instance, the demographic makeup and economic hardships of a community may influence the relative strength of the two parties locally, which in turn may help account for the presence or absence of immigration-related public policies in the city or county. Or to give another example, the economic base of the community likely influences the attractiveness of the locale as a magnet for new immigrants, authorized or unauthorized, thus affecting the rapidity of demographic change, which in turn might shape police practices toward immigrants. The potential ambiguity of the causal relationships involved suggests that we refrain from making strong claims about the various possible influences on immigration policing.[9]

Nevertheless, readers of this chapter will come away with a sense of what factors do and do not shape local police interactions with immigrants. We treat each of them as "suspects" that might move local policy in a more restrictionist or more immigrant-friendly direction. Although we will not be able to "convict" any one of these suspect factors beyond a reasonable doubt, the evidence will help to rule out certain potential influences and focus our attention on others. This chapter concentrates on quantitative evidence from our surveys of law-enforcement executives. Our case-study evidence, discussed in other chapters, augments these findings, enabling us to illuminate the "black box" of local decision making to show how various influences can become implicated in local immigration policing practices.

How We Measure Local Policing Practices Relevant to Immigrants

A key first task is to identify measures of local immigration policing that can serve as reasonable barometers of the priorities and practices of local police. We have found it most useful to focus on three sets of survey questions, the responses to which can serve as shorthand indicators of whether the police department or sheriff agency tends toward strict enforcement or toward a more lenient, immigrant-supportive stance.

The first is a measure of police-enforcement practices, which we call the *Enforcement Count* for short. We asked police chiefs and sheriffs about the circumstances under which their officers or deputies would investigate immigration status when encountering someone they believe might be in the country without authorization—typically someone the officer comes upon for other reasons. Such an escalation involves checking the person's immigration status or reporting them to Immigration and Customs Enforcement (ICE) (or both). This is the type of encounter that many immigrants, legal and unauthorized, have come to fear. The survey asked about seven scenarios that range widely in seriousness, from investigating traffic violations or questioning witnesses or victims, to violent crimes or parole violations (see the top portion of table 4.1).

The *Enforcement Count* can range from zero to seven for city police. This number is the sum of the situations in which respondents indicate that their officers would pursue immigration enforcement. Higher scores represent more aggressive immigration policing. In the sheriff questionnaire, we added a question, asking whether sheriff personnel typically check immigration status or contact ICE when booking a suspect into the county jail. By including the jail scenario, alongside the seven patrol-oriented situations, we arrived at an eight-point immigration enforcement count for sheriffs.[10] Although we lack direct evidence of what officers on the street are actually doing in the surveyed communities, the *Enforcement Count* represents the reports of chiefs or sheriffs about what they *believe* would be the typical practice in their organization when officers or deputies are involved in these situations. Prior research gives good reason to expect that when the chief or sheriff sends a clear message (written or unwritten) about what is expected of officer behavior, those further down the chain of command tend to follow that lead.[11]

Our two other measures of local immigration policing practices focus on survey responses that suggest whether the police department or sheriff unit has a positive or lenient perspective toward unauthorized immigrants. One survey question asked whether it was true of the respondent's agency that "We do *not* participate or assist in ICE immigration-enforcement activities." A "yes" response would tend to indicate a disinclination to engage in immigration policing. We label this measure *No ICE Participation.*[12]

Another survey item, although perhaps somewhat subjective, is quite pointed in inquiring about the agency's posture toward unauthorized immigrants. Respondents were asked to rate, on a five-point scale ranging from "strongly disagree" to "strongly agree," the prevailing view in their agency regarding whether "Gaining the trust of unauthorized immigrants is a priority for my department."[13] Those who gave a response of four or

TABLE 4.1 **Selected Measures of Local Policing Practices Relevant to Immigrants**

	Large-city police departments	Small-city police departments	Sheriff offices[a]
Agencies in which officers would check immigration status and/or report to ICE when encountering suspected unauthorized immigrant who is (%)[b]			
Arrested for a violent crime	87	87	89
Detained for parole violation or failure to appear in court	69	72	80
Arrested for domestic violence	64	66	81
Interviewed as a possible victim of human trafficking	59	54	59
Arrested for a nonviolent crime, with no prior record	51	45	67
Stopped for a traffic violation	21	23	27
Interviewed as crime victim, complainant, or witness	15	14	20
Booked into jail	NA	NA	87
Enforcement Count: No. of above scenarios enforced out of seven (for police departments) or eight (for sheriff offices; includes "booked into jail")	3.6	3.6	4.9
No ICE Participation: "We do *not* participate or assist in ICE immigration-enforcement activities" (% answering "Yes")	14	34	25
"Gaining the trust of unauthorized immigrants is a priority in my" police department/sheriff office (% who "Agree" or "Strongly agree")	52	36	30
Gaining Trust: Mean level of agreement with the statement above, from 1 ("Strongly disagree") to 5 ("Strongly agree")	3.5	3.1	3.1

Note: Items in italics are the three measures of police practices toward immigrants analyzed in chapter 4. ICE, Immigration and Customs Enforcement; NA, not applicable.

[a] Excludes the 9 percent of responding sheriff offices that have no responsibility for patrols and investigations outside of the jails, except for the "booked into the jail" response, which includes all responding sheriffs who have jail responsibilities.

[b] Percentages are calculated as the share of respondents who answered "check immigration status" or "report to ICE," or "both" for each situation. Denominator includes "don't know" responses, but excludes "not applicable" responses and refusals to answer.

five on what we will call the *Gaining Trust* item can be understood as indicating a view of unauthorized immigrants as legitimate members of the
community who are worthy of police concern.

We thus have three dependent variables to be analyzed in this chapter. One of these, the *Enforcement Count*, indicates a restrictive approach
toward immigrants, whereas the other two, *Gaining Trust* and *No ICE Participation*, are indicative of an immigrant-supportive philosophy of policing.
We now turn to the possible external influences on these police practices
and attitudes. We begin with the formal policies of the local government
where the police agency is located.

Do Local Government Policies Act as Constraints on Police Practices toward Immigrants?

Do local governments cue local police and sheriffs as to how they should
go about interacting with immigrants? In a formal organizational sense,
city police departments are administrative units of their municipal government, occupying boxes on an organizational chart similar to the fire department or the public works department. In many municipalities, police
departments are responsible to the elected mayor and city council. Other
communities have a council-manager system, more akin to the structure
of a corporate board of directors and appointed CEO. In the council-
manager form of government, an appointed, full-time executive, the city
manager, is juxtaposed between the city council and municipal departments such as the police department. (Mayors exist but lack true executive authority in council-manager cities.) In either arrangement, the city
council (sometimes called the board of aldermen, selectmen, or city commission) remains the lawmaking body.

The situation for *county sheriffs* is a bit more complicated. In nearly every US county, including 97 percent of those responding to our survey, the
sheriff is an elected position. This gives sheriffs an electoral legitimacy that
appointed municipal police chiefs lack. In essence, the sheriff functions as
an elected public official—a politician—but also as the administrator of
a key agency in county government. This is why we refer to sheriff *offices*,
in contrast to municipal police *departments*.[14] Nevertheless, sheriffs cannot
"make law," at least not in a formal sense; the county legislature makes law
for the county. The name of this legislative body varies across the fifty states:
county commission, county council, board of supervisors, or freeholders, for
example. We refer to it here as the "governing board."

We anticipate that when municipal and county governing boards cre-
ate policies regarding immigration enforcement, those policies will signifi-
cantly shape, although not totally determine, the posture of the local police
agency toward immigrants. A secondary expectation, given the electoral
independence of sheriffs from county governing boards, is that *county*
government policies will bear a weaker relationship to immigration polic-
ing practices than is the case for municipalities.

An important initial question is whether the local governing board
has developed any policy regarding law enforcement's role in detecting
and apprehending unauthorized immigrants. Through our surveys, it is
possible to distinguish five different types of such policies. On the most
immigrant-supportive end of the spectrum, very few localities have passed
what their law-enforcement executives considered "sanctuary" policies toward unauthorized immigrants. However, a larger percentage have "don't
ask, don't tell" policies regarding contacts with immigrants, in which police (and often other city personnel) are instructed not to ask about an individual's immigration status. Such policies are designed to promote open
communication between immigrant residents and city employees.

The form of these policies varies. Often the governing board adopts
an ordinance, but occasionally, the executive issues an order, as when former New York mayor Michael Bloomberg directed city workers not to
inquire about immigration status in the course of their duties.[15] On the
pro-enforcement side, possible responses to our survey question were either that the local governing board "encourages" police to collaborate
with federal immigration enforcement authorities, or that the governing
board expects police to take a "proactive approach in deterring unauthorized immigration in all activities."

Table 4.2 tabulates the results from the three surveys. At the midpoint,
we place those cities and counties where the chief or sheriff indicated that
there is no official local government policy toward immigration enforcement. Indeed, this "no-policy policy" is the most frequent response among
those answering the survey. Altogether, the five possible responses to the
survey question can be considered as an ordinal scale of immigration-
enforcement policies, ranging from sanctuary communities on the low end
to "proactive enforcement" communities on the high end. In this manner,
we constructed a five-point scale of local enforcement policy, with higher
values indicating a tougher posture toward immigrants.

For the most part, the relationships between local government policy
and our three measures of local immigration policing are statistically significant (see table 4.3).[16] These relationships fall in the anticipated direction,

TABLE 4.2 **Policy of Local Government toward Immigration Enforcement According to Police Chief or Sheriff**

	Large-city police departments, %	Small-city police departments, %	Sheriff offices, %
Openly-declared "sanctuary" community for unauthorized immigrants who are not engaged in criminal activities	3.8	2.1	1.6
"Don't ask, don't tell" policy regarding unauthorized immigrants who are not involved in serious crime	15.0	10.6	7.5
No official policy vis-à-vis unauthorized immigrants	47.0	62.9	53.9
Encourages police/sheriff to participate with federal authorities in controlling certain kinds of crime associated with unauthorized immigration	17.5	6.8	11.0
Expects police/sheriff to take a proactive role in deterring unauthorized immigration in all activities	11.5	9.7	13.4

Note: Columns do not sum to 100 percent due to "not sure" responses.

TABLE 4.3 **Correlations between Strictness of Local Government Immigration Policy (Five-Point Scale) and Measures of Police Practices**

	Large cities	Small cities	Sheriffs
Enforcement Count	.34***	.13*	.10
No ICE Participation	−.29***	−.11	−.13*
Gaining Trust	−.15**	−.15**	.13*

Note: ICE, Immigration and Customs Enforcement.
* $p < .10$.
** $p < .05$.
*** $p < .01$.

with police and sheriffs tending to follow the lead of the local governing body. Of interest, however, are the differences regarding the aggressiveness of immigration enforcement between cities and counties. In large and small cities, when the municipality has a more enforcement-oriented policy stance, the *Enforcement Count* is indeed higher—that is, police tend to check immigration status in more of the seven possible situations that chiefs were asked about (see fig. 4.1). County government policies on immigration, on the other hand, do not seem to influence what county sheriffs report as the typical behavior of their personnel when they encounter immigrants. This is probably a reflection of the much greater political independence that elected sheriffs enjoy compared to that of appointed city police chiefs.

This pattern also holds with our question about the importance of *gaining the trust* of unauthorized immigrants. In cities (both large and small) with enforcement-oriented municipal policies, police chiefs are less likely to indicate an interest among their officers in gaining the trust of immigrants. When city councils desire to crack down on unauthorized residents, in other words, police tend to be less interested in gaining the confidence of these residents. Here again, however, sheriff offices are an exception. Where the county governing board has taken an enforcement-oriented stance, the sheriff is more likely to report an inclination to try to *enhance* the trust of unauthorized immigrants among their personnel. This inverse

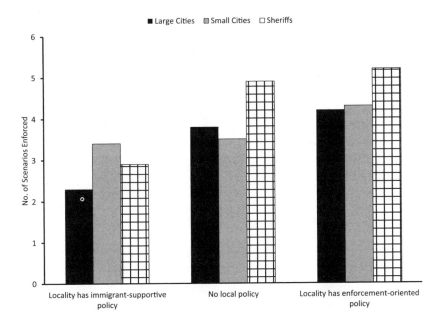

FIGURE 4.1. Mean *Enforcement Count*, by type of local government policy.
Chart shows the mean number of scenarios in which police or sheriff personnel would check immigration status or report a suspected unauthorized immigrant to Immigration and Customs Enforcement. This *Enforcement Count* variable is of a possible seven scenarios for large and small cities, and eight possible scenarios for sheriff offices (including "booked into jail"). Only full-service sheriff offices (those who both patrol communities and supervise jails) are included in the analysis.

relationship between policy and practice is statistically significant, but substantively rather weak.

Regarding the third measure of immigration-policing practices, *No ICE Participation*, there are again fairly strong indications that the behavior of law enforcement tends to align with local government policy. In both large cities and counties where the local government favors immigration enforcement, chiefs and sheriffs tend to say that their police agencies cooperate with ICE. (The relationship is not statistically significant in the case of small cities.) Pro-enforcement, rather than the anti-enforcement, local governments drive this relationship. In other words, where the local governing board has passed policies emphasizing enforcement, chiefs and sheriffs are very unlikely to say they have *No ICE Participation*, but localities with immigrant-supportive policies are not appreciably different in their level of cooperation with ICE than those that have no policy at all. All in all, then, how local police deal with immigrants corresponds fairly substantially, albeit not overwhelmingly, to the posture of the local governing body toward unauthorized immigration. For the most part, this correspondence is closer for large cities than for county sheriffs, who are organizationally more distant from their county governing boards.

Do State Government Policies toward Immigrants Similarly Affect Local Policing?

Municipal police and county sheriff personnel are employees of their local government, not of the state government. Nevertheless, there are at least three reasons to suspect that the policy posture of the state government toward immigrants and immigration also may influence how local police handle the immigration issue. First, local law-enforcement officers are also de facto state peace officers; they enforce state as well as local laws. Indeed, most criminal laws and penalties are defined at the state level. Thus, leaders of police departments may look to the state level for guidance and may view their agencies as part of a statewide system of criminal justice.

Second, state politics and local politics, and the controversies each evokes, are not hermetically sealed off from one another. Local controversies over immigration can prompt state-level legislative activity. Similarly, controversy over immigration in state politics may reverberate in local political contexts as well. Thus, we anticipate that where state governments have been particularly active and punitive with respect to unauthorized immigrants, local police are more likely to take a hard line.

Third, and perhaps most significantly, states ultimately have controlling legal authority over what municipal and county governments can and cannot do, or must do. Under the American legal doctrine known as Dillon's Rule, state law defines the powers and limits of local governments.[17] Some state constitutions allow local governments a substantial degree of home rule, but state law nevertheless determines their right to exist. (The US Constitution makes no mention at all of local governments or their privileges, effectively ceding the question to the states.) With respect to immigration policy, some states have taken actions to limit the discretion of their local governments, for example, by prohibiting the use of local funds for hiring centers for day laborers. More to the point, some states have directly instructed local police agencies on issues of unauthorized immigration.

State instructions may run in pro- or anti-enforcement directions. For example, as discussed in chapter 2, Arizona's SB 1070 and copycat laws in other states attempted to require local police to check the legal status of persons officers encounter whom the officer suspects could be in violation of immigration law, effectively overruling local "don't ask, don't tell" policies. These enforcement mandates have encountered numerous court challenges, but none include challenges to the principle of state power over municipal policing policies. By contrast, California and a few other states have instructed local law enforcement not to ask about immigrants' legal status except under certain limited circumstances. Some states also attempted to limit the scope of the now-defunct Secure Communities program in county jails. Attorneys general in some states have also provided guidance, often taken as legally binding, about the circumstances under which purported immigration violations may or may not be investigated. As we described in chapter 3, local governments are sometimes seriously at odds with their state governments about these attempts to prescribe or proscribe local immigrant-related policy. Nevertheless it is fair to say that, when state governments want to play a role, they can effectively exert some control over certain aspects of local immigration policing.

Chapter 2 described the explosion of state-level legislation on immigration-related topics in the 2000s. Recall figure 3.1 in chapter 3, which shows the number of years in which each state passed anti-immigrant legislation between 2005 and 2013. We have used the same source of information, the annual compendium of state immigration legislation compiled by

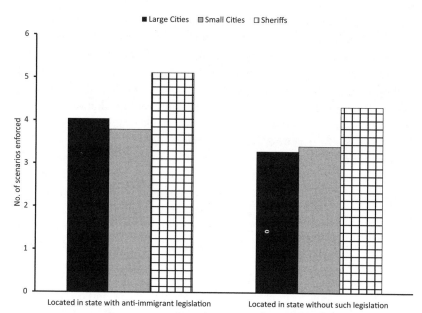

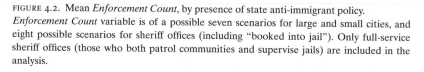

FIGURE 4.2. Mean *Enforcement Count*, by presence of state anti-immigrant policy. *Enforcement Count* variable is of a possible seven scenarios for large and small cities, and eight possible scenarios for sheriff offices (including "booked into jail"). Only full-service sheriff offices (those who both patrol communities and supervise jails) are included in the analysis.

the National Council of State Legislatures (NCSL), to derive a straightforward measure of the policy posture of each state. For this analysis we distinguish between states that did, and did not, enact at least one law restricting benefits or privileges for all immigrants, or for broad classes of immigrants, in the period leading up to our survey.[18] We anticipate that local police departments and sheriff offices will be somewhat more aggressive with respect to immigration violations in states that have recently adopted anti-immigrant legislation. Such legislation is part of the overall political environment that confronts police and sheriffs as they decide how to handle possible immigration-law violators.

Bivariate correlations suggest that there is indeed some connection between state anti-immigrant legislation and a high *Enforcement Count* (see fig. 4.2). Large-city police departments and county sheriff offices tend to engage in more investigation of immigration status violations in states that recently passed such policies, to the tune of about 0.7–0.8 additional scenarios on the *Enforcement Count* scale. (Both relationships are statistically significant at the $p < .05$ level or better.) The relationship is smaller in size, and statistically insignificant, among the small-city police departments.

However, for our two measures of pro-immigrant police practices—*No ICE Participation* and *Gaining Trust*—there is very little evidence of a relationship with state policy, at least in the way we have measured state policy here. Only in the case of large cities is there a statistically significant, negative correlation (a relatively modest –.13) between state anti-immigrant policy and the chief's agreement with the survey statement that "we do not participate or assist in ICE immigration-enforcement activities." It is possible that anti-immigrant politics at the state level constrain any inclination that big-city police departments might have to take a hands-off policy toward immigration violations. In regard to the *Gaining Trust* measure, however, the "effect" of state legislation on the perception of chiefs and sheriffs regarding the importance of gaining the trust of unauthorized immigrants is effectively zero, and not statistically significant in any case. *Gaining Trust* is more likely to reflect a local philosophy of policing, which is less easily controlled by the state than are the more direct operations of local police, such as enforcement practices.

Do High Unemployment and Crime Rates Lead to More Punitive Immigration Policing Practices?

Next we expand the circle of what constitutes the "local context" of policing, moving beyond official state and local policies to consider broader community conditions. A common fear often expressed among native-born Americans is that unauthorized immigrants are "taking our jobs." Particularly during economic downturns, immigrants can easily be framed as a low-wage labor force that successfully competes for scarce jobs once held by native-born residents.[19] It is also frequently alleged that by their illegal residence in the United States, unauthorized immigrants are criminals or have criminal tendencies. There is a widespread assumption, despite strong evidence to the contrary, that immigrants engage in high levels of criminal behavior.[20] These beliefs might be expected to create negative sentiment toward immigration in communities that are experiencing high crime or high unemployment. The popular anxieties, in turn, might provoke the local government and police personnel into punitive policing practices toward newcomers, or be used as a pretext by local politicians or police who want to pursue restrictionist policies.

We find almost no evidence in our data for the hypothesis that local unemployment generates harsher immigration policing. To examine this question, we first obtained estimates of the local unemployment rate from the Census Bureau's American Community Survey for each of the cities and counties that responded to our surveys. In none of the bivariate analyses was there a significant and positive association between the unemployment rate and the degree of restrictiveness in policing practices toward immigrants. In fact, among the small cities, there were significant associations running in the opposite direction, with police chiefs in cities with high unemployment tending to give lower estimates of the *Enforcement Count* and expressing a greater desire to *Gain Trust*.

What about the notion that immigration policing is a response to crime problems? We were able to obtain the violent crime rate for all but a handful of our localities from the FBI's Uniform Crime Reports. Here again, there is virtually no evidence of a connection between crime rates and policing practices. The only exception is among sheriffs, who were less likely to say they had *No ICE Participation* in counties with high crime rates.

It appears, then, that neither crime nor economic malaise is what is motivating tougher immigration policing. These purportedly "objective" conditions in local communities, our evidence suggests, have less impact on how police interact with immigrants than many observers have assumed.

Does Economic Dependence on Immigrant Labor Affect Local Policing Practices?

One might reasonably suspect that the economic contribution of immigrants to a community will affect whether they are welcomed there or treated with special scrutiny. Particular sectors of private industry in some cities and counties have come to depend heavily on immigrant labor. If the industry in question plays a central role in the local economy, then business leaders and elected officials alike might fear the potential economic repercussions of police crackdowns on unauthorized immigrants. Learning to live with newcomers, and indeed perhaps actively integrating them into the community life, might allow the local economy to keep humming along.

Very few systematic studies have considered whether the economic role of immigrants affects local policies relating to immigrants.[21] There is, however, a long vein of academic literature suggesting that business interests play an outsized, if not hegemonic, role in local public affairs, and that local politicians are especially solicitous of business.[22] One hypothesis, then, is that elected officials, and perhaps business leaders themselves, would prevail on the local police agency to avoid targeting or frightening immigrant laborers if the local economy depends heavily on immigrant labor. A countervailing hypothesis, however, holds that the presence of many industries that are attractive to immigrant labor will lead to demographic changes that cause anxiety on the part of native-born workers, who feel their jobs are threatened by competition from immigrants. Populist sentiment might then lead police to be more enforcement-oriented in their interactions with immigrants.[23]

A major challenge in exploring such hypotheses, as in other elements of local public affairs, involves data limitations. It is sometimes possible for knowledgeable observers to identify specific industries or firms in particular cities that rely heavily on immigrant labor (see chap. 6 for examples of this in two communities). Confidentiality restrictions on government-collected employment statistics, however, mean that researchers cannot access detailed data on specific industrial clusters, let alone individual firms in particular localities. We have dealt with these problems by relying on data about local employment in broad industrial classifications that are known to disproportionately rely on immigrant labor.

According to immigration policy analyst Audrey Singer, immigrant workers are overrepresented in certain sectors: private household employment, accommodations, warehousing, agriculture, food services, construction, and management and administration.[24] The last-named sector, however, tends to employ high-skilled immigrants, who are not especially relevant to our investigation of the policing of unauthorized immigrants. Additionally, household employment is so decentralized that it can scarcely be thought of as an "industry" in local political economies.[25] As a consequence we omitted these two categories from our analysis. Using the 2007–11 American Community Survey, we tallied the percentage of all workers in the particular city or county who toiled in the following four sectors, which Singer's work suggests are heavy users of low-skilled immigrant labor:

Agriculture, forestry, fishing, and mining
Construction
Manufacturing
Arts, entertainment, recreation, accommodation, and food services.[26]

Surprisingly, we find no clear evidence that the percentage of local employment in these sectors has any particular connection to immigration policing. Whether we add together the percentage of the local workforce engaged in these industries, or look at the industries individually, we generally do not observe any significant correlation with our three measures of police practices. There is some limited evidence among the small-city police chiefs that a heavier presence of these industries (most specifically, agriculture) leads to a greater prioritization of *Gaining (the) Trust* of unauthorized immigrants.[27] The large-city departments and county sheriffs, however, do not show any such tendency. Moreover, there are some contrary relationships between construction employment and immigration policing: Small-city departments are more likely to participate in federal enforcement activities (i.e., to answer "no" on *No ICE Participation*) in communities where employment in construction is proportionally high.[28] And among sheriff offices, the *Enforcement Count* tends to be higher in counties with high levels of construction employment.[29]

Post hoc, one might propose elaborate explanations for these relationships between the economic structure of a community and its immigration policing. For instance, it is conceivable that immigrant labor in local "export" industries, such as agriculture, is more valued than immigrant labor in local-serving industries, such as construction. Setting aside these complex possible interpretations, however, our overall reading of the bivariate evidence suggests that local industrial structure is not a leading suspect in accounting for harsh (or supportive) immigration policing. This is an area that remains ripe for future research.[30] Our multivariate analysis at the end of this chapter will allow us to consider the role of the industry structure of localities while holding constant for other, potentially related factors.

Does a Community's Size Matter?

Big-city governments and their police agencies may be different creatures, politically and organizationally, than the same agencies in small jurisdictions. Large cities typically have higher percentages of minority residents and higher proportions of Democratic voters than smaller communities. There are also potentially significant differences in policy orientations between large and small communities.[31] Larger local governments often are more active in policy development than smaller localities and have more staff capacity to develop new types of policies. Larger places also tend to have more interest groups and activists of various stripes, sometimes creating pressure for new policies or administrative approaches toward issues such as immigration enforcement or immigrant integration.

There is a high correspondence between the size of the local population and the size of its police agency.[32] For example, among the full-service sheriff offices in our sample, the correlation between county population size and the number of sworn officers is very close ($r = 0.94$). One consequence of this for immigration policing is that bigger communities will have more bureaucratic, and perhaps more professionalized, police agencies. Police chiefs in larger communities are probably more likely to have been hired in competitive, national searches.[33] They thereby may bring more cosmopolitan perspectives to bear on immigration-policing issues and may be more versed in community-policing reforms that stress the importance of opening up a dialogue with all sectors of the community. There is support for this notion from our survey evidence. We asked chiefs and sheriffs whether they used each of eleven different types of community-policing techniques (e.g., bike patrols, regular neighborhood meetings, and community advisory boards). Population size is a highly significant predictor of the number of such techniques used for agencies in all three samples.

The situation is perhaps not quite as clear in the case of elected sheriffs. Counties with larger populations may tend to encourage more active and politicized campaigning for the sheriff office. Depending on political dynamics in the county, these campaign dynamics might push the sheriff's office in either a restrictionist or a lenient direction on immigration issues. Of interest, our data reveal a positive correlation between the size of the county's population and the likelihood that the sheriff identifies as a member of a minority group. Sheriffs from large counties also report a higher percentage of nonwhite deputies.

Given the different policymaking and organizational dynamics in bigger jurisdictions, we anticipated that the population size of cities and counties would be associated with a more immigrant-supportive style of policing. For the most part, results of the bivariate analysis support this expectation.[34] Larger jurisdictions within all three survey samples have significantly lower scores on the *Enforcement Count*, although the relationship is a bit weaker for city police departments than for county sheriffs. To make these relationships more concrete, consider cities in the large-city sample of greater than 250,000 population compared to those at the low end, with fewer than 75,000 residents. The former group enforces an average of 2.9 of the seven scenarios we asked about, whereas the latter group enforces an average of 3.6. Among sheriff offices, the quartile with the largest populations (over 409,000) enforces an average of one fewer scenario than the quartile with the smallest populations (under 43,500).

In addition, in both the large- and small-city samples, local population size is a strong predictor of the chief's level of agreement with *Gaining Trust*.[35] Among each sample of cities, the largest-population quartile averaged about 0.3–0.4 points higher on the five-point scale of agreement with the statement that "gaining the trust of unauthorized immigrants is a priority" for the police department. Overall, then police agencies in large jurisdictions tend to be more immigrant supportive; that is, they are less likely to investigate migrants' legal status and are more interested in gaining the trust of unauthorized residents.

Does a High Proportion of Immigrants Make for More Supportive Policing Practices? Does Rapid Demographic Transition Chill the Atmosphere?

Beyond its sheer size, does the demographic composition of the local population affect how its police force treats immigrants? The relative share of foreign-born residents within the local population, for example, could affect the way police view the immigration issue in several ways. However, one might not expect all these influences to work in the same direction.

On the one hand, a large proportion of immigrants might mean a relatively large number of *unauthorized* immigrants, which could provoke more enforcement. These newcomers might be perceived as a threateningly large proportion of the populace, inspiring nativist sentiments. But, on the other hand, where a large share of the local population is foreign born, local government representatives, including the police, might be more inclined to accept the immigrants as legitimate members of the community, which could lead to more welcoming or lenient practices. There could also be a sense of the inevitable when there are large numbers of immigrants: Local police leaders simply might view restrictionist practices toward immigrants as futile in the face of a very large foreign-born population.

There is also a political dimension to the proportion of immigrants in a locality. Although noncitizen immigrants cannot vote, some of them are likely to have extended families with US citizen members who vote in local elections. These and other citizen coethnics may exert political pressure on local governments to refrain from enforcement and to pursue integrative practices.

Our evidence is consistent with this hypothesis. Bigger immigrant populations, by and large, work in favor of supportive policing practices, par-

TABLE 4.4 **Correlations between Immigrant Percentage of Local Population and Measures of Police Practices**

	Large cities	Small cities	Sheriffs
Enforcement Count	$-.34^{***}$	$-.26^{***}$	$-.11$
No ICE Participation	$.16^{**}$	$-.11^{*}$	$.02$
Gaining Trust	$.22^{***}$	$.18^{***}$	$.18^{**}$

Note: ICE, Immigration and Customs Enforcement.
$^{*} p < .10.$
$^{**} p < .05.$
$^{***} p < .01.$

ticularly among large cities (see table 4.4). Large and small cities with high shares of immigrants tend to have a significantly lower *Enforcement Count* than do cities with low shares of immigrants. The differences are substantial. Police departments in large cities in the top quartile of immigrant composition (21.4 percent foreign born or more) enforce an average of about 2.8 of the seven scenarios we asked about, whereas departments that are in the lowest quartile (less than 7.4 percent foreign born) enforce a much higher 4.7 out of seven.

Regarding *No ICE Participation*, our results are more mixed. Among large cities, those with high shares of immigrants have police departments that are more likely to avoid cooperation with ICE, but the opposite is true of small-city departments, where those with high shares of immigrants tend toward cooperation with the federal agency. On the other hand, the results are clear-cut with respect to *Gaining Trust*: Large- and small-city departments, as well as county sheriff offices, are all more likely to prioritize gaining the trust of unauthorized immigrants when immigrants are a large share of the local population. Familiarity, then, does not seem to breed contempt. On the contrary, the heavy presence of immigrants seems to be accompanied by recognition among law-enforcement leaders that their officers must learn to serve and communicate with newcomers.

One possible concern about these results is that they are not specific regarding the ethnic background of the local immigrants. If Latino immigrants are a more racialized category than Eastern European or Asian immigrants, for example, then patterns of policing may vary based more on the local ethnic makeup than on the simple share of foreign-born residents. On the other hand, as noted above, communities with high percentages of Latinos may well have a political proxy group—nonimmigrant Latinos—who may advocate on behalf of immigrant Latinos and vote with their interests in mind. Taking this concern into account, we reexamined the relationship between ethnicity and immigration policing, but focused instead on the percentage of *Latinos* in the local population rather than the percentage of *immigrants* (although the two variables are quite highly correlated). All the significant relationships reported in table 4.4 were still evident, except that *No ICE Participation* was not significantly correlated with the percentage of Latinos in the large-city sample.

It is also reasonable to wonder whether the current size of the foreign-born or ethnic-minority population is less important than a rapid *increase* in the share of immigrants when it comes to inciting a sense of political threat among native-born residents and perhaps also among politicians.[36] Such threat, perhaps induced by the seeming instability or demographic turnover of the population, might lead, in turn, to more restrictive immigration policing.

Our examination of the bivariate data, however, lends no credence to this argument. We examined the percentage-point change in the share of Latinos in the population of each city or county in the period since 1990. It is not unusual to find cities and counties where the Latino share of the population has doubled or tripled since 1990, or even where Latinos have gone from a relatively small percentage of the population to a numerical majority. If there were a backlash effect from such rapid change, it would be likely to provoke more punitive policing practices. But there is little evidence of this. Most of the relationships between the growth in the Latino share of the population and our policing measures are statistically insignificant. And where the associations are significant, they are primarily in the "wrong" (i.e., unanticipated) direction.

These results generally parallel those for the percentage of immigrants or of Latinos in the population at the time of our surveys. For instance, among cities both large and small, greater increases in the Latino percentage of the population are associated with a lower, not higher, *Enforcement Count*. Indeed, police departments in the quartile of cities with the most rapid increase in the percentage of Latinos tend to enforce about 0.75–1.0 fewer scenarios of the possible seven than police in the quartile of cities with the least increase (see fig. 4.3).[37] By the same token, among the large cities, police departments express more commitment to *Gaining Trust* of unauthorized immigrants in situations where the city has experienced a rapid increase in the Latino share of the population.

In short, then, the evidence suggests that police agencies tend to be more supportive of immigrants as the share of immigrants and Latinos

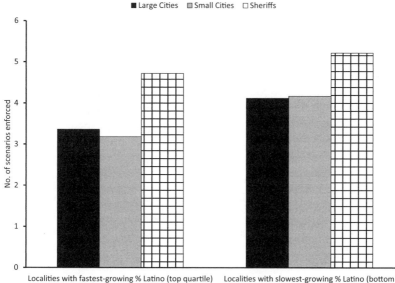

FIGURE 4.3. Mean *Enforcement Count*, by increase in Hispanic population since 1990. "Top quartile" and "bottom quartile" is in reference to the cities or counties responding to each of the three surveys. *Enforcement Count* variable is of a possible seven scenarios for large and small cities, and eight possible scenarios for sheriff offices (including "booked into jail"). Only full-service sheriff offices (those who both patrol communities and supervise jails) are included in the analysis.

in the local population gets larger. Contrary to the notion of rapid demographic change roiling relations among local groups, police agencies in rapidly diversifying communities are less enforcement oriented, perhaps because they are trying to win the trust of newcomers to the community. This might be because of the increasing political weight of Latino voters, or it may simply reflect a desire to better serve the new residents, who often are prone to crime victimization.[38]

Is Immigration Policing Different in Politically Left- and Right-Leaning Communities?

Police practices toward immigrants likely reflect not only local demographics but also local politics. Among the general American public and

political elites alike, conservative ideology and Republican party identification increasingly have been linked to restrictive attitudes and policy
preferences regarding immigration, and unauthorized immigration in particular.[39] Although political entrepreneurs of any persuasion might promote certain narratives about immigrants, most of the loudest voices in
favor of greater restrictions on immigrants and immigration in recent years
have been conservatives and/or Republicans, often associated with the Tea
Party wing of that party. In accordance with these tendencies, a few studies of immigrant-related policies at the state and local level have found
that the measures of partisanship help to explain variations in policy, with
Republican-leaning jurisdictions taking a more restrictionist course. However, the issue remains unsettled in the small literature on the topic.[40]

We explored whether the political leanings of the cities and counties
in our dataset were associated with police practices toward immigrants.
Complicating such investigations at the city level, however, has long been
a lack of available data. Although county-level information on voting in
presidential elections is widely available, no uniform national repository
of municipal-level party registration, election results, or public opinion exists. Many analysts have thus been forced to rely on the county-level presidential election data to characterize the political leanings of cities, a practice that can introduce considerable measurement error, particularly for
those municipalities that comprise only a small proportion of their county's
electorate.[41] Fortunately, in a 2013 study, two political scientists introduced
an innovative way to estimate the ideological leanings of various geographic
units. The authors published standardized estimates of the ideological
placement of all US cities of twenty-five thousand or higher population, on
a left/right scale in which higher values represent more conservative public
opinion.[42] These estimates of local conservatism are available for all the
large cities that responded to our survey and for about half the small cities.
For counties in our sheriff dataset, we simply rely on the percentage Republican vote (of the two-party total) in the closely fought 2004 presidential
election.

When it comes to judging whether politics affects policing practices,
the *Enforcement Count* is perhaps the best measure of police departments
putting their money where their (local electorate's) mouth is, since it represents the aggressiveness with which they look for and investigate unauthorized immigrants. Our measures of local conservatism are associated
in clear and convincing fashion with the *Enforcement Count*. The relationships are not only statistically significant, but the magnitude of these

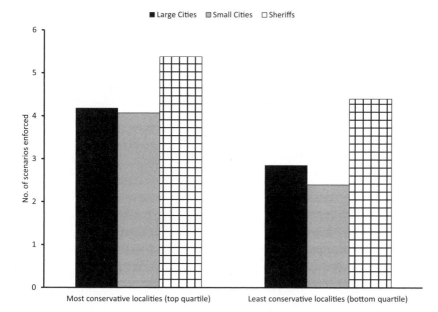

FIGURE 4.4. Mean *Enforcement Count*, by political leanings of local population.
"Top quartile" and "bottom quartile" is in reference to the cities or counties responding to each of the three surveys. For large and small cities, conservatism is measured using the municipal-level estimates of public opinion from Chris Tausanovitch and Christopher Warshaw, "Measuring Constituent Policy Preferences in Congress, State Legislatures, and Cities," *Journal of Politics* 75:2 (2013): 330–42. Conservatism data are unavailable for small cities with populations below twenty-five thousand. For sheriffs, conservatism is measured using the county-level percentage Republican of the two-party vote for president in 2004. *Enforcement Count* variable is of a possible seven scenarios for large and small cities, and eight possible scenarios for sheriff offices (including "booked into jail"). Only full-service sheriff offices (those who both patrol communities and supervise jails) are included in the analysis.

relationships is large (see fig. 4.4).[43] Thus, on average, police are considerably more likely to crack down on suspected unauthorized immigrants in localities where the public leans conservative.

However, the survey data are much less clear on whether the political leanings of cities and counties have a broader impact on police agencies' commitments regarding immigrants. Political leanings do not show any significant influence on the reported desire of police agencies to *Gain Trust* of unauthorized immigrants; this is true for cities large and small and for sheriff offices as well. Police departments in conservative large cities are, as anticipated, less likely to report that they have *No ICE Participation* than their counterparts in liberal large cities. However, this relationship is not statistically significant among the small-city departments or the sheriff offices.

At the street level, however, where officers decide when to detain or question someone they encounter who has questionable legal status, there is a clear relationship between local political leanings and the reported degree of enforcement. It appears, then, that political sentiment may spill over beyond election campaigns and the posturing of politicians to shape the style of immigration policing. This might occur because conservative public opinion and politicians place more pressure on police to engage in immigration enforcement, or because law enforcement personnel in conservative localities are themselves more likely to hold conservative views on immigration.

Borderland Anxieties?

Beyond local policies, local politics, and a community's internal conditions, some police contend with a broader geographic context that may affect the way they approach interactions with immigrants. One of these contextual elements relates to the proximity of the national land border with Mexico. The southern parts of California, Arizona, New Mexico, and Texas have long histories of interactions with Mexico, dating to the days when these regions were part of Mexico. The border separated, and continues to separate, many binational extended families, where parents, siblings, or cousins may live on opposite sides and travel across to visit or to work.

The Latino share of the population tends to be substantial in most border communities. Moreover, in many cases Latinos have long been important political players and voting blocs in these areas. Many local law-enforcement officers in the US border region are themselves Latino; some are immigrants. For all these reasons, one might thus expect a fairly welcoming, tolerant, or lenient posture toward unauthorized immigrants among local police departments located along or near the border. Our case study of El Paso in chapter 6 provides vivid illustration of these points.

At the same time, there are countervailing pressures. Border regions have become a flash point in America's immigration controversies. In some cases local incidents in these regions have inflamed anti-immigrant sentiment. The rise in narco-trafficking and criminal gangs in Mexico, often in areas close to the United States, could potentially incline police in border communities to adopt a stricter posture toward newcomers. The proximity of US Border Patrol agents may be an additional factor encouraging enforcement. The Border Patrol has jurisdiction within a hundred-mile radius of the national border. Local police departments in this area are likely to have a quicker and bureaucratically smoother interaction with federal immigration authorities than in other parts of the nation. Significant experience with illegal border crossing in the area also likely means that police and sheriffs in border areas have procedures in place to deal with unauthorized migrants and to communicate with federal authorities.

Are local police practices regarding immigration highly distinctive in the border region? Here we define "border region" as including counties and municipalities that lie within two hundred linear miles of the Mexican border.[44] Forty of the large-city police departments responding to our survey, as well as seventeen small cities and twenty-four county sheriff offices lie in this area (i.e., a range of from 7 percent to 17 percent of each sample). The fairly small number of border-area agencies in our dataset means that their distinctiveness needs to be fairly pronounced to achieve statistical significance.

The data indicate that local immigration policing in the border region does not appear to be especially distinctive, at least with regard to our three measures of police practices. The *Enforcement Count* is slightly lower for agencies in the border region than elsewhere for all three types of jurisdictions (large cities, small cities, and sheriff offices), but the differences are not statistically significant in any case. Nor is the likelihood of *No ICE Participation* significantly different between border and nonborder agencies. The only significant relationship we found is that sheriff offices in the border region are considerably more likely to report that they seek to gain the trust of unauthorized immigrants than are their counterparts in the rest of the country (with average *Gaining Trust* scores of 3.7 and 2.9, respectively). This suggests that for county sheriffs, finding ways to communicate with and encourage the trust of unauthorized immigrants are more prominent concerns near the border, where a substantial portion of the local population are immigrants without papers. For large- and small-city police departments, however, the differences between border and nonborder respondents on the *Gaining Trust* measure are insignificant.[45]

Putting It All Together

To this point in the chapter, we have examined, in isolation from one another, a variety of contextual factors that might shape police interactions with immigrants. In this section, we take an integrated approach, describing the results of multivariate analyses. This type of statistical model allows us to estimate the relationship between each local characteristic and immigration policing, *while holding each of the other contextual factors constant.* Doing so allows for a more careful and systematic determination of which characteristics of cities and counties are linked to immigration policing practices. The tables detailing the results may be found in the appendix. We summarize the key findings here.

We once again consider our three "outcomes" of interest: the *Enforcement Count*, the reported level of interest in *Gaining the Trust* of unauthorized immigrants, and the reports of chiefs or sheriffs as to whether there is *No ICE Participation* by their agency.[46] The multivariate models include as independent (predictor) variables all the "suspects" we have described thus far:

Policy of the city or county governing board regarding immigration enforcement
Presence of state anti-immigration legislation
Local unemployment rate
Violent crime rate
Percentage of employment in the key immigrant-employing sectors related to agriculture, construction, manufacturing, and accommodations
Population size
Percentage of foreign-born residents
Growth in the percentage of Latinos in the locality since 1990
Political conservatism, either the measure of local public opinion (for cities) or the percentage of Republican presidential voting (for counties)
Border proximity (the indicator of localities that lie less than two hundred miles from Mexico).

We again examine big cities, small cities, and county sheriff offices separately.[47] For the small cities, our sample size is unfortunately limited to those communities for which conservatism scores were available (generally those of populations above twenty-five thousand). Because this missing data problem causes us to lose a significant number of cases among the small cities, we primarily focus on the results regarding the large cities and the county sheriffs.

Regarding the *Enforcement Count*, the clearest finding, at least among municipalities, is that the stance that the mayor and council take toward immigration has an important bearing on police enforcement. Where elected city officials have instructed police to be more aggressive in seeking out immigration-law violators, the police (according to their chief) tend to investigate legal status in a greater number of situations in which they encounter immigrants, other things being equal. This relationship is statistically significant for large- and small-city departments alike, but not for sheriff agencies. We suspect, as noted earlier, that this is because sheriffs are elected independently, and thus may be less likely to take cues or direction from county legislators owing to their own base of political power.

A second finding of note in the multivariate analysis concerns the political leanings of the community. For our (limited) sample of small cities, as well as among the sheriffs, more conservative or Republican-leaning populations are associated with higher levels of enforcement. This relationship lacks statistical significance among the large cities. However, it is possible that conservatism also operates indirectly, by influencing city government policy, a point that we return to below.

Thirdly, among *large cities*, enforcement tends to be less aggressive where the proportion of immigrants is high. In a similar vein, in *counties* where the share of Latinos grew considerably after 1990, sheriff offices also tend to have a lower *Enforcement Count*. These findings once again suggest that the diversification of the population does not increase the tendency of police to go after possible immigration-law violators, but rather reduces that tendency.

The multivariate results for the *Gaining Trust* variable are harder to interpret. Among large cities, a more restrictionist policy toward immigrants on the part of the mayor and council is associated, perhaps not surprisingly, with less interest among police in *Gaining Trust*. Among sheriff offices, oddly, the estimated results, although statistically weaker, suggest the opposite: Counties with restrictive policies promulgated by their governing boards tend to have sheriffs who report *more* interest in *Gaining Trust*. The only other variables of possible importance for *Gaining Trust* are population size and proximity to the Mexican border. Large population size appears to increase the perceived desire among big-city police to *Gain Trust*, while close proximity to the border inclines sheriff offices to try to gain trust. Borderland counties, of course, frequently tend to have heavy immigrant populations, a significant number of whom lack legal status. Thus, for sheriffs in border counties, the desire for smooth community relations may lead them to work to increase the level of trust among unauthorized residents.

We turn next to the models for *No ICE Participation*. What contextual

factors influence whether police cooperate with raids and other enforcement activities launched by Immigrations and Customs Enforcement?
Once again, the local government's policy stance is key. Where the local governing board has adopted a more restrictionist position, the police
chief or sheriff is significantly less likely to report noncooperation with
ICE. This is true for large cities, small cities, and sheriff offices alike. For
the cities, no other factors have any clear relationship with *No ICE Participation* when controlling for all the other variables.

Among county sheriffs, where there may be more opportunity and
more federal pressure to work with ICE, two additional factors may play
a role. A higher share of Republican voters tends to increase engagement
with federal immigration officials. Or to put it another way, it is heavily
Democratic counties in which sheriff offices tend to have *No ICE Participation*. High levels of employment in the industry sectors that rely heavily
on immigrant labor also tend to reduce sheriffs' participation with ICE. It
should not be surprising that in places where the county's economy rests
heavily on agriculture, manufacturing, or accommodations—all reliant
on immigrant labor—sheriffs would be less likely to rock the economic
boat by participating in ICE enforcement activities. Indeed, in chapter 6
we describe the case of Dodge City, Kansas, where there has been a special arrangement between the sheriff's office and ICE that is geared to
avoiding disruption of the local meatpacking industry, which depends
heavily on immigrant workers.

As we have shown, local governing boards' policies toward immigration have proven important for all three measures of immigration policing. If a "tough" city or county government policy strongly predicts police
practices that are restrictive toward immigrants, then what predicts local
government policy? In the appendix, we show results from an additional
multivariate model that estimates local policy restrictiveness, using each
of the other city or county characteristics as independent variables. The
results provide some clarity on this matter. Only one local characteristic
clearly and significantly predicts a restrictive city policy across large cities,
small cities, and counties alike: the political leanings of the local populace.
A politically conservative public (or, in the case of counties, a Republican-
voting public) tends to beget more restrictive policies emerging from the
local governing board. These restrictive policies, in turn, tend to increase
the readiness of police to report immigrants whom they suspect are in the
country without authorization. In short, local politics has an impact on
immigration policing practices both through indirect and (in some cases)

direct mechanisms. While this conclusion finds support in the quantitative analysis presented here, it also resonates with findings from the case studies described in chapters 3 and 6.

Conclusion

Counties and municipalities are not simply the lowest level of the federal system, doing the bidding of states and the national government. Rather, they are live wires politically, economically, and sociologically—active arenas where a variety of actors seek to advance their own goals and careers by using the not inconsiderable powers and discretion of local government. To the extent that devolution allows localities to decide on their own immigration policies and practices, we should not be surprised that they choose disparate paths, creating what we have termed the patchwork of immigration enforcement. Local public officials will tend to pursue policies that make political and economic sense to them, given the community's particular combination of demographic trends, industrial composition, and ideological leanings.[48]

This chapter has provided a somewhat extended tour through the contextual characteristics that might influence local police either to scrutinize immigrants or, by contrast, to seek their trust and confidence. To generate our list of "suspects" that might be responsible for differences in immigration policing, we have relied on the growing literature about attitudes and policies toward immigrants, as well as on some common intuitions about what factors might arouse suspicion or sympathy toward newcomers.

Our statistical analyses suggest several conclusions about what precipitates different styles of immigration policing. First, we can, with some confidence, dismiss some suspects from further consideration. For instance, high unemployment or crime rates do not seem to motivate tougher immigration policing. And demographic diversification (namely, a high percentage of immigrants in the population or a rapid recent increase in Latino residents) seems to soften, rather than harden, the local police posture toward immigrants. Location near the Mexican border, similarly, does not seem to increase the tendency for police to investigate immigration status under the scenarios we asked about in our surveys. If anything, borderland location may lead sheriffs to seek to gain greater trust among undocumented residents.

On the other hand, it is fairly clear from these findings that the stance toward illegal immigration adopted by the city council or the county governing board sends strong signals to local police agencies about how they should interact with immigrants. Restrictive local policies tend to accompany restrictive policing practices. We cannot be entirely sure whether legislative policies generate policing practices or whether the police agency's posture precipitates legislation.[49] It is important to bear in mind, too, that *a plurality of local governments has no stated policy on immigration enforcement*. These localities appear to be leaving such matters to the discretion of the police, an issue we discuss in the next chapter.

Our evidence also suggests that the political leanings of the local population affect immigration policing. Conservative communities tend to be more oriented toward enforcement. Our statistical analyses suggest that much of this relationship is indirect: Conservative voters influence the policies adopted by the local governing board, which in turn set the bounds for policing practices toward immigrants.

The importance of the ideological variable is worth emphasizing. Local immigration policing seems to be shaped as much by whether local populations hold liberal or conservative attitudes as it is by ostensibly more objective community conditions. This ideological patterning suggests that the patchwork we described in chapter 3 arises, to a large degree, from the particular political framing and narrative that emerges about immigrants in each city or county. One might be tempted to say that the national ideological and partisan debate over immigration policy has been inserted into and nested within thousands of local communities in the United States and is shaping how police in those communities deal with immigrants on a day-to-day basis.[50] However, it seems just as likely that a politics of immigration arose first at the local (and state) level, where the community changes generated by immigration had most visibility and political resonance, and then filtered up to help define the national debate. Unfortunately, our mostly cross-sectional data are unsuited to resolve the sequence of these events.

The quantitative findings in this chapter challenge much of the conventional wisdom regarding immigration policing. Our findings suggest that some factors that have long been assumed to provoke local hostility to immigrants, such as high crime, unemployment, or rapid demographic shifts, cannot account for interlocal differences in immigration policing. Instead, political ideology and the framework of state and local policy toward immigrants seem to be the major factors shaping how local police deal with immigrants. And the growth of Latinos or of immigrants as a share of the local population tends to bode well, rather than ill, for the supportiveness of local police toward immigrants.

With that said, much about the choices that local police make is not fully accounted for by the factors that we examined in this chapter. Chapter 3 showed that the conflicting preferences and motivations of various local actors can create a complex patchwork of immigration policing practices within a single state, or even within one metropolitan area. Only by looking in some detail at particular communities can one begin to piece together the events that have produced current patterns of police/immigrant relations. We do this in chapter 6, which describes how law enforcement agencies in several communities have accommodated conflicting local perspectives and pressures to begin to define their own approach to immigrants. First, however, in chapter 5 we deploy our surveys and other research to look inside law-enforcement agencies, seeking to better understand how individual discretion and agency policy shape immigration enforcement at the street level. The combination of evidence drawn from national surveys that illuminate basic relationships, and case studies that illustrate how communities arrive at their own understandings, provides, we believe, unique insight into immigration policing.

CHAPTER FIVE

Discretion on the Front Lines: Immigrant Policing in Action

A s states and localities have become increasingly involved in immigration enforcement, police chiefs and sheriffs have faced the unprecedented challenge of crafting policy for a wide and complex array of immigration-related encounters. They do so with relatively few legal guideposts, with the potential for enormous public controversy, and with frequent shifts in local, state, and federal policy. This new responsibility also challenges the well-established tenet among law-enforcement professionals that developing and nurturing trusting relationships with local residents—community-oriented policing—is the most effective route to public safety.

Chiefs and sheriffs who fully embrace the norm and practice of community policing and understand its potential for conflict with immigration enforcement must weigh their options in light of the basic realities of police work. The law-enforcement agents they supervise have wide discretion in carrying out their duties, making crucial, sometimes life-and-death decisions within the context of loosely conceived, or often nonexistent, departmental regulations, and out of public view. As such, the role of departmental policy in determining frontline decisions is not always clear. This chapter sheds light on how the sometimes conflicting and contradictory forces at work shape immigration-related enforcement at the local level.

Community Policing and Immigration Enforcement: Conflicting Mandates

Community-oriented policing is based on the belief that members of the community are the most effective informants about criminal activity. If

a law-enforcement organization can gain the trust and confidence of local residents, its work will be more effective. The idea of prioritizing increased communication with local residents emerged in the 1970s as an
alternative to a less engaged and more distant professional stance that had
proved ineffective in dealing with urban rioting in the waning days of the
civil rights movement.[1] Since then it has become the standard for professional policing, endorsed by every national-level professional police organization as well as the Department of Justice (DOJ), which maintains
an Office of Community Oriented Policing Services (COPS) as a compo-
nent of its agency.[2] In debates about the quality of policing in poor, urban
communities of color, for example, it is the standard against which police
performance is measured.

Community-oriented policing includes all residents in its ambit, especially those most vulnerable to victimization.[3] The relationship-building
aspect of community policing extends to unauthorized immigrants whom
the police are mandated to protect as residents in the communities they
serve. Indeed, maintaining positive relationships with these residents is
especially critical because of their high levels of victimization and, often,
their tendency to mistrust police and government authorities based on experiences in their former country of residence.[4]

In the case of immigrants, community policing involves not only encouraging trust and confidence in the police but also taking the steps necessary to communicate effectively with this somewhat isolated constituency.[5]
This dilemma has prompted professional policing organizations to advocate strongly for more bilingual officers.[6] Police departments and sheriff's
offices have good reason to take these issues seriously, and the available
empirical evidence suggests that they do. Paul Lewis and Karthick Ramakrishnan, drawing on data collected in 2003, found that California police
departments were typically ahead of elected city officials in taking steps
to assist immigrants, for example, by hiring bilingual officers to help these
residents communicate with police.[7] In our surveys we also found a high
level of agreement that having officers proficient in foreign languages is
an effective way to improve community policing, and a relatively high proportion of personnel policies that give advantages to bilingual officers or
applicants.[8] However, only a minority of chiefs and sheriffs reported they
actually had enough officers who spoke a foreign language to be effective
in their communities.

While community policing remains the prevailing wisdom in policing
literature, over time there has been some divergence in what is considered
within its proper scope.[9] Wesley Skogan argues that four general principles

are integral to community policing: (1) community engagement—meeting with community groups, attending events, etc.; (2) problem solving—working with community representatives to improve services; (3) organizational transformation—making the changes necessary to communicate with all segments of the community, for example, through incentivizing language training; and (4) crime prevention—steps that involve police and citizens working together, e.g. neighborhood watch.[10]

Our surveys reveal a high level of commitment to all these elements of community policing. The majority of large-city and small-city departments reported activities like bike patrols and foot patrols, as well as maintaining a phone line for crime tips. Other common community-policing activities include communicating with local residents informally and keeping them "in the loop" with information. Meetings with residents and sharing of crime data, we found, are nearly ubiquitous in larger cities, though meetings specifically with immigrant advocacy groups are not as common. Sheriffs, with their countywide territorial base, rely less than police departments on foot and bike patrols. Table 5.1 sums up these findings, which are quite similar among all three law-enforcement groups.

The engagement of local law enforcement with federal immigration mandates clearly has the potential to undermine the basic trust-enhancing goal of these organizational initiatives. As San Antonio Police Chief William McManus argued in opposition to a Texas law that would require local police to enforce immigration law: "We depend on the community to work with us to identify crimes in their neighborhood. We would not get that kind of collaboration from the community if, all of a sudden, our officers were out there enforcing immigration laws."[11] Federal mandates present the same problem: They have been introduced without clear policy, protocol and standards that respect the need for maintaining trusting relationships with local communities.[12] The DOJ, for example, has promoted trust-building policing without confronting the potential for conflict that the Department of Homeland Security created in pushing to engage local law enforcement in immigration policing. In a November 2014 DOJ publication, Ronald Davis, director of COPS, stated: "Effective law enforcement requires trust and mutual respect between law enforcement agencies and the communities they serve. Progress has been made in enhancing these relationships as a result of community policing efforts over the past several decades."[13] Significantly, this publication never mentions the word "immigration" or "immigrant."

The federal government's increasingly insistent effort to involve local

TABLE 5.1 **Police Agency Usage of Various Community-Policing Approaches**

	Large cities, %	Small cities, %	County sheriffs, %
Foot patrols	76	68	29
Bike patrols	90	76	40
Regular neighborhood meetings	94	85	81
Phone line for anonymous crime tips	76	72	86
Regular visits to schools, churches, and neighborhood organizations	97	90	92
Regular meetings with immigrant-advocacy organizations	53	27	46
Citizen access to crime statistics/maps	86	69	62
Community advisory committee/board	60	35	41
Public hearings on topics of community concern	76	63	57
Having officers proficient in foreign languages	95	75	80
Cooperation/coordination with nongovernmental organizations	93	78	85

Note: Denominator for calculating percentages includes "don't know" responses, but excludes refusals to answer. Sheriff tabulations include only those sheriff offices that are responsible for patrols and investigations outside of the jails.

law enforcement with immigration enforcement suggests its fundamental incompatibility with community policing. At the most basic level, the duty of police and sheriffs to "protect and serve" their communities extends to everyone within the jurisdiction, including people with problematic or nonexistent legal status. Immigrant residents, law-enforcement officials believe, are less likely to report crimes than other victims, a finding that is supported by research on immigrant victims.[14] Law enforcement thus loses a potentially valuable source of information about criminal activities if it fails to cultivate trusting relationships with immigrants. Dayton police chief Richard Biehl sounds this theme of community safety in arguing that, "Having state and local law enforcement take on the work of federal immigration officials undermines community policing and is counterproductive," citing the fear of reporting crime among immigrant groups fearful that their immigration status, or that of friends and family members will be revealed and that dangerous criminals will prey on immigrant communities and the community at large.[15] The issue, as Biehl notes, extends beyond people who have entered illegally or overstayed visas. Many families are of mixed legal status, and in light of the nation's complex immigration laws, it is not unusual for police to confront "liminal legality" and "semi-legality" in their work.[16]

Acutely aware of the negative public mood about illegal immigration that Congress and federal agencies have cultivated and hyped, many immigrant residents have become distrustful of police and avoid contact with them, even as victims of crime. Reports from the field indicate that police and sheriffs face many challenges in this area. Kercher and Kuo's survey of immigrant victimization found that of 538 respondents who reported being victimized, nearly half of whom had been victimized multiple times, only 57 percent called the police.[17] A 2012 survey in four major cities found widespread reluctance to contact police as victims or witnesses to crime. Nearly half of the more than two thousand Latinos surveyed reported that they were less likely to contact police as a crime victim or if they had information about a crime because they feared that this will be used as an opportunity to inquire into their immigration status or that of people they know. Almost two-thirds of those surveyed stated that they believed that police stop Latinos without cause.[18]

This reluctance gives their victimizers a sense of impunity that puts the entire community at risk of more crime. As Angela Garcia and David Keyes note from their 2012 study of the experiences of undocumented immigrants, whole communities are affected by exclusionary policies and ramped-up enforcement: "Immigrants react to legal threats and hostile reception by going underground: They hold negative perceptions of local law enforcement, associate routine activities such as driving and walking with anxiety and the risk of deportation, and develop strategies of avoidance and fitting in to mitigate the discovery of their unauthorized status."[19] Community-policing principles are clearly at risk in this environment.

The national emphasis on enforcement and the highly discretionary nature of policing create a sense of peril everywhere, even in cities that resist full cooperation with federal efforts to engage local police in immigration enforcement. But how did this "race to the bottom" occur? The rollout of Operation Secure Communities, a national program to link local police and sheriffs to the federal enforcement effort, was a key element in sharpening the conflict between community policing principles and local engagement in immigration enforcement.

Secure Communities: Saga of a Failed Federal-Local Partnership

The federal government's much-touted Operation Secure Communities was designed to increase federal enforcement capacity by using the everyday law-enforcement activities of local police and sheriffs to detect undocumented immigrants and those legal permanent residents with outstanding warrants against them. The idea was to effectively harness the local level to federal enforcement. A 2006 Congressional Research Service report notes the problem of strengthening interior enforcement "with only a limited number of interior investigators charged with enforcing immigration, customs, and other federal law within the interior of the country, compared to over 600,000 state and local law enforcement officers."[20] The idea was to maintain normal law-enforcement standards for stops, arrests, and bookings, but add an extra immigration-related step after an arrest and transport to jail for booking. At this point Immigration and Customs Enforcement (ICE) would take action based on its own enforcement priorities.

This was a bold move that for the first time made the enforcement of federal immigration law depend in significant part on local personnel largely outside of federal control. Loss of a "locus of control" through devolution of the initial intake to the local level, however, inevitably made implementation of federal policy less consistent and less transparent. Earlier federal/local partnership programs have operated with much the same devolutionary logic, but were much less extensive. The Criminal Alien Program (CAP) targets only immigrants with outstanding criminal warrants. The 287(g) program, which was established in 1996, was conceived to focus on aliens who had failed to appear in immigration court, though it soon grew more diffuse, with some agencies by 2008 "seeking to apprehend as many unauthorized immigrants as possible."[21]

Nevertheless, the number of localities participating in 287(g) agreements was fairly small, in part because the program required local police agencies to sign up for federal training, a prospect that did not appeal to many. The 287(g) program had no adopters for the first five years of its existence and at its height included only seventy sheriffs' offices and police departments out of nearly eighteen thousand law-enforcement agencies in the United States. By February 2014, thirty-five agreements were still in effect, but a complete phase-out was in prospect. In the words of John Sandweg, former acting ICE director, "The 287(g) task forces had proved to be too costly, too inefficient and too problematic" to support.[22]

Operation Secure Communities was misleadingly simple in its requirements. The stated goal was to identify and detain suspected unauthorized immigrants who had committed crimes sufficiently serious to require booking in a local jail for later prosecution. Under Secure Communities, fingerprints of all arrestees brought in for booking were to be run, not just through FBI databases, which had long been customary, but also through immigration databases, which contain a wealth of information about outstanding immigration warrants, past violations, and other matters. Those identified as having an immigration violation were subject to a seventy-two–hour detainer issued by ICE. The idea was to prevent release until ICE could decide whether to pick up the person for possible removal proceedings.

The federal government's rather naive assumption in initiating this program was that police and sheriffs on patrol would make surveillance, stop, and arrest decisions without regard to the possibility that an immigration violation might be uncovered during the booking process. There were no special safeguards against racial profiling and pretextual stops targeted at suspected unauthorized immigrants. Yet, as legal scholar Hiroshi Motomura has noted, the decision to arrest sets the stage for all subsequent government action in connection with removal.[23] Reports about the implementation of Secure Communities suggest that racial profiling and pretextual stops were frequent. In 2011 Kohli, Markowitz, and Chavez analyzed how Secure Communities was working in the 44 states and 1,595 jurisdictions in which it was then operating. They found a disproportionate number of Latinos (93 percent) had been arrested and that an unusually high proportion of them had been detained; the average detention was nearly a month.[24]

It was also clear that Secure Communities was *not* achieving its stated goal of focusing on criminal offenders. A 2011 study revealed that more than half of those detained under this program had no prior arrests or only minor past infractions.[25] Many cases classified as criminal involved only illegal re-entry. Between fiscal year 2008 and 2012, ICE agents issued nearly one million immigration detainers. Only 22.6 percent of the time did the individual have any criminal conviction, and only 8.6 percent of the time was a serious crime involved. A total of 834 US citizens were mistakenly detained.[26] Among those deported in 2013, only 12 percent had committed a serious crime; for half, the most serious charge was an immigration or traffic violation.[27] In Baltimore, Maryland, for example, over 40 percent of those deported in 2013 had no criminal record at all.[28] In the exercise of officer discretion on the frontlines, it seemed that Latino appearance, rather than criminal misbehavior, must have guided many enforcement decisions.[29] This pattern appears to be continuing despite changes at the federal level designed to focus enforcement on immigrants who have committed serious crimes.

The Department of Homeland Security had promised an internal civil rights review of the Secure Communities program in June 2011, but over a year later, in November, 2012, announced that data collection challenges had delayed conclusions as to whether the program facilitated racial profiling.[30] No further announcements were forthcoming, though the DOJ undertook its own investigation of a few high-profile cases. In December 2012, for example, it accused the Alamance County North Carolina Sheriff's Office of targeting Latinos with unwarranted arrests to maximize deportations.[31]

In short, Secure Communities only exacerbated fears among immigrants that any contact with local law-enforcement officials could result in deportation. The efforts of some big city chiefs to opt out of the program were rebuffed by ICE officials, despite earlier promises that participation would be voluntary. As the Immigration Policy Center complained in a 2010 press release: "In the current environment confusion and the lack of transparency undermine the trust necessary to properly implement the program and achieve legitimate goals."[32] Relations with Latino communities in some areas had been strained even before the emergence of Secure Communities. In a massive study of community policing in Chicago that monitored community-policing efforts between 1992 and 2004, Skogan found that, while community policing had greatly benefited African Americans in the city, it had utterly failed to engage and assist Latinos, the city's second largest demographic group.[33]

For evidence of why Secure Communities went awry, the implementation of the 287(g) program offers useful insights. Though not nearly as extensive in relation to the overall number of sheriffs and police departments as later federal partnering programs like Secure Communities, the 287(g) program nevertheless had enough adopters to provide a kind of test case on the issue of racial profiling. Amada Armenta examined the implementation of a 287(g) agreement in a Nashville, Tennessee, jail and found that some desk officers assigned to processing immigrants bound for deportation were aware of cases involving suspiciously minor offenses that normally do not result in arrest; the officers she interviewed nevertheless felt constrained to move these cases forward.[34] Mathew Coleman studied the implementation of a 287(g) agreement in Raleigh, North Carolina.[35] Consistent with our findings regarding Raleigh in chapter 3, Coleman found that everyone involved felt relieved of responsibility to avoid racial profiling by the arrangements adopted there. The county sheriff's office ran the jail and booked arrestees, but did not make arrests, and so was not directly involved in instances of racial or immigrant profiling. The municipal police, environmental police, and other law enforcement agencies that did make arrests were not involved in booking cases, and so felt no obligation to consider possible deportation consequences.[36]

Resistance to Secure Communities, which had begun to take shape as the program was rolled out, grew more determined after a series of lawsuits in 2014 held that federal detainers were not sufficient to justify holding suspected immigration violators. Honoring these holds without an underlying justification would subject local authorities to legal liability. At this point Secure Communities was en route to becoming a failed federal initiative. In his November 2014 memo explaining that the Department of Homeland Security had decided to end Secure Communities, Acting Director Thomas Winkowski noted that its very name had become a negative symbol and that some local public officials were taking active steps against it: "Governors, mayors, and state and local law enforcement officials around the country have increasingly refused to cooperate with the program, and many have issued executive orders or signed laws prohibiting such cooperation."[37]

To replace Secure Communities, in November 2014, the Department of Homeland Security unveiled a new, ostensibly more restrained, federal/local partnership arrangement. The Priority Enforcement Program contains some safeguards against arrests undertaken mainly or solely to provoke deportation proceedings. Two of the most significant are the requirement of a conviction before federal authorities become involved and the requirement that the conviction be for a specified offense on the federal list.[38] All these are more serious than a traffic violation or minor misdemeanor. At this writing it is unclear how much the pattern of arrests will change under the new approach. As legal scholar Juliet Stumpf has observed, the key question is whether the federal government will require adherence to its new standards: "If immigration enforcement is to avoid repeating the self-immolation of Secure Communities, DHS must fundamentally transform how it regulates its own immigration enforcement discretion."[39]

The die, however, appears to have been cast. Years of experience with the virtually unregulated engagement of local police in immigration enforcement have helped to implicitly criminalize residence without legal status. Other factors have contributed to this trend, including legal changes that criminalize immigration offenses and harsh public rhetoric about the supposed criminogenic character of "illegals." The result of this multipronged trend has been counterproductive from a policing perspective. Like the extraordinary security measures directed at Muslim residents after the 9/11 attack, local immigration policing has undermined fragile relationships that police depend on to fight and solve crime. This impact, however, appears more generally understood by law-enforcement leaders than by the public at large.

Gaps between Law Enforcement and Community Perspectives

Police chiefs and sheriffs face constant pressure to "do something about crime." In many places this is understood to include arresting unauthorized immigrants. Unlawful presence in the country is widely, but mistakenly, assumed to be a crime. Nor is immigration enforcement by local police within the scope of traditional local law-enforcement activities, which focus on public safety. There is, in fact, a perverse relationship between immigration enforcement by local police and sheriffs and suppression of criminal behavior, as we have noted, because fear of deportation silences witnesses and victims of crime. These considerations, however, appear to weigh more heavily on law-enforcement professionals than on the general public.

We found evidence of significant differences in perspective between law-enforcement leaders and the communities they serve. Our surveys reveal that policing professionals see the community at large as more aroused than they or their colleagues are by immigration issues, and more likely to oversimplify the issues involved in detecting unauthorized immigrants. The only respect in which these leaders see similarities between their departments and the general public concerns the victimization of immigrants. Table 5.2 illustrates these patterns, which vary somewhat by the type of policing agency involved.

In jurisdictions where there is strong support for detecting and deporting immigrants, police chiefs must engage in a difficult balancing act to maintain effective working relations with the city councils and city managers that employ them. As professionals, they are responsible for public safety and for developing effective internal controls against abuses in immigration enforcement, as in other policing activities. Yet committing to a written policy or particular training regime risks political controversy. Given the political sensitivity of the issue, perhaps not surprisingly, we found that police departments and sheriff's offices tend to avoid the spotlight. Our surveys reveal that during the period when Secure Communities

TABLE 5.2 **Immigration-Related Perceptions, as Reported by Local Law-Enforcement Executives**

	Mean agreement score		
Statement	Large-city police chiefs	Small-city police chiefs	Sheriffs
Unauthorized immigration is a controversial topic in my department/office	2.90	2.69	3.05
Unauthorized immigration is a controversial topic in this locality/county	3.58	3.11	3.60
Gaining the trust of unauthorized immigrants is a priority in my department/office	3.50	3.08	3.01
Gaining the trust of unauthorized immigrants is a priority in this locality/county	2.86	2.63	2.70
Victimization of immigrants is considered a significant problem in my department/office	2.82	2.30	2.49
Victimization of immigrants is considered a significant problem in this locality/county	2.66	2.25	2.49
People believe that it is relatively easy to determine who is in this country without authorization in my department/office	2.52	2.56	2.74
People believe that it is relatively easy to determine who is in this country without authorization in this locality/county	3.26	3.13	3.19

Note: Data are *means* of responses that are on a five-point scale, where 1 is "strongly disagree" and 5 is "strongly agree." Sheriff sample is limited to full-service sheriff offices —those engaging both in patrol and in jailing.

was being implemented at a nationwide level, fewer than half of all departments and sheriffs' offices had any written policy on how to handle interactions with suspected unauthorized immigrants. Fewer than half offered training related to incidents or calls involving these immigrants.[40] In the absence of explicit guidance and rules from their superiors, it is quite likely that individual officers on patrol either develop their own standard operating procedures when they confront this situation, or that they absorb an unofficial "norm" from their colleagues and superiors regarding how to act in such situations. This may involve the targeting of Latinos, the prototypical unauthorized immigrants in many minds.

The understandable reluctance of police chiefs or sheriffs to commit to a written policy also opens the door to uneven enforcement. A consensus among public administrators and scholars in the field developed around the early 1970s that, "while externally imposed legal rules are usually ineffective in regulating administrative action (and may be very counterproductive), internally developed rules are likely to be professionally accepted and influential."[41] But even such clear-cut rules may be difficult to enforce in the highly discretionary environment that characterizes policing. Consider profiling of African American citizens, a long-standing problem not associated with immigration. Almost every law-enforcement agency that we surveyed has a written policy forbidding racial profiling, but persistent complaints by African American citizens that racial profiling is occurring remain, and social science studies support that claim.[42] The same, of course, can be said of racial profiling of Latinos to achieve immigration arrests. We know little, however, about what considerations may be operating when sheriff's deputies and police officers encounter people they suspect of being in the country without authorization.

Discretion at the Street Level

Local law enforcement is intensely individualistic work in which officers on the street are generally beyond the view of their supervising officers and enjoy wide discretion regarding what to investigate, and whom to question, stop, and arrest. Often the real reason for a stop differs from the violation for which someone is cited. Armenta's research in Tennessee found, for example, that "traffic stops are never about the traffic offense—they are about checking for warrants and discouraging criminals from being in the neighborhood." Nor, she asserts, can there ever be too many stops from an officer's point of view because days off and preferred shifts depend on making sufficient stops. The emphasis on stops also encourages stops for technical violations—a broken taillight or dirty license plate—because they are much easier than catching someone speeding or disobeying a traffic signal. Police and sheriffs also often exercise discretion concerning whether to issue a citation or to make an arrest, and whether to accept the identification a person offers as sufficient. Inadequate self-identification is grounds for taking a person in for booking to confirm identity.[43]

How do law-enforcement officers flex their discretionary muscle in the context of immigration? The scholarly literature on police discretion has not yet much engaged with this new frontier of law enforcement, but there is a great deal of research on a related topic, the exercise of discretion in the day-to-day enforcement of the penal law by police, an activity that lies squarely within the traditional duties of local law-enforcement personnel. Michael Lipsky's seminal *Street Level Bureaucracy* (1980) has given rise to a substantial empirical literature on the power of police and other street-level bureaucrats, such as teachers, counselors, and social workers, to shape outcomes.[44] Those workers who occupy the front lines of contact with the public on a day-to-day basis, Lipsky argued, are more than *implementers* of policy—they are policy *makers* whose decisions ultimately "add up to agency behavior": "[P]ublic policy is not best understood as made in legislatures or top-floor suites of high-ranking administrators . . ."[45] "To the mix of places where policies are made, one must add the crowded offices and daily encounters of street-level workers."[46]

What we know of police discretion reminds us that nonenforcement of the law is very often an option. As James Wilson has observed: "With respect to routine police matters, the normal tendency of the police is to under-enforce the law."[47] Kenneth Davis similarly emphasizes nonenforcement based on prudence and an officer's own sense of justice.[48] Situations involving mentally disturbed or disoriented individuals offer an obvious case in point.[49] These decisions, however, must often be made quickly and without consultation. In his interviews with police officers, Michael Brown found that they repeatedly cited instinct and judgment and repeated that "you can't go by what the book says" in describing their decisions.[50] Immigration enforcement raises the issue of discretion in a special way because of the potentially weighty consequences of an arrest.[51]

Making an arrest that will ultimately revolve around an individual's lack of immigration status does not sit comfortably with the profession's core mission of making communities safer. The policing literature stresses this commitment to getting "bad guys" off the streets, which suggests that law-enforcement decisions are often made according to a moral calculus, not a legal one.[52] Conflicts between legal and nonlegal frames are not uncommon in police work or in other frontline public service occupations.[53] As Steve Herbert observes: "What an officer defines as 'the right thing to do' may in fact, violate legal rules. In these situations, officers must choose which framing to use in defining the situation, and their decisions might differ from those of other officers. Organizational conflict is the inevitable result."[54] This problem was evident among the booking officers whom Armenta interviewed in her research on local immigration enforcement in Nashville. She learned that some officers expressed guilt when processing for possible deportation immigrants who had been arrested for very minor violations.[55]

Our own data, as we noted in earlier chapters, reveals a nuanced understanding among law-enforcement personnel of when to contact federal immigration authorities. Our surveys provide indirect evidence that law-enforcement officers—whether police in large or small metropolitan areas or sheriff's deputies—do not necessarily deploy all the legal instruments available to them. Consider the *Enforcement Count* measure introduced in chapter 4. We asked each group of law-enforcement executives to reflect on the divide between policy and practice in their departments by responding to seven scenarios, ranging in seriousness from an interview with a crime victim or witness to an arrest for a violent crime. The likelihood of officers checking immigration status or reporting the person to ICE (as estimated by their chiefs), it will be recalled, was directly related to the seriousness of the suspected offense. This normative calculus appears to be common to various types of law-enforcement agencies, whether they work in large or small cities or in countywide sheriff offices. There were no statistically significant differences at all between large and small municipal police units; among sheriffs there was only a slightly higher inclination to report to immigration authorities.

An example of how police officers weigh their options comes from a 2009 *Arizona Republic* article by reporter Daniel Gonzalez, who describes his "ride along" with a Phoenix police officer. The officer stopped a vehicle because it was going much slower than the speed limit, which made him suspicious. He ran a check, finding no warrants. But the driver, it turned out, had no license to drive. Both of the stopped vehicle's occupants, who spoke only Spanish, appeared to be on their way home from work. The officer let the men go without a citation or a question about legal status, explaining to Gonzalez: "Those are just a couple of hard-working dudes." The department's policy at the time was consistent with the officer's decision because it discouraged immigration enforcement in noncriminal situations. As the officer explained to Gonzales: "We have that discretion. Our main concern is whether a crime has been committed."[56]

Pressure to report suspected immigration violators to federal officials probably has increased since this incident. As we discussed in chapter 2, a number of states, following Arizona's lead in 2010, considered or adopted legislation requiring officers to inform ICE whenever they encounter a person whom they believe lacks the legal status to remain in the country. All these state laws were met by legal challenges, with Arizona's law reaching the US Supreme Court. As with *Arizona v. United States* (2012),[57] the federal government generally succeeded in its effort to roll back state laws creating their own immigration-enforcement protocols, although the right to inquire about immigration status in the context of a nonimmigration-related stop remains, as long as the detainment is not prolonged. While the cool response of the courts to these statutes has discouraged further state-level legislation of this type, the problem of racial profiling and pretextual stops remains a sore point in relations between law enforcement and immigrant communities.

The moral calculus that operates in immigration-related arrests can cut two ways. It can either encourage deportation-oriented arrests or discourage them. For officers who interpret illegal presence or residence as a quasi-criminal act, the moral question is whether to bend the rules about stops in order to check immigration status. An unauthorized immigrant will not have a valid driver's license in most states because proof of legal status is required. Lack of sufficient identification, even in the case of a minor traffic violation, becomes grounds for arrest and transport to the local jail for booking, ostensibly to confirm identity. This type of immigration enforcement, which has been dubbed "shadow immigration enforcement," has become more common as the lines between civil and criminal liability have blurred. In this situation, as legal scholar Maureen Sweeney has observed, neither the arresting officer nor the Department of Homeland Security personnel are held accountable for the constitutional violations that have occurred.[58] How such arrests will be handled in light of recent changes at the federal level remains unclear.

What is clear is that racial profiling to achieve deportation outcomes has occurred and is likely to continue unless it is no longer effective. Lawsuits challenging police stops have become common around the country and are sometimes successful, as in a suit brought by the American Civil Liberties Union and other organizations and individual plaintiffs charging Maricopa County, Arizona, Sheriff Joseph Arpaio with racial profiling. As discussed in chapter 3, in May 2013 federal district judge Murray Snow issued a permanent injunction barring the sheriff and his deputies from continuing past enforcement practices and mandating extensive remedial action; he backed up this decision with a 142-page opinion finding a long-standing pattern of racial profiling and abuse of legal authority.[59] The case continued, however, because the sheriff failed to comply with the judge's order. Charged with contempt of court, it is unclear at this time whether he will be held criminally liable.

Racial Profiling in the Enforcement of Immigration Laws

Reliance on racial criteria to make stops and arrests, always a simmering concern, emerged as a widely discussed issue in light of the post-9/11 policies that the administration implemented to assist with its investigations of terrorist organizations.[60] The Patriot Act, adopted within weeks of these attacks, was criticized as specifically targeting Arabs and Muslims.[61] In addition to impositions on the civil liberties of specific groups, immigration and terrorism soon became linked in the political landscape because some of the 9/11 terrorists had overstayed their visas and were in the country illegally. Soon thereafter, the linkage between immigration and terrorism was extended to other immigrants, including those arriving from Mexico.[62] Ironically, at the very moment of the terrorist attacks, the United States and Mexico had been in negotiations to allow for increased immigration and a new guest-worker program. The events of 9/11 abruptly ended this negotiation.

In the wake of aroused fears about national security, racial profiling, which had once been condemned in the law-enforcement community, was slowly being legitimized as an appropriate mechanism to deal with terrorism. Racial profiling's quasi respectability in one realm has had radiating effects in others. Michael Wishnie argues that the institutionalization of racial profiling that occurred in response to the 9/11 terrorist attacks has contributed to the deterioration of relationships between immigrant communities and local law enforcement.[63]

Racial profiling has also long been cited as a reason for strained relationships with African American communities, an issue that took on new salience after a series of killings of unarmed black males by white police officers in fall 2014. The high-profile deaths in Ferguson, Missouri, and New York City, in fact, may have precipitated the release of new DOJ guidelines on racial profiling in December 2014. These new guidelines, the first the department had issued in more than a decade, were the product of a five-year review. They largely condemn racial profiling as a federal law-enforcement tool in light of the need to maintain unbiased policing and community trust.[64] In a statement that Attorney General Eric Holder released with the new guidelines, he stated: "As Attorney General, I have repeatedly made clear that profiling by law enforcement is not only wrong, it is profoundly misguided and ineffective."[65] Significantly for this discussion, however, the Border Patrol, an agency of the Department of Homeland Security, asserted that it is exempt from the DOJ guidelines, citing its need for ethnic profiling in its work, and noting its administrative independence from the DOJ. The impact of this exemption is broad because the jurisdiction of the Border Patrol extends, not just to immediate border areas and ports of entry, but also to all areas within one hundred miles of the border, where two thirds of the US population resides.[66]

The Border Patrol's assertion of a right to racially profile as a key element in its work raises a yet-unaddressed question: Do local police and sheriffs who cooperate with federal immigration agents, and who work with them on taskforces to control gangs and other problems, also have authority to racially profile the people they encounter? The issue also arises in Arizona and Georgia where law-enforcement officers have been given authority to detain suspected illegal immigrants whom they stop based on their evaluation of the probability that they are in the country illegally. What leads an officer to become suspicious that the person stopped is in the country illegally? At the height of the furor over SB1070 in Arizona then-Governor Jan Brewer's response to this question was, "I do not know what an illegal immigrant looks like." Clearly local law-enforcement officers do not know either. In each of our three surveys, fewer than 27 percent of chiefs or sheriffs said their officers found it "relatively easy" to determine who is in this country without authorization. Yet statistics suggest that an unauthorized immigrant, in most minds, is Mexican. In 2010 Latinos, over half of them from Mexico, made up 97 percent of deportees, well above their estimated 81 percent of the unauthorized population; most of the difference is attributable to disproportionate deportation of Mexican immigrants.[67]

Anger about racial profiling has shaped minority perceptions of law enforcement. For example, African Americans, followed by Latinos, perceive that they experience more bias than whites, with perceptions of bias increasing after minorities have had contact with law enforcement.[68] While Latinos appear to have more positive overall perceptions, these views may be souring in light of more aggressive immigration enforcement. Latinos, including citizens and legal permanent residents, are reporting that they feel they are stopped more frequently, think more negatively of the police, and are less likely to report crimes than they had been before immigration enforcement became a politicized issue.[69] In many cases, Cecilia Menjívar and Cynthia Bejarano report, direct experiences with American law enforcement, in tandem with past experiences in countries of origin, tend to paint a picture of local law enforcement as dangerously powerful and without restraint.[70] When combined with the confusing patchwork of enforcement, the effect is increased mistrust of local law enforcement everywhere.

Interpreting the Federal Mandate

The federal government has issued mixed messages about the desirability of deporting residents who have lived in their communities without incident. Shortly after taking office in 2009, President Obama increased resources directed at enforcement, a decision that resulted in record numbers of deportations, the number exceeding four hundred thousand in one year and earning Obama the title "deporter in chief." In June 2012, however, President Obama announced a massive program of deferred action for young people who had come to the United States as children and satisfied other criteria as members of society in good standing. The Deferred Action for Childhood Arrivals (DACA) program, which provided a two-year reprieve from the threat of deportation and work permits, was estimated to have the potential to affect up to 1.7 million young people. President Obama also announced "parole in place" for families of military personnel with unauthorized parents, children, and spouses.[71] In November 2014, President Obama again used executive action to extend DACA to more young people and to add temporary relief from deportation for parents and spouses of citizens and legal residents. The 2014 initiative may allow over four million people lacking legal authorization to stay in the country temporarily if court challenges can be resolved.

The case for inaction in the public eye and in the law is strongest for people with deep roots in the United States. The president's 2012 and 2014 executive actions targeted this most-sympathetic population of long-term residents. These are the cases that often get media attention. In immigration proceedings that arise in the normal course of enforcement, the rootedness criterion also plays a role, underlying most requests for suspension of deportation. Immigration law has historically counted connection to the United States and its citizens as a positive factor that can lead to relief from removal. Even after the 1996 toughening of those standards, a small window of possibility remains in cases of extreme hardship when a US citizen would be adversely affected by deportation.[72]

Both Department of Homeland Security and ICE have acknowledged inconsistencies in identifying eligible cases when local law-enforcement agencies partner with federal authorities through 287(g) agreements.[73] A fundamental problem was the failure of either the 287(g) program or its now-defunct successor, the Secure Communities program, to live up to their common mandate of making communities safer through deportation of dangerous individuals. Stana's report to the US Government Accountability Office noted the prevalence of minor offenses in cases brought to the attention of federal immigration officials.[74] In a study for the American Immigration Lawyers Association that covered Secure Communities, the 287(g) program and the Criminal Alien Program, Alexsa Alonzo et al.

found that Department of Homeland Security was often taking cases with no criminal element and ignoring strong ties to the local community; it also took cases from local agencies and individuals already under investigation for racial profiling and other improper police practices.[75] Adam Cox and Thomas Miles, after a comprehensive study of the roll out of Secure Communities in three thousand counties, concluded that the program has not served its central objective of making communities safer.[76] Elina Treyger, Aaron Chalfin, and Charles Loeffler came to a similar conclusion in their analysis of Secure Communities, finding no evidence that participation in the program by local law enforcement agencies led to reduced crime or increased arrests.[77]

Our surveys suggest that part of the disconnect between levels of law enforcement can be blamed on lack of oversight and guidance from federal authorities. Among the respondents to our surveys, many more reported that more useful information flowed upward from their agencies to ICE, rather than downward from ICE to the local level (although the modal response was that useful information flowed "about equally" between the two levels).[78] And as we described above, even within police departments and sheriff's offices, more often than not, there is no written policy and little or no opportunity for training regarding interactions with immigrants.

In the current environment, communication failures are a particular problem for immigrants, regardless of their legal status. Legal immigrants and US-born Latinos feel the pressure of aggressive policing to detect and remove unauthorized immigrants because of racial profiling.[79] Some legal immigrants and citizens also have family members vulnerable to deportation. Even in the wake of President Obama's initiatives, more than half the estimated eleven million unauthorized immigrants in the United States remain at risk of deportation. This dynamic extends beyond undocumented immigrants, as local immigration policing also targets legal immigrants with criminal records.

The Patchwork of Immigration Enforcement in Action: Evidence from the Front Lines

An unauthorized immigrant's vulnerability to deportation depends, to a surprising extent, on where he or she lives. As earlier chapters have suggested, we are faced with a complicated scenario in which state, county, and local law-enforcement agencies are being asked to enforce federal law in a contentious political context that sometimes includes directives from local legislators. Some cities and counties are eager for more immigration enforcement for political reasons, and some have come to depend on federal reimbursements for detainees in local jails in order to cover expenses.[80] Others have adopted policies that prevent police agencies from asking people who have not been arrested to prove their legal immigration status. Since 1979, for example, Los Angeles has prohibited police officers from inquiring about the immigration status of people not suspected of crimes.[81]

The determination of organizations at the front lines of enforcement to resist federal pressure should not be underestimated. Over three hundred cities and counties, according to one report, do not fully cooperate with ICE.[82] Shared norms and knowledge helps police agencies, city councils, and county governments resist efforts from the outside to change their form and function. Professional organizations also provide something of a bulwark against even determined federal initiatives that appear to violate settled professional norms, much as academic professionals defend academic freedom.[83] When the US House of Representatives in July 2015 voted to deny funding to cities that do not report unauthorized immigrants to federal authorities, the outcry came not only from the White House and immigration advocates but also from the National Fraternal Order of Police and the Major County Sheriffs' Association and the National League of Cities.

As we have noted earlier, the relevant law is also a patchwork of conflicting and changing requirements, with courts at all levels involved in reviewing state statutes and local ordinances. Federal requirements and incentives are also subject to change. In March 2015, for example, a presidential task force to reform US policing recommended ending the use of communication of information about the immigration status of individuals to local police and sheriffs because it has "exacerbated the fear that immigrant communities feel towards local police and remains a significant impediment to effective community policing."[84] Whether that recommendation will be adopted was unclear at the time of this writing.

Local law-enforcement leaders must translate the sometimes-vague mandates they receive into policies that reflect local political, demographic, and institutional realities, and at the same time take account of the relatively broad discretion that individual officers exercise in their work. Their administrative actions mark the point where laws are, in Jenness and Grattet's terms, "operationalized," or turned into rules and directives that are meant to govern the actions of frontline officers.[85] Chiefs and bureaucrats create, in Jenness and Grattet's terms, a law "in between" statutes and implementation. This is not to suggest that implementation of departmental or office mandates is a clear-cut matter. As this chapter has shown, frontline officers are also policymakers, translating the mandates they receive into their own individual plans and actions. As Jenness and Grattet suggest, we must "move beyond a simplistic understanding of law-on-the-books and law-in-action" and speak to "a larger process of lawmaking and implementation."[86]

A number of scholars have started to explore this dynamic. Coleman, in his investigation of local immigration-enforcement practices in Raleigh, North Carolina, notes the influence of "specific political, legal, policing, and biographic contexts" in determining the strategies officials follow.[87] Eagly describes such differences in terms of three competing paradigms of enforcement, relying on evidence from three localities. She categorizes the criminal justice system in Maricopa County (Phoenix, AZ) as an "illegal alien punishment" model that makes immigration enforcement a central part of local policing, and, with the help of immigrant-specific state laws, attempts to maximize the likelihood of deportation. Los Angeles County exemplifies an "alienage neutral" model, which reaches in the opposite direction to try to limit the possible effects of immigration status and enforcement in criminal adjudication. Harris County (Houston, TX) exemplifies an "immigrant enforcement" model that treats undocumented immigrants charged with crime more harshly than other criminal defendants with respect to bail eligibility, plea-bargaining, and sentencing.[88] A similar pattern of significant local variation within a single national-level policy appears pervasive in other immigrant-receiving nations.[89]

Conclusion

The local level is clearly not the unambiguous "force multiplier" that Congress envisioned in 1996 when it set up the 287(g) program that initiated the process of formal devolution to local policing agencies.[90] It is more accurate, we have argued, to view local enforcement of immigration law as a patchwork of variations on a broad federal theme. Discretion to enforce—or not to enforce—immigration law is the working principle behind the patchwork of immigration policy and practice that prevails in the United States. This discretion, as we have shown in this and earlier chapters, exists at every level, including at the individual level among frontline officers.

Some of this diversity of views is obvious and transparent. At the same time that some sheriff's offices were signing 287(g) agreements to assist the federal government in its enforcement role, chiefs of police in large US cities were publishing statements against it.[91] During 2014, according to the *New York Times*, local police agencies declined to respond to 10,182 detention orders according to Department of Homeland Security officials, and 270 jurisdictions were refusing to honor detainers.[92] Twenty-seven police chiefs and sheriffs and two national police chiefs organizations signed on to a brief supporting President Obama's executive actions on immigration in litigation brought by twenty-six states to block the president's action.[93]

Discretion operates, not just within law-enforcement agencies and among officers on the street, but also in city council chambers and mayors' offices, as evidenced by the variety of legislation that has emerged from state legislatures and municipal governments. All these local decision makers act against a backdrop of increasing federal efforts to manage immigration through enforcement in the nation's interior. But even in regional ICE offices, discretion operates to prioritize the processing of some immigration "hits" over others, depending on a variety of factors, both judgmental and practical, such as case overload. In a recent example of this phenomenon, a March 2015 report in the *Houston Chronicle* described lawyers around the country reporting that federal authorities are inconsistent in adhering to ICE guidelines designed to protect immigrants with deep roots in the country.[94]

Discretion at the local level operates in the context of changing federal priorities, which reminds us that it also operates at the very top of the enforcement pyramid. Anna Pratt suggests that we see discretion in the administration of immigration law, not as "the unruly shadow of law that allows for the expression of individual agency," but rather as "a productive form of power in modern systems of liberal rule."[95] The multilayered *discretionary* patchwork of immigration enforcement allows the system as a whole to operate without undue internal conflict and, at the same time, reduces opportunities for informed critique from outside the system.

A sort of lowest common denominator has emerged in this ever-shifting, nontransparent process because of the decision to take action against longtime residents who come into contact with local law enforcement in mundane ways, usually through traffic offenses. In targeting this population, racial profiling and pretextual stops have become part of immigration enforcement. The involvement of local police in detecting these immigrants has also added to the general trend toward crimmigration, that is, the criminalization of the processes and rules that can lead to deportation.[96] Legal scholar Kevin Johnson asserts that racial profiling has become the "Law of the Land" in the United States, at least with respect to immigration violations.[97] Mat Coleman and Angela Stuesse describe the historic transformation that has made "deportability" a real possibility for millions of resident immigrants:

> For most of the twentieth century, U.S. immigration enforcement was nearly exclusively about border enforcement in the U.S. Southwest. This is no longer the case. Although the U.S.-Mexico border remains an important site for federal immigration authorities, over the past decade immigration policing has extended deep into the U.S. interior. Indeed, today's landscape is characterized by a complex proliferation and intensification of state and local immigration enforcement initiatives. . . . . Some of these operate in partnership with federal immigration authorities, while others do not. Collectively, these initiatives have transformed immigration enforcement from a federally-managed and outward-looking power, located at the territorial margins of the U.S., into an operationally diffuse and inward-looking power focused on resident immigrant populations deep within the country's heartlands.[98]

The introduction of a new, less extensive and less intrusive federal partnership (the Priority Enforcement Program) is unlikely to eliminate these problems, especially with the ability of the Border Patrol to continue profiling.

Is this what American communities want for their immigrant residents? Here too, as we showed in chapters 3 and 4, there is a patchwork. Localities and their law-enforcement agencies are highly varied in their thinking and behavior. Recent executive actions expanding deferred action, reducing federal pressure on local law enforcement, and encouraging citizenship among legal permanent residents and immigrant integration are unlikely to reduce this variation significantly, though they do provide a roadmap for a more positive approach toward all immigrants. The following chapter looks at this issue from another angle, examining individual cities to ask how community leaders and activist organizations struggle to shape the response of their communities to the federal government's increasingly insistent call for local participation in immigration enforcement.

CHAPTER SIX

Negotiated Understandings between Law Enforcement and Local Communities

P olice, sheriffs, political officials, and activists of all stripes have moved into the space created by the federal government's offer to devolve immigration enforcement to the local level. These actors negotiate their relationship with immigrants in the context of the political environment in which they live and work. The previous chapters lay the foundation for the focus in this chapter on the local decisions that help to determine the way cities approach resident immigrants and, specifically, how they police these residents. In chapter 3 the emphasis was on the patchwork of responses, while chapter 4 sought reasons for this variation in local policy in environmental and institutional terms. Chapter 5 elaborated this theme of variation by describing the discretion that operates at each level of the immigration-control network.

This chapter looks closely at four municipalities to examine how members of communities customize federal immigration policy to suit their own local needs and preferences. Relying heavily on our case-study research in El Paso (Texas), Allentown (Pennsylvania), Dodge City (Kansas), and Salem (Oregon), we describe the complex web of economic and political power that determines local policy and its response to the housing, education, and demographic challenges posed by the arrival of new immigrants and the accommodation of those long-settled in the community. We selected these particular communities because they vary significantly in their responses, and yet they are all of a size that allows one to see relatively clearly the relevant forces and issues in play. Our key concern is with the relationship between local police and immigrants, whether documented or not. We begin therefore with a brief review of the issues at stake from the perspective of each side of this relationship.

From the Vantage Point of Local Law Enforcement

The push to enforce federal immigration law has in many cases compromised older norms that law enforcement once relied on for determining the meaning of "community" in community policing, as we noted in chapter 5. The need to connect directly with all segments of the local population in order to build trustful relationships conflicts with demands to act as enforcers of immigration law, particularly in communities with large numbers of unauthorized immigrants. The crux of the problem is that the enforcement of immigration law depends on a static situation—a person's legal *status*—rather than that person's illegal *behavior*. To detain a person based on status is inconsistent with the basic premise of conventional law enforcement: that a person has nothing to fear from police if he or she has committed no crime. Proactive enforcement of a status-based law also sends a message that the presence of some residents is inherently problematic and deserves a forceful response from law enforcement, undermining any sense of entitlement to police protection in parts of the community where persons without solid legal status might be found.

Partnerships between local and federal law enforcement designed to detect and remove unauthorized immigrants or legal residents with outstanding warrants also run the risk of undermining vital local relationships. As we discussed in chapter 3, the situation becomes even more fraught when adjacent law-enforcement organizations take opposing approaches to these arrangements. The conflict between the city of Mesa, Arizona, and the Maricopa County sheriff who shares jurisdiction over the city offers another apt illustration of the difficulties police face in negotiating a workable relationship with immigrants. Two of the cases discussed in this chapter, Dodge City and El Paso, involve a slightly different policy dilemma: the mismatch between a reluctant local government and a state government that wants to encourage its municipalities to undertake immigration enforcement.

The case studies in this chapter bring into focus two previously unacknowledged factors in decisions related to immigrant integration and enforcement: the economic well-being of the community when it is heavily reliant on immigrant labor, and, in the case of El Paso, the need to acknowledge cross-border economic and social relationships built over a long period of time. In these situations especially, local enforcement of immigration law imposes a tremendous burden on the entire community. The racial profiling, decreased reporting of crimes, greater vulnerability to crime, and negative consequences of deportation threaten the social and economic fabric of communities whose wellbeing depends on positive relationships with immigrants and their families. The individual police officer faced with making decisions about custody, counsel or release must somehow take these issues into account, often without much explicit guidance from superiors.

Police and sheriffs do not have the benefit of a strong preexisting understanding of the cultural issues they may encounter in dealing with Latino residents, even in the absence of immediate concerns about deportation. As Ronald Weitzer notes, this is a neglected area in the policing literature and in the training of new officers.[1] This lack of attention to the potential for miscommunication is particularly puzzling in light of the large number of Latino citizens and their growing political and social importance. Latinos also lack information about police. Weitzer reports that many draw their impressions from "indirect experiences" through media, friends, and other such sources.[2] The experience of or perception of racial or ethnically biased policing also shapes attitudes toward law enforcement. The shortage of Latino officers in most communities exacerbates this situation. Lack of mutual understanding challenges the ability of law enforcement to build strong, positive relationships with Latinos, even apart from the very real fear of deportation of members of families and friends who lack legal status. This can easily stand in the way of successful community-oriented policing, even in law-enforcement agencies strongly committed to its principles.[3]

From the Vantage Point of Immigrants
with and without Legal Status

As local law enforcement has become increasingly connected to federal immigration enforcement efforts, immigrants are finding that they have no place to turn when they are victimized or witness crimes. Fears that they or their friends and family will have their immigration status checked if they contact law enforcement mean that they rarely involve the police when they are victimized.[4] This fact is well known to many offenders. Intimate partner violence is another source of vulnerability for immigrant women with insecure legal status.[5] Reticence to call on local police can lead to repeat victimizations, while calling carries with it the threat of retribution from the abuser who can threaten to call immigration authorities.

Interviews that Jacqueline Hagan, Briana Castro, and Nestor Rodriguez conducted with unauthorized immigrants in the 1990s and 2000s reveal some of the fears that prevail in this population.[6] Nearly 16 percent reported being questioned by immigration officials over citizenship status. Some stated they had been questioned while walking to work or to school. About 40 percent reported being arrested. Fears of confrontations with local and federal law enforcement led them to avoid contacts with strangers and social agencies. These immigrants tended to avoid health services, government projects, schools, and driving to work. Immigrants in one county "reported that they were particularly concerned about local police acting as ICE agents through the 287(g) program" and felt they were unable to contact law enforcement as a result.[7]

The consequences of deportation are severe, and not just for the person(s) deported. The removal of family members results in "fear, stress, family separation, and economic hardship" for those who remain in the United States.[8] "Mixed-status" households, where one or more family members lack legal status, further complicate the effects of deportation, as US-born children may face one or both parents being deported or may themselves be forced to relocate quickly to a country they have never seen.[9] These effects have been felt more widely as the number of removals has soared. In 2011, Immigration and Customs Enforcement (ICE) Director John Morton announced that during fiscal year 2010 the agency had deported more immigrants than ever before.[10] Nearly half had no criminal conviction, and many others were low-level offenders. In some communities, the quantity of deportations impact whole neighborhoods, with apartments vacated and businesses with Latino patrons experiencing declines. Established ties to employment are weakened by deportations. Those who remain are constrained as consumers by the need to send more money home to assist displaced family members.

The irony is that nearly 50 percent of deportees remain committed to returning to the United States.[11] Deportees leave families and employment opportunities in the United States. These are strong magnets for attempted returns. The prospect of being caught and deported again is not a sufficient deterrent to change this desire to reunite with family and work opportunities.[12] This remains true even at a time when federal prosecutions and deportations are at record levels.

Policing Practices in El Paso, Texas: "All Hat and No Cattle"

El Paso, Texas, is an important city for understanding immigration and immigration enforcement for many reasons. Directly across the Rio Grande River, on the Mexican side, lies Ciudad Juárez (see fig. 6.1). El Paso and Ciudad Juárez were, in fact, one city until the US border divided them. The two communities have a long history of relationships that involve commerce, families, shopping, and employment. El Paso deals with issues of immigration in light of its efforts to maintain family connections, promote cross-border commerce, and encourage employment opportunities. Because of its history, El Paso is quite distinctive from the "new destination" cities—Dodge City, Salem, and Allentown—discussed later in this chapter.

El Paso is, in many respects, a binational city. The Latino presence dominates the city, comprising 81 percent of the total population of 670,000. Just over one-quarter of this population is foreign born. African Americans comprise just over 4 percent of the population. El Paso is not a wealthy city. The median household income is $32,124 and per capita

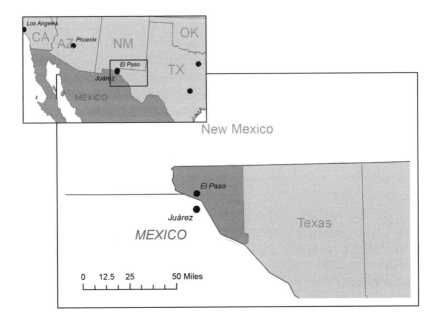

FIGURE 6.1. El Paso, Texas, and surrounding jurisdictions

income is $14,388. Roughly 19 percent of families and 22 percent of the total population live below the poverty level.

There is a significant federal presence in the El Paso area, including the large military base at Fort Bliss and an Air Force base and military medical facility. International trade, government civil service, the defense industry, and petroleum are the key industries. The city has a council-manager government, with strong leadership from the city manager. The Catholic Church is also a strong presence in El Paso County, with the local diocese headed by a bishop. Despite its relatively high poverty rate, El Paso has very low rates of crime and typically ranks among the safest largest cities in America. This is especially true of violent crime, including murder. El Paso's record of public safety stands in stark contrast to its neighbor across the river: Ciudad Juárez has become famous for its very high rates of crime and violence.

El Paso's approach to immigration enforcement reflects, to a large degree, its own political and practical realities. During the course of our case study, we interviewed individuals representing eight agencies, including law enforcement, nongovernmental organizations, government social-service agencies, and faith-based groups. Many of these individuals attempted to "explain" El Paso as a unique place, an isolated community that felt itself to be "far away" from the politics of Texas. To these observers, that distance, emotionally felt, but also real in terms of miles and access, made El Paso different from the rest of Texas. Its remoteness from the state capitol removed El Paso from much of the political discourse of the state, which was to some extent a matter of regret, but that distance also enabled El Paso to operate "under the radar" in many ways.

The ethnic composition of El Paso's population is a critical aspect of its identity, but our study did not suggest that demography is destiny. A number of other factors influence the practices and philosophy of law enforcement in El Paso as it responds to the challenges of undocumented immigration. One significant fact is that, while an overwhelming majority of the population are Latinos, they are not especially well-represented in positions of power in the city, either in elected or appointed positions in government, or in the fields of education, business, and law enforcement. Another important consideration in adjusting enforcement policy to local conditions is the economics of the border, particularly as it affects commerce and employment.

There is a symbiosis between El Paso and Ciudad Juárez across the river. This relationship reflects the historical relationship between the two, which for decades included free travel (across a bridge and with a trolley) and free trade. Tending to undermine this historical relationship, however, is the explosion of drug violence in Ciudad Juárez, particularly since 2008. The violence and lack of accountability has changed perceptions of life in Ciudad Juárez on both sides of the border. Not surprisingly, it has propelled an increasing number of Ciudad Juárez residents to seek asylum or residence across the river in El Paso.

The difference in the number of murders experienced by each city is instructive. In 2008 there were fewer than twenty homicides in El Paso, but over two thousand in Ciudad Juárez. As El Paso County Sheriff Richard Wiles told us, the dynamic that threatened to change immigration-enforcement practices and policy in El Paso was not the 9/11 terror attack, but rather the violence of powerful drug cartels in Mexico. The city's low crime rate, however, has held despite the threat posed by these cartels. The low number of violent incidents makes it possible to pursue a restrained immigration-enforcement policy without encountering much political flack. In the city of El Paso, individuals are not stopped for identification purposes. El Paso remains a city of entry, not only for residents of Mexico but also for large numbers of Central Americans. For local police and sheriffs, the challenge is to balance the need for commerce and human communication between nations with the need to protect public safety.

We spent considerable time interviewing Sheriff Wiles, who formerly served as chief of police in the city of El Paso. Although the sheriff's office has countywide jurisdiction that theoretically would allow him to police the city of El Paso, Sheriff Wiles explained that he does not have sufficient resources to do that. He decided to run for his current position because of his own and public dissatisfaction with the former sheriff, who had authorized traffic stops for the purpose of determining identity. The stops involved a request for Social Security numbers from the driver and passengers in the car. This policy produced an outcry of protest that culminated in the county board of supervisors voting to prohibit traffic stops for the purpose of determining identity. Sheriff Wiles promised to implement this new policy and was elected with over 70 percent of the vote.

Sheriff Wiles also limits his interactions with ICE. Only in incidents in which the charge is a low-level misdemeanor or something more serious does his office forward fingerprint and other identity information to federal authorities. This eliminates most of the traffic stops from ICE oversight and blunts the possibility that a sheriff's deputy will be accused of making pretextual stops for the purpose of *sub rosa* immigration enforcement. The sheriff supports an increased federal—and reduced local—role in immigration enforcement. He campaigned with Bill White, the former Democratic candidate for Texas governor. Both argued for expanded federal border enforcement that would free local enforcement entities to concentrate on local crime.[13] This platform spoke both to the need for trust in local police and to the dangers posed by the extremely high levels of violence in Ciudad Juárez.

Sheriff Wiles is committed to the philosophy, strategies, and management associated with community policing. He followed the same approach while chief of the El Paso police department. In his adherence to community policing, Wiles stands out from his fellow sheriffs, as community-policing principles are far more prevalent among police departments than among sheriff offices, as our survey data indicate. Sheriff Wiles explained that, in the service of enhanced public safety, he had made it his mission to implement large-scale policy and personnel changes to infuse the agency with the principles of community policing and to professionalize its operation.

The sheriff's commitment to community policing extended back to his early years as chief of police in the city of El Paso. At that time he worked with a local group, the Border Network for Human Rights (BNHR), and became a member of its board of directors. He became involved with BNHR because the organization filed complaints about the police targeting immigrants. At first, then-Chief Wiles didn't think these complaints were credible. When he investigated, however, he found them to have merit, which inspired him to join the BNHR board. He has worked with them since. More recently he created citizen advisory committees at each of the regional command centers and established a committee that advises him about community issues. His efforts to create community linkages also include the establishment of citizens' police academies and regular hosting of an extensive list of community meetings. He also worked to open a jointly staffed community center in a disadvantaged part of the county.

From this sheriff's perspective, federal law enforcement fulfills a different mandate than local law enforcement, a mandate that does not require the same intense level of involvement with citizens and does not include community policing. As a representative of Border City Chiefs on the Major Cities Chiefs Immigration Committee of the International Association of Chiefs of Police, he argued that local enforcement of federal immigration law undermines the community trust that must be the basis for effective local law enforcement. He also defines his commitment to local law enforcement in practical terms. He told us that his question to local law enforcement is, "When you do the job of federal law enforcement, who is doing your job?" The sheriff elaborated on his view about the proper role of local law enforcement with regard to immigration.

> In a community like El Paso local residents don't want to be stopped for identity verification. During a lawful stop during a criminal investigation identity can be checked and Border Patrol can be contacted to determine identity. It's very irritating to be stopped over and over because of how you look, especially since over eighty percent of the population in this area is Hispanic.[14]

One of the challenges Sheriff Wiles faces is that people unfamiliar with his policies often fail to distinguish between federal and local law enforcement, which can make it difficult to secure cooperation from persons with insecure or nonexistent legal status. This was confirmed in a subsequent interview with a member of the Inter-Faith Alliance (IFA) who told us that, despite the fact that targeted stops no longer took place in El Paso (city or county), undocumented individuals still fear the police; local citizens, however, do not. Sheriff Wiles voiced concern about the tendency of people to group all law enforcement together: "Distinguishing local police from federal law enforcement is not easy to do, especially by first generation immigrants. The way forward is through interaction with people who have been in the city for a while and to communicate with immigrants."[15]

Sheriff Wiles identified the very large federal presence in the city and county of El Paso as a key to understanding the broader context of law enforcement in the area. The large number of officers representing Customs and Border Patrol, ICE, the Drug Enforcement Agency, and the FBI, as well as an exceptionally large military presence provides an important resource for local law enforcement and a buffer against movement across the US/Mexican border by drug cartels.

Although we were unable to interview the current chief of police, we were able to learn a good deal about the department from our interviews in the community and by reviewing relevant documents. We learned that the department does not participate with ICE in immigration-enforcement activities, continuing the policy that Sheriff Wiles described when he was chief of police. The city council has not passed any legislation directly addressing this issue, but the police department does have a nonparticipation policy in their general orders.

We spoke with representatives from a number of advocacy groups.

These groups represented a broad spectrum in the services they provided, in their level of advocacy, and in the amount of their direct contact with unauthorized immigrants. Some, such as *Las Americas*, provide few direct services, but are active in providing information and advocacy about the needs of refugees, asylum seekers, and immigrants, particularly families and children from Central America who have been victims of domestic violence.

Immigration enforcement is clearly an issue for these advocates. We asked each of our interviewees how their perceptions of local policing policy comported with what Sheriff Wiles described as his policies. For the most part, these interviewees confirmed what we had heard from the sheriff. Louie Gilot, executive director of *Las Americas*, for example, focused on trust: "The Chief and Sheriff have taken strong stands against doing immigration policing by local police. They have also not gone on joint raids; they don't work with Border Patrol."[16] She told us that the former sheriff had acted much differently and had even welcomed the minutemen to the area. When he began to conduct raids and establish checkpoints, he encountered "a big push back" from the community. This was the point at which Mr. Wiles, then chief of police, initiated his campaign for sheriff.

The BNHR, which has been in existence since 1998, led the campaign against the former sheriff's tactics. BNHR was instrumental in getting the Social Security number removed from the traffic stop form. They continue to protest on behalf of immigrants and are committed to raising the level of information available to the immigrant community about its rights. The organization maintains an open dialogue in pursuit of its principles with Customs and Border Patrol, as well as local police. As a local watchdog, it has surveyed neighborhoods about mistreatment on the part of Customs and Border Protection and the El Paso Sheriff's departments, but found little to report.[17] Expressing doubt about their findings, the group extended its data collection for two additional weeks, but still was unable to turn up any verifiable cases of abuse. Members also actively participate in the Border State Coalition and are engaged in voter registration drives. Their primary hope for change lies with federal reform, particularly the DREAM Act. The fact that Sheriff Wiles has served as a member of their executive board suggests the uniqueness of the situation in El Paso as a border city with a majority Latino population. The El Paso case shows how Latino economic and political power is translated into policy and practice.

Another activist group that seeks to organize Latino residents and encourage higher levels of civic participation, including voting, is the IFA. A representative explained that there is still a tendency for undocumented residents to fear the police, even though people no longer need to worry about being stopped for identification. Members of the group hope to build trust and empowerment among their clientele and to maintain El Paso as a uniquely safe place for immigrants in Texas.

We also spoke with providers of direct services to immigrants and families, including Annunciation House. The agency is located near the El Paso federal detention facility. While Annunciation House does not work in concert with the detention facility, it fulfills the needs of individuals who have a family member housed there or who are displaced for other reasons. Diocesan Migrant and Refugee Services, another local organization, does work in detention centers, providing asylum assistance for people fleeing violence in their home country.

In short, El Paso is well served by agencies and organizations dedicated to helping vulnerable immigrants. This level of institutional support and the countywide commitment of law enforcement to a robust vision of community policing that protects immigrants with problematic legal status are unique among the cities we studied. The presence of the Sheriff on the executive board of an immigrant-rights organization also sends a strong signal of support. It is noteworthy that this linking of community policing to unwillingness to undertake immigration enforcement has occurred in a conservative state.

Geography and the demographic make-up of the population help to explain El Paso's distinctive approach to immigration enforcement. The city's proximity to the border has fostered a long history of relationships that span the Rio Grande, intertwining family, religious organizations, and the commercial and employment sectors. It is also significant that, as locals say, El Paso is a long way from the rest of Texas, and it is poor enough to often be ignored in state politics. Politically, too, El Paso is somewhat of an outlier within a "red" state, as it leans Democratic and liberal. Low crime rates and the presence of a large number of federal law-enforcement agents further protect El Paso from critical scrutiny. These conditions combine to allow law enforcement to function differently than in other jurisdictions in Texas or many other parts of the United States.

It must be noted that things were not always this way in the sheriff's office. The dramatic change of policy under Sheriff Wiles is remarkable in light of the usual practice in jails that sheriffs manage, which is to verify the identity of all individuals in their custody. In El Paso, however, reflecting the need for positive relationships between police and community, Sheriff Wiles has limited the identification information his deputies provide to ICE. This case is thus a reminder that, while demography, history, and space play a role in determining how a locality will respond to immigrants, the decisions that local law-enforcement leaders make about their role in the community are the sine qua non of a positive climate for these residents.

Policing Practices in a New Destination: Allentown, Pennsylvania

Allentown is located in the northeast United States and is the third largest city in Pennsylvania, considerably smaller than Philadelphia (with 1.5 million people) and half the size of Pittsburgh (with just over 300,000 inhabitants), but still a significantly sized metropolis, with approximately 118,000 people in the city, and approximately 350,000 people total in Lehigh County, in which Allentown is located (see fig. 6.2). For many years, the "Pennsylvania Dutch," descendants of settlers from Germany and Switzerland who arrived in the seventeenth and eighteenth centuries, dominated Allentown's population.

During the twentieth century, the city became increasingly diverse, with the establishment of Puerto Rican, African, Irish, Italian, Arab, Ukrainian, and Polish neighborhoods. In the last several decades, however, two events played a significant role in shaping Allentown's current demographics: the completion in the 1980s of Interstate Highway 78 (I-78), running from New York City through Allentown and beyond, and the 9/11 terrorist attacks on New York City.

The completion of the highway made Allentown, for the first time, a plausible commute from New York City. Allentown lies ninety miles due west of New York City and sixty miles northwest of Philadelphia. With housing prices skyrocketing in the New York metropolitan area, I-78 provided the means by which Allentown and its environs became, in essence, commuter suburbs of the greater New York and Philadelphia regions (despite the two-hour, one-way commute). This trend accelerated after the 9/11 terrorist attacks. Seeking affordable housing and a sense of peace and safety, an even larger group of households made the move from the New York area to Allentown and the broader Lehigh Valley. Many of those who settled in the city over the last two decades are of Latino origin.

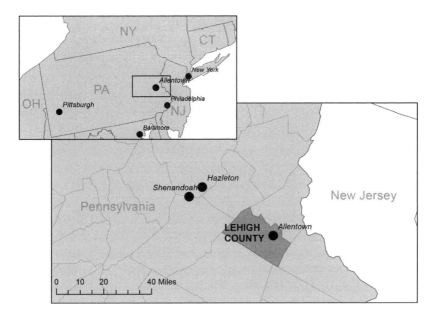

FIGURE 6.2. Allentown, Pennsylvania, and surrounding jurisdictions

Allentown is now home to a diverse population with Mexican, Domini-can, Puerto Rican, Venezuelan, and Colombian heritage, as well as first-generation immigrants from those nations.

Allentown thus represents one of the "new immigrant destinations" that have emerged across the United States in the past quarter century. In 1980, only 5.1 percent of Allentown's population was Hispanic. In the en-suing decades, the number of Latinos living in the city rapidly expanded. In 1990, Allentown was 82 percent non-Hispanic white and approximately 12 percent Hispanic. By the 2010 census, however, the proportion of non-Hispanic white Allentown residents had fallen to 43 percent, whereas the proportion of Hispanic residents had risen to 25 percent, with 10 percent foreign born. In this respect it is quite distinctive from Pennsylvania as a whole. Only 4 percent of Pennsylvania's total population is Latino, and 5 percent of the state's population is foreign born. The Latino popula-tion of Allentown is relatively young: the public school district, once pre-dominantly non-Hispanic white, is now approximately 75 percent Latino. These are the classic markers of a new immigrant destination.

Tensions surrounding the city's shifting demographics started to emerge in the late 1980s and early 1990s, and were mainly given voice by Emma

Tropiano, a controversial city councilmember. In the mid-1980s, the Allentown city council had passed a nonbinding resolution declaring the city a sanctuary for Central American refugees. Though Tropiano initially voted for the resolution, she quickly changed her mind and tried to rescind it. Her resolution stressed that the city had no legitimate role in passing judgment on the foreign affairs of the federal government of the United States and, furthermore, that actually enforcing the sanctuary resolution would be a violation of federal law:

> However laudable the goals of the Lehigh Valley Sanctuary Support Group and the Lehigh Valley Friends Meeting might be, the attainment of those goals, i.e. the provision of sanctuary to illegal aliens, nevertheless involves the violation of federal criminal statutes and a determination by some that the end justifies the means.[18]

Her attempt to repeal the sanctuary resolution failed in 1986, two votes to four, but she again revisited the sanctuary policy in 1991, this time expressing her concern that the city's sanctuary status might hasten the spread of the AIDS virus throughout the community,[19] as well as stating, "We have to start worrying about native Allentonians who have lived here all their lives, not the people who come here from New York and New Jersey."[20] In 1988, she also publicly accused Latinos of being responsible for 99 percent of crime in the city.[21] Finally, in her waning years on the city council, in 1993, she tried to pass a local ordinance banning the "outdoor" use of "indoor" furniture. This was widely understood to be a protest against Latino families in Allentown who sat and socialized on sofas on their front porches, and hence another protest against the changing demographics of the city. Tropiano died in 2002. Many of the people whom we interviewed for this project viewed her as the public face of nativism during her tenure on the city council, as well as a voice for intergroup tensions simmering in the community.

Tropiano's anti-immigrant activism resonates with attitudes around the state. Pennsylvania has played a leading role in the huge jump in immigration policymaking at the local and state level that began around 2005. It was a national leader in the number of local anti-immigrant ordinances passed and 287g agreements signed.[22] Hazleton, Pennsylvania, for example, was one of the birthplaces of the "Illegal Immigration Relief Act," an anti-immigrant local ordinance that went on to be considered and/or adopted by 140 localities across the United States. Hazleton is approximately fifty miles northwest of Allentown.[23] High-profile immigration-related crimes also have taken place near Allentown. In 2008 several white teenagers were accused (though later acquitted, controversially, by an all-white, non-Latino jury) of fatally beating an undocumented Mexican immigrant in Shenandoah, Pennsylvania, a town near Hazleton.

As this anti-immigrant environment was evolving, Lou Hershman, an Allentown city councilmember, proposed an ordinance that would have required the Allentown police department to sign a 287(g) agreement with the federal government. As Hershman recounted, he had talked with constituents who complained of long waits in the hospital emergency room, union members who described cuts to wages and benefits as well as unemployment, and teachers who mentioned how the schools were increasingly overcrowded. So he decided to take on the issue in order to look out for "the residents of Allentown . . . the *legal* residents of Allentown."[24] While the proposal caused much controversy, it was ultimately defeated because it did not garner support from the broader community, other members of the local government, or the police force. As then-Assistant Police Chief Joe Hanna told us, "We work with all agencies equally and we assist them, but it's not one of those things where we have campaigns . . . that we need to 'clean up the city of illegal immigrants,' you know? We have a lot of things that, quite frankly, are more pressing."[25] The mayor of Allentown, Edward Pawlowksi—a former community organizer—also opposed the measure.

Crime, however, is a matter of serious concern in Allentown. Accompanying the demographic transition of the last twenty years has been a significant increase in gang activity and drug-related violence. Members of the police force with whom we talked linked this increase directly to the completion of I-78 and the easy connection between New York City and Allentown. By the time of our research, the connection between the New York police department and the Allentown police department was so tight that officers from one force would regularly spend time in the other city in pursuit of suspects.

When asked about his opposition to Hershman's 287(g) proposal and the broader question of police involvement in immigration enforcement, Police Chief Roger Maclean stated,

> I thought, you know, if we're breaking down doors looking for immigrants, how in the world are we going to get information on the bad guys? You know? A lot [of immigrants] don't trust us to begin with, and then if we're starting to kick

doors down and looking for green cards, you know, it makes it even harder. So, my thought process was, "Wait a minute, this is a federal issue. We'll continue to do *our* job and let the federal government do *their* job."[26]

Chief Maclean's words, it should be noted, closely parallel the sentiments of Sheriff Wiles in El Paso.

However, unlike the situation in El Paso, the practice (though not policy) of the Allentown police department is *not* one of "noncooperation," or an unwillingness to cooperate with federal immigration authorities. The Allentown police *do* cooperate with federal immigration authorities by sharing national origin and citizenship information (as best they can determine) of everyone brought in to the local jail for booking. The department's relationship with ICE is informal and ad hoc having evolved from long-standing professional relationships between members of the police force and former Immigration and Naturalization Service (INS) agents who had been stationed in Allentown in the past. The department does not, however, seek immigration status of individuals who are stopped, but not arrested.

That said, despite the insistence by police leadership that frontline officers were not specifically targeting immigrants, a number of community leaders whom we interviewed claimed that some Allentown police officers practiced racial profiling. As one respondent complained, "driving while brown" was a real problem in the city.[27] Another prominent Latino community leader downplayed this concern, however, and argued that the police did follow an immigrant-neutral protocol, and that community fears were based more on what was happening at that time regionally—in Shenandoah and Hazleton, for example—and nationally, than on any local behaviors.

While a number of the migrants to the Allentown region are, indeed, first-generation immigrants, many are actually legal permanent residents and citizens, albeit of a variety of nonwhite ethnic groups. Deportation is often not of particular concern to this demographic, though it is possible that a legal permanent resident's criminal conviction can create the possibility of deportation, depending on the crime involved. As the city's population has changed, therefore, the Allentown police department has developed a set of practices regarding engagement with these new communities. It seems that the most significant challenge to the Allentown police lay in managing the fears of immigrants who, despite years of legal residence in the United States, did not feel themselves fully accepted or assimilated with local traditions. Local police in this situation, wholly apart from their internal policies and practices, had the potential to become a focal point for fears in the immigrant community.

The informal practices of the police force—mainly the desire to avoid local immigration policing, as well as to recognize the importance of strong relationships with immigrant and Latino communities—were eventually formalized in official city policy. By 2013 the city had opened a Mayor's Office of Immigrant Affairs. As stated on its website, the office "promotes the well-being of immigrant communities by providing information and programs that facilitate successful integration of immigrants into the civic, economic, and cultural life of the City."[28]

The opening of this office follows a small, but growing, nationwide trend in which local governments recognize the value of an office dedicated specifically to fostering the incorporation of immigrants into their communities.[29] Allentown, like these other cities, is seeking to develop innovative, forward-thinking practices to incorporate its new residents— with bureaucracies such as the police leading the way. In Allentown this effort even included a recent resolution by the Allentown city council calling for federal action on immigration in light of the fact that 11 to 14 million immigrants "contribute to our communities, the economy and the country—yet are denied essential rights."[30]

The story in Allentown, then, is one of tensions over demographic change and racial transition that was briefly wrapped in an anti-immigrant banner. While the anti-immigrant constituency in the city has tried to capitalize on tensions surrounding demographic change, all of these attempts have fallen flat, as the majority of the city's population seems uninspired by nativist rhetoric. As Alan Jennings, a local community activist, told us:

> I don't really think immigration is a big issue for the vast majority of people in the Lehigh Valley. I think there are a lot of ignorant people who think that Puerto Ricans are illegals; they don't understand that Puerto Ricans are Americans. There is a lot of that but not nearly enough to prevail on the policy making structure and the law enforcement agencies to stand up and fight back.[31]

Dodge City, Kansas: Protecting Industry, Protecting Immigrants

Dodge City is located in Ford County, Kansas (see fig. 6.3). There are just over twenty-five thousand residents in Dodge City, 55 percent of whom

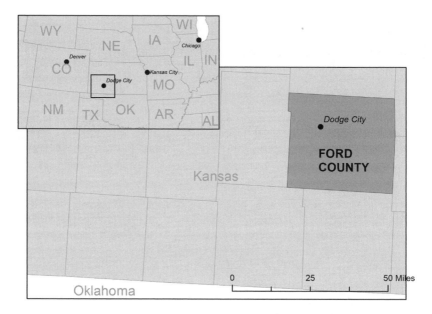

FIGURE 6.3. Dodge City, Kansas, and surrounding jurisdictions

are Latino and 25 percent foreign born. The median household income is $41,540 per year. This is slightly below the average for the state, but well above the national average. The median age of city residents, twenty-nine, is considerably lower than that of the median in the state of Kansas, which is forty-three. This younger median age reflects the preponderance of Latino residents attracted by work opportunities in the area's meat-processing plants. The city's financial well-being is largely connected to its dependence on the meat packing industry, the major employer in the city and county. Approximately thirty thousand cattle are slaughtered weekly in Dodge City. Tens of thousands of beef cattle wait in nearby holding lots to be processed, giving the city a faint animal odor.

Many of the individuals whom we interviewed described Dodge City as an "island" because of its lack of connection to major transportation hubs. There are no interstate highways that pass within fifty miles of Dodge City, and the area is isolated from media and other cultural influences. Despite its isolation, the city has prospered in recent years, in contrast to much of the nation. Housing prices have not declined and unemployment has remained low (3 percent). The city's relative prosperity can be largely attributed to the presence of the two enormous meat-processing and meatpacking plants in the city and the low-wage immigrants who staff these operations.

There is a long history of immigrants in Dodge City. In the nineteenth century, Chinese and Mexican laborers helped to build the rail lines that run through the city. Some stayed and played a role in city politics. During the past two decades, the "Mexican Village" that housed railroad workers has grown enormously. As we found in our research, the city has welcomed these new residents as workers and consumers, but not as full-fledged members of the community needing specific kinds of support. Many of the newest arrivals are crowded into the poorer parts of town, where housing-code enforcement is weak to nonexistent. Affordable housing is limited, but there are no major initiatives to change that situation.

The schools are 75 percent Latino, crowded, and not oriented to the shifting demographics. There are few Latino teachers and the curriculum takes little account of Latino culture and history. Most teachers do not speak Spanish. At the time of our visit, the seven-member school board included one person with a Latino surname. The school website is only in English, though pictures of students include many Latinos. These observations reinforce the role that Latinos play in the community—providing labor for the key industry, their presence acknowledged in some ways—but not being actively incorporated into civic life.

The Anglo and Latino populations live quite separate lives in Dodge City. Sporting events and social and residential life tend to segregate by ethnic group. There is some resentment of the newcomers, who are poorer and less able to speak English. The Methodist church offers a service each week in Spanish, but there is not much activism from the churches on behalf of immigrants and the church leadership and its outreach efforts remain dominated by Anglos.

This separation is also visible in city government. The city has a commissioner-manager form of government. The commission, basically the legislative chamber, consists of five elected members from whom the mayor and vice mayor are selected. Despite the fact that over half of the residents of the city are Latinos, all the commissioners are currently Anglos. In its long history the city has had only one Latino mayor, no Latino school superintendents or principals, and no Latino chiefs of police or sheriffs. The city's website was in English only.

We spent considerable time speaking with law-enforcement officials, including the police chief of Dodge City and the sheriff of Ford County, which surrounds Dodge City. Police Chief Robin James took office in

June 2010, and we interviewed him a few months later, in November 2010. He lost his job in the month following our meeting with him, due to an allegation of illegal deer hunting. This unusual dismissal, we believe, reflects the tensions that Chief James encountered in trying to promote a more community-oriented approach to law enforcement in the city. His brief tenure also illustrates the challenges facing an individual from outside a police department who tries to make wholesale changes in a time of high anxiety about unauthorized immigration.

The appointment of Chief James was met with considerable public and civic acclaim. The local paper identified him as someone who had lived in Central America and would work to improve the relationship between the Dodge City police department and the Latino community. The city commissioners who selected him as chief viewed positively his fluency in Spanish and his marriage to a woman from Central America, information that was covered favorably in local news accounts. This positive view of his qualifications extended to the faith-based community, including Father Juan Guerra, director of Hispanic Ministries for the Catholic Dioceses of Dodge City.

That said, Chief James sought to be a change agent in the Dodge City police department. The previous police chief had served for twenty years, came from within the department, and had devoted little effort to community outreach. Chief James broke with this tradition by taking steps to implement community policing. He reorganized the department through promotions and assignments in order to foster better community relations. He made an effort to hire more Latinos and officers who spoke Spanish, but was frustrated in his efforts to do so by the lack of applicants with the necessary qualifications. He was able, however, to establish a multicultural focus group that met monthly. These meetings revealed the perception within the Latino community that the police were targeting them. This perception was supported by an analysis of departmental traffic stop data that showed Latinos were twice as likely to be stopped as members of other race/ethnic groups. The prior response to this problem had been to encourage minority residents not to violate traffic laws. Chief James took a more active approach, initiating an education campaign that underscored the rationale for traffic enforcement and the protocols that guide vehicle stops in order to help the immigrant community understand why the stops occurred and to teach these drivers ways to avoid drawing a police officer's attention. In all these actions Chief James felt that he was acting in accordance with a mandate from the city's leadership who seemed to want to do something to better integrate their immigrant residents in the community, but did not know what to do. In his words: "Cultural knowledge is more than language. When you start seeing culture as different, rather than right or wrong, you can make progress."[32]

Chief James saw cooperation with Immigration and Customs Enforcement (ICE) as important in dealing with the city's criminal element, but he refused to allow his officers to inquire about citizenship or to contact ICE. As he explained, 90 percent of the workers in Dodge City are Hispanic and about the same percentage are undocumented. To take an active role in seeking out unauthorized immigrants would wreak havoc with the workforce and threaten the local economy. The chief's reluctance to share information about citizenship underscores the role of the meatpacking industry in the town and its importance as an economic engine for the city and Ford County. The statistical analysis in chapter 4 suggested that, on average, the amount of employment in immigrant-heavy sectors does not alter immigration policing to a large extent. That said, when economic and political interests intersect they can exert powerful influences on the way that immigration enforcement is negotiated.

Sheriff Dean Bush, in contrast to Chief James, is a longtime Ford County resident who first joined the sheriff's department in 1974. He manages a new jail facility that has 230 beds, and he supervises 24 sworn deputies, managing a total of 85 employees. Sheriff Bush, like Chief James, is an advocate of community policing, and like his counterpart, Sheriff Bush has had difficulty finding Spanish-speaking personnel. Unlike Chief James, he has been able to implement community-policing principles without encountering opposition from county officials.

Sheriff's deputies respond to a large number of calls for service in Dodge City itself, reflecting the high level of cooperation that exists between the city and county. All the special units on the sheriff's staff were cross-deputized in the city and vice-versa. It is almost as if the lines between the city and county law enforcement do not exist in Ford County, which distinguishes this county from most others in Kansas and elsewhere.

The relationship between the sheriff's department and ICE is also unusual. It illustrates the role that demography, geography, and economics together play in shaping local law-enforcement practices toward immigrants. In Ford County, ICE officials and the sheriff reached an agreement by which the sheriff or his deputies (not ICE agents) would serve all immigration warrants and papers. ICE agents agreed not even to enter Ford County except under exigent circumstances. The sheriff's office

agreed to notify ICE personnel when any self-reported, foreign-born pris-
oner was processed through the jail, but any transfer of a detainee would
be handled by the sheriff's personnel. As Sheriff Bush told us: "We have
a gentleman's agreement with ICE. The Sheriff serves ICE warrants or
contacts individuals that ICE wants to speak with. There is a great relationship between the Sheriff's department and ICE; but ICE is 150 miles
away."[33] The goal of this arrangement is clearly to avoid arousing fears
that an immigration raid is imminent, a situation that might prompt dis-
ruptions to the work force at the meat processing plants.

Sheriff Bush underscored that immigration status is never a topic for
inquiry during a traffic stop, and that questions regarding legal status
arise only during the booking process at the jail. It is striking that this
unique arrangement arose in a conservative state that is widely regarded
as strongly in favor of vigorous enforcement of immigration laws. The
Kansas secretary of state, Kris Kobach, is a nationally recognized figure
in the effort to push for more immigration enforcement at the state and
local level, and he was reportedly a key draftsperson of Arizona's SB 1070,
which attempted to create state-level immigration crimes and higher levels of local immigration enforcement. Dodge City, like El Paso, appears
to have benefitted from its isolation in ways permitting it to respond to
immigration enforcement in ways that work to its advantage.

The local economy and its dependence on meatpacking and immigrant
labor was the subject of much of our conversation with the then-city manager for Dodge City, Ken Stroebel. (Stroebel retired in 2014.) He began
with what he called "a little cattle talk" about the two plants, Cargill and
National Beef, their history in the area, and their role in the relatively robust local economy. He noted that the expansion of the plants, even during
the recession, had kept the unemployment rate low, and that business was
continuing to grow. At the time, each plant employed roughly 2,500 individuals. The odor of beef and blood lingering in the air, he told us, was "the
smell of money."

We were told that neither Cargill nor National Beef had spoken out
publicly about issues directly affecting the resident Latino population (such
as the DREAM Act or drivers' licenses for unauthorized immigrants). The
official story is that all their workers have legal status. When we discussed
law-enforcement issues, Mr. Stroebel also avoided the issue of legal status. He expressed concern about excessive traffic stops and mentioned
that it was not good for business to stop people on their way to work. In a
city that is majority Latino and with a major industry in which 90 percent

of the workers are Latino, most of whom are believed to be unauthorized, it is not hard to understand what kind of drivers he had in mind.

Mr. Stroebel, a Dodge City native, was a veteran of forty-two years in law practice. He had earlier served as the city's attorney and the attorney for area schools. He was an active participant in the selection of Chief James. He was, in short, an excellent source for learning more about the low level of civic participation among Latinos. His conclusion was that the Latino community was hard to engage in civic issues. He did, however, underscore the important role that schools play in a city's future, and he noted that this meant that Dodge City needed to invest in its overwhelmingly Latino school population. That investment, we learned, would not be forthcoming, at least in the short run. While we were conducting interviews in Dodge City, a major school bond issue failed badly at the ballot box for the second time.

We also interviewed Sister Angela, director of Hispanic Ministry for the Catholic Church in Dodge City. [34] She was optimistic about the new police chief and impressed with his background and credentials. She had been included in his community outreach efforts. She agreed with the changes he was implementing, including reassignment of some officers, enhanced training for dealing with members of the public, and the appointment of a community liaison within the department to conduct seminars for Latino residents. Like Chief James, she was anxious to see more Latino and Spanish-speaking officers on the police force. Sister Angela noted the isolation and insulation of Dodge City from the rest of the state. As she put it, you had to come to Dodge City "on purpose and intentionally." Unlike some other informants, she expressed concern over the lack of equity in the city's treatment of its Latino residents. There was money to build a new arena, to subsidize a new casino, and to refurbish the downtown historic district, but not for schools, which hold the key to the future of Dodge City. She also bemoaned the lack of Latino teachers, counselors, and administrators in the local schools.

Bianca Alvarez, the school system's Parent Involvement coordinator, also echoed this concern about the lack of Latino personnel in the schools. Though married to a Latino and fluent in Spanish, Ms. Alvarez herself is Anglo. She was the only person with whom we spoke who had worked in a processing plant and described the work as very hot, very difficult, and exhausting. Ms. Alvarez cited a litany of struggles that the schools face, including an outdated curriculum, lack of parental participation, an inadequate number of Spanish-speaking employees, crowded classes, and inadequate Latino representation among teachers and staff. She regarded the new chief of police as a good start for the city but pointed to the general failure to integrate the Latino population into civic life. She also recounted her own experience with racial profiling. She reported being stopped several times riding in the car with her (Latino) husband or members of his family. She said that there is fear in the immigrant community that reporting victimizations to the police will lead to unwanted police investigation of the legal status of the victim.

In sum, Dodge City is a place of contrasts. Its isolation allows it to shield its largely undocumented workforce from intervention by federal immigration agents, despite being in a state that actively seeks to restrict the rights of undocumented immigrants. Dodge City and Ford County have done this, not to increase civic participation or to empower Latino residents, but rather to accommodate the needs of local industry and to protect the local economy. The failure of the school bond issue, twice, and the ouster of Chief James suggests that the spirit of accommodation has implicit limits that are perhaps better understood by insiders like Sheriff Bush.

Salem, Oregon: Quietly Avoiding the Pandora's Box of Immigration Enforcement

Salem is the second largest city in Oregon, the state's capital, as well as the county seat of Marion County (see fig. 6.4). Salem lies in the center of the lush Willamette River valley, forty-seven miles from Portland. It is one of the state's oldest cities; the first European Americans, working as trappers, arrived in the area in 1812. Salem has more recently become a city of prisons, with five in the vicinity.

The backdrop against which the immigration debate has occurred in Salem includes a long and complicated racial history. As a territory, Oregon banned slavery and required that anyone who brought slaves must remove them within three years or the government would release them from servitude. Territorial leaders, however, did not want these freedmen to live in Oregon—they were required to leave or face punishment, including, for a time, whipping. The small Chinese American population was confined to menial jobs and obliged to live in a two-block section of downtown. Until 1926 African Americans were prohibited from living anywhere in the state, and the state did not ratify the Fifteenth Amendment granting voting

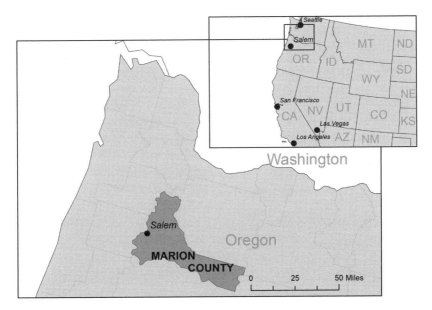

FIGURE 6.4. Salem, Oregon, and surrounding jurisdictions

rights to African American men until 1959. Several interviewees noted that the local Greyhound bus station had for a time a sign boasting that Salem was 99.9 percent white.

During World War II, Japanese Americans in the area were removed from their homes and sent to internment camps, most never to return. The *Bracero* program helped farmers to replace these workers; Oregon absorbed fifteen thousand of the estimated four million Mexican contract laborers that came to the United States to work between 1942 and 1964. When the *Bracero* camps shut down, laborers were asked to return to Mexico or face deportation, but many stayed, and new workers came into the state at a rate of forty thousand per year.[35]

Despite the state's long history of racial animosity, Salem became more ethnically and racially diverse during the 1980s and 1990s. The city's Hispanic and Asian communities grew and migration from the former Soviet bloc brought numerous Eastern European families to Marion County. Tokyo International University of America opened a Salem campus in conjunction with Willamette University in 1989. An estimated 21 percent of persons aged five years and older speak a language other than English at home, the vast majority of them speaking Spanish (72 percent). There are many restaurants and retail stores catering to Salem's immigrant communities.

Even today, however, the African American community remains small, comprising only 1.5 percent of the Salem population, according to the 2010 census. As one local resident stated in a 1995 interview, Blacks and Latinos face the same problem of gaining recognition and respect: "Salem has not accepted minority populations, period."[36] Local journalist Tim King describes his efforts to fight racism and promote civil rights in the state as "a lonely job."[37]

Nevertheless, much has changed since the 1980s when local law-enforcement agencies throughout the state carried out immigration raids and set up roadblocks in collaboration with federal immigration agents. Legal residents as well as US citizens were swept up in these raids. The resulting outcry led to a state statute in 1987 that prohibits police and sheriffs from using their resources to detect or apprehend foreign citizens, except in connection with arrests for ordinary (nonimmigration) crimes.[38] In 1997 both Marion County and the city of Salem followed this lead, adopting policies that prohibit all city and county employees, including law-enforcement officers, from enforcing immigration law.[39] Demographic change continues to create anxieties, however. A 1994 state law directed mainly toward the rising number of Latino gangs imposed a mandatory minimum sentence of five years on teenagers who commit certain types of crimes.

In 1999 parents and school administrators in Salem and nearby Keizer, Oregon, founded an organization to help Latino parents have more impact on school policies, an area of serious concern to these parents. The schools had accepted federal money based on the number of their minority students, but reportedly had not spent it on their behalf. Instead, Black and Latino children were drastically overrepresented in school suspension cases and among low-level academic performers. The Salem-Keizer Coalition for Equality (SKCFE) is a very active presence, even at the state level. In addition to lobbying, helping minority parents become more vocal, and advocating for better treatment of minority students, the group has succeeded in diversifying the historically white and conservative school board.

Local police treat immigration enforcement with caution. The Salem police department, with nearly two hundred sworn officers, appears to have an informal policy of avoiding immigration-based arrests, but has not taken a public stand on the issue. The Marion County sheriff's office, which is nearly double the size of the Salem police department, has been more open about its policies. In 2009, then sheriff Russ Isham rejected a proposal from ICE to use the county jail as a regional holding place for undocumented immigrants, arguing that there was no room for them. In keeping with county policy, the sheriff's office prohibits deputies from inquiring about immigration status. Yet deputies in the county jail facility nevertheless report to ICE all those booked who are foreign born, including naturalized citizens. In 2008, for example, the sheriff's office booked between 120 and 220 foreign-born persons per month, about a third of whom were issued an ICE detainer, with a slightly smaller proportion being transported by ICE to its facility in Medford.

Latino immigrants in Salem thus remain vulnerable to federal enforcement actions. They also suffer from a lack of clout in state or local government. Though local services are provided without inquiries into immigration status, none of the members of the city council or other top officials have Latino surnames. The problem of lack of meaningful political connections at all levels was evident in 2010 when a small group dominated by retired people, Oregonians for Immigration Reform, pushed to end the availability of drivers' licenses for persons who could not prove legal status. Oregon at that time was an outlier among the states in providing drivers' licenses without proof of citizenship; only two other states had similar liberal provisions. Pressure to change the law was building, both from the persistent lobbying efforts of Oregonians for Immigration Reform and from federal officials intent on implementing the REAL ID Act, which requires evidence of lawful status. When the issue came up for a vote by the state legislature, it aroused a strong showing from pro–drivers' license groups of Latinos and sympathizers. Despite a turnout of several thousand people favoring continuation of the state's drivers' license policy, when the members of the legislature voted on the bill to restrict licenses to legal residents and citizens, the measure was adopted. The governor, who had campaigned hard for Latino votes, signed the measure into law.

This was not, however, the end of the matter. In 2013 the pro–drivers' license forces scored a temporary win with S833, which permitted the issuing of a drivers' card to unauthorized immigrants. By this time, ten states and the District of Columbia had decided to issue licenses without evidence of legal status. Opponents of Oregon's new "driver's card" law, however, were able to gather nearly seventy-one thousand signatures, enough to force the issue to a statewide referendum. Supporters of the referendum argued that providing a driver's card rewards illegal actions and might encourage more people without legal documents to come to the state to live.[40]

Voters evidently agreed, rescinding S833 by a margin of 67 to 33 percent in November 2014.[41]

In the rural/suburban milieu in which many immigrants work, the loss of driving privileges creates a significant problem. When workers lose the right to have licenses, some growers and farmers are forced to pick up workers in vans at their homes. Driving without a license is too dangerous for most wage earners because of the county sheriff's policy of sending the names of all foreign-born people to ICE, which has meant that any unauthorized immigrant who drives without a license is at risk of deportation.

The back-and-forth policies on drivers' licenses are an indication that the role of unauthorized immigrants in Oregon communities remains unsettled. In the struggle over who belongs in the state and in Salem, unauthorized immigrants have some articulate and well-organized advocates. Two organizations, *Mano a Mano* and CAUSA, operate English classes and offer various services to individuals and families. Many Latino agricultural workers are members of a union of orchard and agricultural workers focused on immigrant rights and working conditions, *Piñeros y Campesinos Unidos del Noroeste* (PCUN). Another pro-immigrant group is the Coalition for a Working Oregon, comprised of twenty different business groups, including orchard owners, managers of local businesses, church leaders, and farmers. The group formed with the goal of defeating anti-immigrant policies in the area and nationally. Representatives of these organizations have worked with local law enforcement to come to at least an informal understanding about the need to avoid racial profiling and pretextual stops, but the contours of that understanding remain unclear to most residents, and perhaps to many patrol officers and sheriff's deputies.

One of the lessons of Salem is that unauthorized immigrants can be vulnerable to deportation, even in the absence of a 287(g) agreement and even in the presence of policies against assisting in immigration enforcement. The lack of a clear consensus about how to respond to the significant numbers of unauthorized residents in the community makes for an uneasy peace in Salem. The white establishment has kept its silence at all levels, except in the schools, where there has been some response to the demographic changes that have occurred. The rule of silence prevailed even in our attempts to gain interviews with key city officials. The city manager and most council members refused to meet with us. The Salem police chief expressed a willingness to meet, but the city manager intervened and ordered him not to do so. The picture that emerges from Salem is one of reluctance to integrate unauthorized immigrants into the community, but also reluctance to take active steps to remove them. We suspect that the lack of overt pursuit of anti-immigrant policies arises partially because of the economic importance of foreign-born workers to the largely agricultural economy, and partially because of the articulate political interests that have organized to hold the line against nativism.

Salem, in short, lacks the elite consensus that was evident in Dodge City and El Paso, where it was understood by everyone in authority that the city must protect its resident immigrant workers in order to remain economically healthy. Nor is it like Allentown, where the minority community is also marginalized, but not because of lack of legal status. In none of these communities, however, is there a widespread public consensus about the importance of unauthorized immigrants as members of the civil, political, and social community. Immigrants, whether legally present or not, are appreciated for their work, particularly as that work benefits an economic and political elite. They are less appreciated for the cultural diversity they bring to the community or for the fact that in each of the cities we studied, they are a significant proportion of the population.

Conclusion

The pressures on local police to "deal with" immigration come from many directions and are shifting. This suggests that the contours and fabric of the immigration-policing patchwork are dynamic. This issue is likely to remain dynamic, as global terror threats, increased mobility, challenges to economic security, and high levels of immigration undermine conventional understandings of who is a member of urban communities. The policies and practices that we discussed in this chapter are therefore subject to change. In each case they reflect the outcomes of informal negotiations or mutual adjustment between the police and the many publics that have an influence on their work. Practical realities of the local context also influence these negotiations, as these case studies indicate. The local economy is a major determinant of immigration enforcement in Dodge City, for example. Long-standing community ties and the sheer size of the immigrant population are significant conditioning factors in El Paso. Allentown and Salem are more mixed cases. In each of these cases federal policy also plays a role, but, from the local perspective, it is a surprisingly limited and malleable role. Still, as federal law and policy changes, community responses are likely to be affected. But our evidence suggests that local leaders will filter any change in federal law through the prism of their particular needs and aspirations.

Just as we believe that demography is not destiny, neither is geography destiny. Significantly, the local arrangements we describe here do not arise out of a statewide or even an area-wide ethos. Kansas and Texas are well known as states committed to very strong enforcement-oriented policies designed to detect and remove unauthorized immigrants. Yet, as we have shown, local enforcement policies in Dodge City and El Paso do not reflect that approach. Geography, however, does make its weight felt in other respects. El Paso could not realistically cut the ties that bind it to Ciudad Juárez and still thrive economically. Economic power also makes its weight felt, as the situation in Dodge City illustrates. The needs of the meat-processing plants, we found, are strong enough to limit immigration enforcement to situations of serious criminal offending, even in the absence of any significant political participation by resident immigrants.

What each of these communities lack is a comprehensive strategy that would enhance assimilation and integration of immigrants into the fabric of their communities, though Allentown has taken steps in a positive direction with the recent founding of its Mayor's Office of Immigrant Affairs. Local law enforcement is buffeted between demands for "enforcing the law" and protecting (but not interfering with) large numbers of unauthorized individuals who play key roles in the community, particularly as labor, but also as consumers who spend money and as students who fill the public schools. Commitments to the ideals of community policing, we found, must also be factored into the policies that local law enforcement develops. Each of the law-enforcement organizations we encountered in our case studies adheres to some degree to the basic principle that trust among all members of the community is important for effective policing. With little guidance on how to balance this principle against federal and state entreaties to cooperate in immigration enforcement, they must find their own way forward. The result is the richly diverse patchwork that is immigration federalism.

CHAPTER SEVEN

Conclusions and Recommendations: Finding the Way Forward

Fourteen percent of the United States population was born outside the United States. Eleven percent are children of immigrants. One-quarter of the US population has been in the country two generations or less.[1] A significant proportion, over eleven million people, have either overstayed a visa or entered the country illegally. In a few states over 10 percent of schoolchildren have at least one unauthorized parent. Unauthorized residents are, to varying degrees, married, employed, parents, students, and contributors to their communities. The immigration issue is not small, it is not new, and despite recent federal efforts to provide administrative relief from deportation, it is not going away any time soon.

The central theme of this book is that immigration enforcement is a "patchwork" of policy, legislation, and enforcement. Much enforcement activity occurs in the space between the law on the books and the law in action, a space that is often invisible to scrutiny and review. Standards are unclear, and guidelines for enforcing immigration law are changing and often vague. This problem is growing. Indeed, the response to immigration has been a "spreading patchwork" as law enforcement and government at all levels move forward in a sometimes-uncoordinated fashion to meet the dynamic challenges posed by immigration.

This spreading patchwork has a number of consequences for immigrants, citizens, and law enforcement. The patchwork creates uncertainty about how officials—especially law-enforcement officers—will respond to persons, actions, and circumstances. The lack of clear expectations feeds suspicion of officials and undermines faith in the legal system. A growing body of work emphasizes the importance of trust and confidence in frontline personnel and in procedural justice within the legal system. The absence of that trust and confidence endangers public safety, as has been recently observed in many poor neighborhoods with large African American populations with a history of harsh policing. The goal, if the system is to work effectively and fairly in a democratic system, must be to create a broad-based consensus that the system is legitimate, that is, that the law has moral power, not just coercive capacity.

We organize our conclusions about immigration enforcement around four general observations, followed by several policy recommendations.

We observe *first* that local immigration enforcement is a recent phenomenon. In the 1968 Kerner Report on race and civil disorders, for example, one of the authors remarked on the federal government's notable lack of enforcement of its immigration laws.[2] As late as the 1990s, border control was lax, and interior enforcement of immigration was almost nonexistent. The impetus for change came from the grassroots and cannot be attributed simply to the growing number of immigrants without legal authorization residing in the United States. What developed over time, sometimes aided by political rhetoric, was the perceived "threat" of illegal immigrants and the challenge to national sovereignty that this population was thought to represent, particularly following the events of 9/11. Advocacy groups, law enforcement, and legislators at all levels reacted to growing public anxiety about unauthorized immigrants, rather than proactively engaging with their growing numbers. Law enforcement was required to deal with immigration from the front lines, often without much political support.

This situation has not changed. Because of the rapidly changing dynamics of immigration, law enforcement often finds itself playing from behind. Training, policies, practices, and relationships are forged out of necessity and often based on old data and old models. For example, experts did not anticipate or plan for the surge in Central American youth across the southwest border in the early months of the summer of 2014. Every level of government was ill prepared to deal with the legal, humanitarian, and practical challenges presented by this unanticipated migration. Clearly, a more nuanced approach would involve investigation and planning, and to the extent possible, should anticipate changes in migratory flows before they occur.

Our *second* observation begins with the fact that the federal government and state and local governments all answer to a different set of constituencies, mandates, and funding priorities. They do not all look the same way at the opportunities and challenges posed by legal and unauthorized immigration. In the realm of enforcement in the nation's interior, the federal government has always prioritized its own concerns, most recently with achieving high, and unprecedented, numbers of deportations. The 287(g) program and Secure Communities assert the federal view of local police and sheriffs as "force multipliers" in the federal effort to detect and remove immigrants subject to deportation.

This blurring of functions between the federal and local levels has met with resistance in some places and a warm embrace in others. A recent *New York Times* editorial took note of the growing local resistance to the "force multiplier" perspective: "Both states and cities are rejecting the blurring of a once-bright line that separated local cops and federal immigration agencies. For the local police, it's a costly and dangerous diversion from their main job, preventing crime and catching criminals."[3] As we noted in earlier chapters, this is the position taken by the Major Cities Chiefs Section of the International Association of Chiefs of Police, and most recently by the President's Task Force on 21st Century Policing, which asserts that "Law enforcement agencies should build relationships based on trust with immigrant communities. This is central to overall public safety."[4] One of its action items is to "Decouple federal immigration enforcement from routine local policing for civil enforcement and nonserious crime."[5] These sentiments are not shared by everyone, however, as we have seen. Chiefs of small- or medium-sized departments and sheriffs are often more amenable to federal partnerships to enforce immigration law.

Even in places amenable to federal priorities, local politics determine how programs will be implemented. At its peak, for example, there were more 287(g) agreements between the federal government and law-enforcement groups in North Carolina than in any other state. This emphasis arose less from the migration challenges North Carolina was facing at the time than from local political pressures and preferences. The power of local politics is also evident in the upsurge of state and local action to deter or detect unauthorized immigrants. Most of this activity has been through state legislation, but executive orders from governors, decisions of state attorneys general, and city ordinances have also played a role.

These efforts have not been well coordinated with federal actions or among local governments. Within states, the actions of various governmental units have sometimes moved at cross-purposes, with law enforcement agencies caught in the middle. For example, the Maricopa County sheriff, with 287(g) powers and an aggressive stance toward immigration enforcement, conducted raids in the City Hall in Mesa, Arizona, without consultation with Mesa's own police department. The raid highlighted troubling jurisdictional and public-safety issues, as well as important questions about varying local priorities and coordination of effort.

Part of the problem is that immigration enforcement is not a good candidate for devolving formerly federal responsibilities to local agencies. Enforcement of immigration laws against settled, otherwise law-abiding immigrants who arrived or stayed without legal authorization arouses strong emotions on all sides and almost inevitably invites racial profiling. The cooperative relationships envisioned by the "force multiplier" approach are, in practice, hard to manage and are limited by constitutional considerations that separate federal and local law enforcement from each other.

This brings us to our *third* observation: that the patchwork—the disconnectedness among levels of government and units of government across the country—has been increasing and is unlikely to end soon. The move toward more engagement across levels has not been accompanied by better communication. Consider, for example, the cool reception in many of the nation's largest cities to the Secure Communities program. Despite objections voiced shortly after the program was rolled out in 2008, not until November 2014, after a series of lawsuits and many refusals to participate, did the Department of Homeland Security finally acknowledge the need to change course. In the meantime, local law enforcement was left with little guidance, no fiscal support, and a lack of leadership by federal law enforcement and elected leaders at all levels.

Lack of clear policy guidance, especially in an area of controversy, creates a wide space for law-enforcement officers to act as street-level bureaucrats making crucial decisions, in this case, life-changing decisions that can propel an immigrant toward deportation. The essentially unreviewable decisions by law-enforcement officers, social-services administrators, prosecutors, and other frontline personnel make government authority less transparent. This does not always work to the disadvantage of immigrants. Some local agencies and staff have used their discretion to take actions that support the integration or welcoming of immigrants into the community, a process that scholars have dubbed *bureaucratic incorporation*.[6] From a governance perspective, however, these types of discretionary actions, whether supportive or punitive toward immigrants, mean that bureaucratic agents and agencies—not elected officials and laws—become the critical dynamic in forging responses to immigration.[7]

Those public officials who work on the front lines of enforcement or service provision will only become more important as the patchwork continues its fragmentary trajectory. These officials do not have the luxury of "waiting and watching" to see what is going to happen on the legislative front. This is particularly true for police officers and sheriffs' deputies, who must respond to the challenges posed by large volumes of 911 calls. They cannot pick and choose their issues, deflecting cases and conflicts they do not want to deal with to other units. The majority of these calls are for service, usually not for violations of criminal law, but instead for matters of public safety and public information. The "impossible mandate" faced by law enforcement means they must juggle competing demands for action or inaction, arrest or no arrest, and responsiveness or unresponsiveness in situations of ambiguity and personal conflict.

Our *fourth* observation arises from the narrow focus on enforcement at the federal level, which finds its parallel at the local level in states like Arizona, Kansas, and Texas. The emphasis on enforcement has occurred at the expense of the need to educate the public about both the costs and the benefits of immigration, and to engage with and promote productive integration strategies at the local level. Education, health services, and housing are real concerns where new immigrants settle. Neglect of the many issues associated with settlement of these new residents has helped to frame immigration in many minds as a burden imposed by the federal government on local governments.

The entanglement of police and sheriffs in detecting unauthorized immigrants has sent a particularly powerful negative message, helping to cast these newcomers as quasi criminals with no place in American society. The extent to which these residents contribute labor, form families, and participate in civic life tend to stay out of the public spotlight. In this pernicious atmosphere, advocacy groups and nongovernmental organizations must perforce adopt a defensive posture, focusing on the hardships of deportation rather than the powerful integrative role they could otherwise play. Most significantly for our analysis, the enforcement-based approach that the federal government has taken since the late 1990s directly challenges local law-enforcement's commitment to the principle of community-oriented policing, which seeks to build a foundation of broad-based trust in law enforcement in the community at large.[8]

In the face of the daily challenges of maintaining order and enforcing the law, local law-enforcement agencies have looked to their national leadership for guidance. The relevant national organizations include the

Major Cities Chiefs Section of the International Association of Chiefs of Police, the Police Executive Research Forum, the Police Foundation, and the National Sheriffs' Association. These groups have responded variously to calls for greater local involvement in immigration enforcement. But even if there were consistency, there are inherent limits to broad policy statements. Often local law enforcement encounters unauthorized immigrants as victims, which necessarily complicates enforcement issues. Difficult questions arise about whether to arrest possible victims of human trafficking, how to deal with undocumented children and their parents, whether to arrest undocumented witnesses of crime, how to identify and respond to victims of sex trafficking, and how to manage a host of heretofore unanticipated decisions, each of which has little or no precedent or antecedent in training or policy. These decisions call for the exercise of broad powers of discretion, often in the face of little or no policy or legal guidance. Neither government nor law enforcement leaders have attempted to provide a playbook to guide officers as they face these real-life situations. So the patchwork continues to spread, with life-changing inconsistencies in the responses of law enforcement within geographic jurisdictions and among individual officers.

Limitations of This Study

This is a study of the perceptions of law-enforcement leaders, advocates within communities who support immigrant rights, and local political leaders as they confront immigration in their communities. They respond to this essentially local issue in the context of a federal policy of enhanced local participation in enforcing federal immigration laws. To understand how local leaders are resolving the challenges they face, we rely on quantitative (survey) and qualitative (case study) evidence. There are significant limitations in both sources of data. Our survey evidence is confined to chiefs and sheriffs who administer law-enforcement agencies across the nation. Some of our questions ask chiefs and sheriffs to make inferences about what is happening on the street as their officers confront suspected unauthorized immigrants. We cannot assume that these inferences will be accurate. The case studies provide an important supplement to this material. Our interviews with immigrant advocates, political leaders, and other observers in seven communities added considerable depth and reliability to our survey findings. Nevertheless, the number of case studies was not large and this phase of the work, like the surveys, occurred within a relatively short space of time. We are not, therefore, in a position to assess the long-term impacts of policies, legislation, and practices.

We should also note that policy changes at the executive and local level are frequent, creating a moving target for study. While Congress remains caught up in a seemingly intractable stalemate concerning federal immigration policy, the federal executive sometimes has taken action on its own. Our study began during the period when congressionally authorized 287(g) agreements were the main avenue for local/federal cooperation in immigration enforcement. Within two years, 287(g) agreements had been supplemented and would soon be entirely upstaged by the Secure Communities program, a creation of the Department of Homeland Security under Secretary Janet Napolitano. Secure Communities became the dominant program across the United States during the latter phases of our field research. In November 2014, Napolitano's replacement, Jeh Johnson, announced the discontinuance of Secure Communities and its replacement with the Priority Enforcement Program, which is supposed to focus enforcement efforts on immigrants who have committed serious crimes and to significantly reduce requests for detaining arrested immigrants.

Many states and some localities were also active in creating laws designed to deter or support unauthorized immigrants during the period of our research. We have attempted to take account of the general direction of these laws to the extent they are relevant to what cities and towns are doing. Still, this is an on-going process and changes of direction are possible. Despite the limitations imposed by time and resource constraints, our research remains the most detailed and comprehensive yet undertaken to understand the response of local law-enforcement agencies to pressure to enforce federal immigration law.

Recommendations

It has been astutely observed that strategies that emphasize community connection over arrests and prosecution are vulnerable to change when crime rates increase or new challenges to community order arise.[9] Immigration may well be just such a challenge. For this reason it is important that research on the role of local law enforcement continue as executive policies and state laws continue to change in light of shifting public opinion and political realities. It is also important to target for research the specific populations that become a focus of national-security and public-safety concerns. These shift from time to time, vis-à-vis the Muslim residents who were subjected to heightened scrutiny after the 9/11 terrorist attacks.

With the challenges posed by immigration-related law enforcement also come opportunities. There is growing evidence that immigration is a driving force in innovation within the ranks of law enforcement and, apparently, among immigrants. Law-enforcement agencies in California, researchers found, responded to immigration in their communities with language training and other programs, and did so more adeptly than their city governments.[10] At the same time, new immigrants and the groups they form bring their values, practices, and relationships to their new setting. Angela Stuesse and Mathew Coleman found that, in the face of possible deportation, networks among immigrants formed, often based on the use of social media.[11] Sharing information about police checkpoints and saturation patrols enhanced feelings of solidarity and helped create ties with more established immigrants and the general community.

Nor are all the consequences of the patchwork that we have described problematic. The ability to tailor a response to local circumstances is one benefit of the loose reins that the federal government is obliged to maintain under the American system of divided powers. The circumstances in Nogales, Arizona, and Bemidji, Minnesota, are quite different, despite their close proximity to an international border. The patchwork allows communities to craft a response that accommodates local circumstances, capabilities, and history. Our case studies document the important role that local context plays in immigration enforcement. The differences between East Haven and New Haven (despite their many similarities, including a shared border), the role of powerful economic interests in Dodge City, and the historical cultural and economic connections between El Paso and Ciudad Juárez are three examples of how local context shapes immigration policy and enforcement.

What is missing is a broadly shared sense that immigrants who have settled in the United States have some moral claim to remain that law and policy should honor. There has been some effort to take length of residence into account in administrative policies the federal government has developed to guide prosecutorial discretion, but such directives remain a matter of executive grace, not law. The Supreme Court, in several sharply divided cases decided over a century ago, deemed even immigrants with long roots in the United States to be vulnerable to deportation. These decisions, reached after openly racist arguments alluding to the evils of racial mixing and the dangers of alien races, do not stand critical scrutiny in an era that rejects racism and embraces basic human rights. The United States may be moving slowly to acknowledging this lack of fit with contemporary values. Length of residence and evidence of connections to American citizens were key criteria in President Obama's executive actions to defer deportation to selected groups of unauthorized immigrants.

An enforcement policy acknowledges the need to accept long-term unauthorized residents as legitimate members of the American community, combined with federal policy that respects community policing, are key elements in any plan for going forward. This means that federal engagement of local police and sheriffs must be limited to cases where the threat to public safety and security is real. Any other approach may be self-defeating, as recent research on the effect of aggressive enforcement on "self-deportation" shows.[12] To do otherwise is to reshape the mission of local police and sheriffs to federal priorities, which raises constitutional and political issues that should be avoided in a robust federal system. Such an approach also undermines trust in local law enforcement, a key element in engaging communities and enhancing public safety.

These broad principles, however, leave a lot of room for policy development. To achieve a comprehensive approach to immigration enforcement in the nation's interior, all the relevant parties should be involved, and the inquiry should be broad-based, even to the point of including the possibility of state-level participation in some admissions decisions, as occurs in Canada.[13] The relevant participants include, at a minimum, law-enforcement agencies at all levels, representatives of immigrants' rights groups, municipal leaders familiar with immigrant incorporation issues, and academic and think-tank scholars who can provide relevant insights and research. The federal government, whether through executive action or congressional legislation, should not attempt to resolve the policy paradox of interior enforcement by itself. That approach, our study shows, ignores the complexity of our federal system and the diversity of responses to immigration across the nation. Devolution in this realm must work from a shared understanding of the principles and priorities at stake.

This approach to reshaping law-enforcement priorities has sound precedent behind it. National commissions with a broad range of voices have been convened at comparable points in the history of American law enforcement. In 1929 the National Commission on Law Observance and Enforcement was formed. Better known as the Wickersham Commission, this group was critical of the role of law enforcement in its response to Prohibition. The National Advisory Commission on Civil Disorders (better known as the Kerner Commission) was formed in 1967 to investigate the causes of the urban riots of the 1960s. The role of law enforcement in responding to urban disorder was a key focus of the Kerner Report. President Carter created the Select Commission on Immigration and Refugee Policy (SCIRP), also known as the Hesburgh Commission in 1979, and its findings served as the foundation for all major immigration legislation that followed over the next decade. The challenges faced by local law enforcement in the face of immigration make this an appropriate time for a new national commission to sort out the best way forward in the context of continued immigration and a changing, challenging, and increasingly globalized environment.

Appendix

Multivariate Analyses of Policing Practices and Local Government Policies

This appendix reports the results of the multivariate analyses described in chapter 4 (reported in the section "Putting It All Together"). Table A.1 provides results for the large-city sample, table A.2 for the small-city sample, and table A.3 for the county sheriffs. Within each of the tables, the first three columns of results show estimates from analyses of the three policing practices examined in chapter 4:

> *Enforcement Count*: The number of scenarios in which identification is checked or federal immigration authorities are contacted;
> *Gaining Trust*: The five-point scale of agreement with the statement that "gaining the trust of unauthorized immigrants is a priority" for the police department or sheriff office; and
> *No ICE Involvement*: The chief or sheriff's response of "yes" to the statement, "We do not participate or assist in ICE immigration-enforcement activities." (Recall that ICE is the federal Immigration and Customs Enforcement agency.)

Thus, positive and significant coefficients for the *Enforcement Count* column indicate variables that are associated with *restrictive* policing practices toward unauthorized immigrants. By contrast, positive and significant coefficients for the next two columns indicate variables associated with *supportive* practices toward unauthorized immigrants.

The fourth column of results in each table relates not to policing practices, but to the policy established by the elected governing board of the

TABLE A.1 **Large-City Multivariate Results**

| | Policing practices | | City government policy |
	Enforcement Count	Gaining Trust	No ICE Involvement	Strictness of City Policy
Strictness of city government policy (five-point scale)	.558 (.118)***	-.302 (.127)**	-.482 (.142)***	—
State passed anti-immigrant policy, 2005–7	.445 (.269)*	-.187 (.285)	-.340 (.250)	-.392 (.283)
City within 200 miles of Mexico	-.240 (.339)	-.053 (.447)	-.048 (.343)	.412 (.353)
Population size (in thousands), 2005	-.001 (.001)	.002 (.001)***	.000 (.000)	.001 (.001)
Population foreign born, 2005, %	-.038 (.013)***	.020 (.013)	.009 (.010)	-.012 (.014)
Percentage-point change in Latino population, 1990–2005	-.004 (.016)	.022 (.017)	.009 (.017)	-.022 (.014)
Employment in immigrant-heavy sectors, %	.001 (.027)	.008 (.024)	-.001 (.025)	.039 (.026)
Unemployment rate, 2005, %	.089 (.109)	-.100 (.120)	-.091 (.114)	-.112 (.129)
Violent crime rate per 10,000 population, 2005	-.002 (.004)	.001 (.003)	-.000 (.003)	-.002 (.004)
Political conservatism scale	.632 (.576)	.560 (.520)	-.408 (.532)	2.468 (.715)***
Constant	2.099 (.839)**	—	.643 (.790)	—
N	220	219	222	222
Type of analysis	OLS	Ordered logit	Probit	Ordered logit
R²	0.233	—	—	—
Pseudo R²	—	0.041	0.150	0.065

Note: Data are unstandardized coefficients, with robust standard errors in parentheses, unless otherwise noted.

*p < .10.

**p < .05.

***p < .01.

TABLE A.2 **Small-City Multivariate Results**

	Policing practices			City government policy
	Enforcement Count	Gaining Trust	No ICE Involvement	Strictness of City Policy
Strictness of city government policy (five-point scale)	.515 (.189)***	-.060 (.298)	-.372 (.180)**	—
State passed anti-immigrant policy, 2005–10	.210 (.457)	-.520 (.499)	.348 (.345)	.733 (.565)
City within 200 miles of Mexico	.336 (.686)	-.363 (.690)	-.510 (.517)	-.583 (.915)
Population size (in thousands), 2008	-.014 (.015)	.001 (.016)	.006 (.012)	-.014 (.019)
Population foreign born, 2008, %	-.020 (.024)	.013 (.024)	-.018 (.017)	.017 (.040)
Percentage-point change in Latino population, 1990–2008	-.032 (.027)	-.006 (.028)	.021 (.026)	.016 (.039)
Employment in immigrant-heavy sectors, %	.035 (.047)	.024 (.045)	-.034 (.036)	-.082 (.047)*
Unemployment rate, 2008, %	-.266 (.175)	.086 (.148)	-.032 (.117)	.265 (.168)
Violent crime rate per 10,000 population, 2005	.009 (.006)	-.004 (.006)	-.006 (.004)	-.004 (.008)
Political conservatism scale	2.058 (.866)**	-.228 (.837)	-.817 (.732)	2.546 (1.214)**
Constant	2.874 (1.403)**	—	1.713 (1.187)	—
N	95	95	95	95
Type of analysis	OLS	Ordered logit	Probit	Ordered logit
R^2	0.240	—	—	—
Pseudo R^2	—	0.016	0.113	0.077

Note: Data are unstandardized coefficients, with robust standard errors in parentheses, unless otherwise noted.

*$p < .10$.
**$p < .05$.
***$p < .01$.

TABLE A.3 **County Sheriff Multivariate Results**

	Policing practices			County government policy
	Enforcement Count[a]	Gaining Trust	No ICE Involvement	Strictness of County Policy
Strictness of county government policy (five-point scale)	.174 (.196)	.295 (.167)*	-.310 (.111)***	—
State passed anti-immigrant policy, 2005–9	.344 (.385)	.270 (.308)	.097 (.192)	.486 (.327)
County within 200 miles of Mexico	.258 (.694)	.959 (.429)**	-.357 (.332)	-.979 (.734)
Population size (in thousands), 2008	-.001 (.000)***	-.000 (.000)	.000 (.000)	.000 (.000)
Population foreign born, 2008, %	.038 (.034)	.030 (.026)	.009 (.016)	.017 (.041)
Percentage-point change in Latino population, 1990–2008	-.105 (.045)**	.009 (.034)	-.010 (.022)	-.045 (.048)
Employment in immigrant-heavy sectors, %	.038 (.029)	-.024 (.022)	.036 (.016)**	-.004 (.025)
Unemployment rate, 2008, %	.066 (.173)	.041 (.131)	-.106 (.096)	.086 (.131)
Violent crime rate per 10,000 population, 2007	.008 (.010)	-.002 (.006)	-.005 (.004)	.002 (.006)
Republican of two-party presidential vote, 2004, %	.030 (.016)*	-.009 (.011)	-.015 (.008)*	.037 (.014)***
Constant	1.246 (1.513)	—	.601 (.772)	—
N	194	241	251	251
Type of analysis	OLS	Ordered logit	Probit	Ordered logit
R^2	0.123	—	—	—
Pseudo R^2	—	0.026	0.075	0.033

Note: Data are unstandardized coefficients, with robust standard errors in parentheses, unless otherwise noted.

[a] Includes full-service sheriff offices only (i.e., those providing both jail and patrol services).

*$p < .10$.
**$p < .05$.
***$p < .01$.

city or county (as reported by the chief or sheriff). Here the dependent variable is *Strictness of City (or County) Policy*, which is a five-point, ordered scale regarding how "tough" the local government's posture is regarding immigration policing. It ranges from officially declared "sanctuary" communities (a score of 1 on the scale) to local governments that "expect the police department [sheriff's office] to take a proactive role in deterring unauthorized immigration in all . . . activities" (a score of 5). Local governments that have no official policy regarding unauthorized immigrants, or where the chief or sheriff is unsure whether such a policy exists, are given the intermediate score of 3.[1] For the *Strictness* column, positive and significant coefficients indicate variables that are associated with more restrictive local government policies regarding unauthorized immigrants.

Thus, there are four columns of multivariate results for each sample (large cities, small cities, sheriff offices). Because the dependent variables differ in format (relatively continuous scales, ordered categories, dichotomous categories), the appropriate estimation strategy also differs (ordinary least-squares [OLS], ordered logit, and probit regression, respectively).

Each of the independent variables used in these analyses is described in chapter 4. The year of data collection for several of these independent variables (e.g., unemployment rate) varies, due to the different years in which we surveyed the sample in question. The large-city survey was conducted in 2007–8, the small-city survey in 2010, and the sheriff survey in 2009–10. The multivariate analysis of small cities is limited to those for which a score on the political conservatism index is available; as described in chapter 4, this generally limits the sample to communities of twenty-five thousand or greater population. For that reason, in describing the multivariate results in chapter 4, we place more emphasis on the large-city and sheriff-office estimates.

Notes

Chapter One

1. SB 1070, the Support our Law Enforcement and Safe Neighborhoods Act, requires local law enforcement to inquire about immigration status during any lawful stop if the officer suspects the individual lacks legal status. It also creates a misdemeanor for failure to carry immigration documents, makes it illegal to solicit work, permits warrantless arrest of suspected unauthorized immigrants, penalizes transporting an unauthorized immigrant, prohibits jurisdictions in the state from limiting this law, and allows private citizens to sue law enforcement agencies if they believe the agency is not aggressively enforcing the law. AZ Statutes 2010, Chapter 113, http://www.azleg.gov/legtext/49leg/2r/bills/sb1070h.pdf.

2. See statement by the Legal Law Enforcement Engagement Initiative, an organization of police officials who favor federal immigration reform, July 20, 2010, http://ndn.org/blog/2010/07/law-enforcement-officials-support-partial-injunction-sb1070. The Arizona Association of Chiefs of Police predicted that SB 1070 will "negatively affect the ability of law enforcement agencies across the state to fulfill their many responsibilities in a timely matter," http://www.readbag.com/leei-us-main-media-aacop-statement-on-senate-bill-1070.

3. Angela Stuesse and Mathew Coleman, "Automobility, Immobility, Altermobility: Surviving and Resisting the Intensification of Immigrant Policing," *City & Society* 26:1 (2014): 105–26, 106.

4. David B. Robertson and Dennis R. Judd, *The Development of American Public Policy: The Structure of Policy Restraint* (Glenview: Scott Foresman, 1989).

5. Nor are the opportunities for affecting policies the same at every level, as Lisa L. Miller demonstrates in *The Perils of Federalism, Race, Poverty, and the Politics of Crime Control* (New York: Oxford University Press, 2008).

6. See, e.g., Kitty Calavita, *Inside the State: The Bracero Program, Immigration, and the I.N.S.* (New York: Routledge, 1992); and Daniel J. Tichenor, *Dividing Lines: The Politics of Immigration Control in America,* Princeton: Princeton University Press, 2002.

7. Hiroshi Motomura is credited with coining the term "immigration federalism" in a 1999 paper in which he asks what role should states and localities play in making and implementing law and policy relating to immigration and immigrants ("Federalism, International Human Rights, and Immigration Exceptionalism," *University of Colorado Law Review* 70 (1999): 1361–94. 1361). See also Alesandra Filindra and Daniel Tichenor, "Raising *Arizona v. United States*: The Origins and Development of Immigration Federalism," *Lewis and Clark Law Review* 16:4 (2012–13): 1215–47.

8. See, e.g., Frank Baumgartner and Bryan Jones, *Agendas and Instability in American Politics* (Chicago: University of Chicago Press, 1993), who show that, in many controversial policy areas, "each institutional venue is home to a different image of the same question" (34).

9. Sally Falk Moore, "Law and Social Change: The Semi-Autonomous Social Field as an Appropriate Subject of Study," *Law & Society Review* 7:4 (1973): 719–46.

10. Malcolm Feeley summarizes and critiques this perspective in "The Concept of Laws in Social Science: A Critique and Notes on an Expanded View," *Law & Society Review* 10:4 (1976): 497–523.

11. Valerie Jenness and Ryken Grattet, "The Law-In-Between: The Effects of Organizational Perviousness on the Policing of Hate Crime," *Social Problems* 52:3 (2005): 337–59.

12. David Garland, *The Culture of Control: Crime and Social Order in Contemporary Society* (Chicago: University of Chicago Press, 2001); and Katherine Beckett, *Making Crime Pay: Law and Order in Contemporary American Politics* (New York: Oxford University Press, 1997).

13. Stephen H. Legomsky, "The New Path of Immigration Law: Asymmetric Incorporation of Criminal Justice Norms," *Washington and Lee Law Review* 64 (2007): 469–528.

14. See, particularly, Juliet Stumpf, "The Crimmigration Crisis: Immigrants, Crime, and Sovereign Power," *American University Law Review* 56 (2006): 367–419.

15. Leanne Weber and Benjamin Bowling, "Policing Migration: A Framework for Investigating the Regulation of Global Mobility," *Policing & Society* 14:3 (2004): 195–212.

16. Suzanne Mettler and Joe Soss, "The Consequences of Public Policy for Democratic Citizenship: Bridging Policy Studies and Mass Politics," *Perspectives on Politics* 2:1 (2004): 55–73.

17. Murray Edelman, *Constructing the Political Spectacle* (Chicago: University of Chicago Press, 1988), 7–8. Political rhetoric can also contribute to fear of immigrants; see Daniel J. Hopkins, "Politicized Places: Explaining Where and When Immigrants Provoke Local Opposition," *American Political Science Review* 104:1 (2010): 40–60.

18. Hiroshi Motomura, "The Discretion that Matters: Federal Immigration Enforcement, State and Local Arrests, and the Civil-Criminal Line," *UCLA Law Review* 58:6 (August 2011): 1819–58, 1819.

19. The association of illegal status and other undesirable characteristics with Mexican origins has a long history. See Mae Ngai, *Impossible Subjects: Illegal Aliens and the Making of Modern America* (Princeton: Princeton University Press, 2003); see also Leo Chavez, *The Latino Threat: Constructing Immigrants, Citizens, and the Nation* (Stanford: Stanford University Press, 2008).

20. On the significance of prosecutorial discretion in immigration cases, see Marjorie S. Zatz and Nancy Rodriguez, *Dreams and Nightmares: Immigration Policy, Youth, and Families* (Oakland: University of California Press, 2015).

21. Our work speaks indirectly to the argument that has been advanced by de Genova, Calavita, and others suggesting that this condition of deportability keeps wage rates low, thus working to the advantage of some business interests. Kitty Calavita describes them as "useful invaders" (*Immigrants at the Margins: Race and Exclusion in Southern Europe* [Cambridge: Cambridge University Press, 2005]). See also Nicholas De Genova, *Working the Boundaries: Race, Space, and "Illegality" in Mexican Chicago* (Durham: Duke University Press, 2005).

22. The problems associated with an immigrant's "perilous" or nonexistent legal status and "liminal legality" have spawned a large literature. For a recent example, see Geoffrey Heeren, "The Status of Nonstatus," *American University Law Review* 64 (2015), 1115–81.

23. Chiamaka Nwosu, Jeanne Batalova, and Gregory Auclair, "Frequently Requested Statistics on Immigrants and Immigration in the United States," Migration Policy Institute, April 28, 2014, http://www.migrationpolicy.org/article/frequently -requested-statistics-immigrants-and-immigration-united-states.

24. Jeffrey S. Passel, D'Vera Cohn, Jens Manuel Krogstad, and Ana Gonzalez-Barrera, "As Growth Stalls, Unauthorized Immigrant Population Becomes More Settled," Pew Research Hispanic Trends Project, September 3, 2014, http://www .pewhispanic.org/2014/09/03/as-growth-stalls-unauthorized-immigrant-population -becomes-more-settled/.

25. Beginning with a list of all municipalities with populations of less than 65,000 in the counties that meet the criteria above, we assigned each community to its region (Northeast, Midwest, South, or West) and to its population size range (0–4,999; 5,000–9,999; 10,000–19,999; 20,000–34,999; 35,000–49,999; and 50,000–64,999). We then determined what percentage of the total population of the overall set of cities lived in each stratum (i.e., region by size range), and randomly selected the correct number of cities in each stratum to attain this percentage within our sample. Because we focused on "where the population is" within the overall set of small cities, larger-population communities were more likely to be selected for the sample than smaller ones. Municipalities without their own police departments (typically because they contract for police service with a neighboring town or a county sheriff) were excluded and replaced by another city of similar size from the same region.

26. Daniel J. Tichenor and Alexandra Filindra, "Raising *Arizona v. United States*: Historical Patterns of American Immigration Federalism," *Lewis and Clark Law Review* 16:4 (201): 1215–47.

27. Monica W. Varsanyi, ed., *Taking Local Control: Immigration Policy Activism in U.S. Cities and States* (Stanford: Stanford University Press, 2010).

28. David A. Harris, "The War on Terror, Local Police, and Immigration Enforcement: A Curious Tale of Police Power in Post-9/11 America," *Rutgers Law Journal* 38 (2006): 1.

29. Anne Schneider and Helen Ingram, "Social Construction of Target Populations: Implications for Politics and Policy," *American Political Science Review* 87 (1993), 334–47; Andrea Louise Campbell, *How Policies Make Citizens* (Princeton: Princeton University Press, 2003); Suzanne Mettler and Joe Soss, "The Consequences of Public Policy for Democratic Citizenship: Bridging Policy Studies and Mass Politics," *Perspectives on Politics* 2 (2004): 55–73; and, more generally, James G. March and Johan P. Olsen, "The New Institutionalism: Organizational Factors in Political Life," *American Political Science Review* 73 (1984): 735–49.

Chapter Two

1. Anna O. Law, "Lunatics, Idiots, Paupers, and Negro Seamen: Immigration Federalism and the Early American Republic," *Studies in American Political Development* 28 (October 2014): 107.

2. Will Maslow, "Recasting our Deportation Law: Proposals for Reform," *Columbia Law Review* 56 (March 1956): 309.

3. See, e.g., Desmond S. King and Rogers M. Smith, "Racial Orders in American Political Development," *American Political Science Review* 99:1 (2005): 75–92. The authors criticize the tendency to analyze immigration policies separately from domestic racial issues (88).

4. Mai Ngai, *Impossible Subjects: Illegal Aliens and the Making of Modern America* (Princeton: Princeton University Press, 2005).

5. On the era of state and local control, broadly speaking, see Gerald Neuman, *Strangers to the Constitution: Immigrants, Borders, and Fundamental Law* (Princeton: Princeton University Press, 1996); Aristide R. Zolberg, *A Nation By Design: Immigration Policy in the Fashioning of America* (New York: Russell Sage Foundation; Cambridge: Harvard University Press, 2006); Benjamin J. Klebaner, "State and Local Immigration Regulation in the United States before 1882," *International Review of Social History* 3 (1958): 269–95; and Law, "Lunatics, Idiots, Paupers."

6. Castle Garden, operating from 1855 to 1890, was the first official immigration center in the United States. It was a pioneering collaboration between the state of New York and New York City and now is a national monument. See http://www.castlegarden.org/.

7. Law "Lunatics, Idiots, Paupers."

8. Neuman, *Strangers to the Constitution.*

9. Ibid., 51.

10. Benjamin J. Klebaner, "State and Local Immigration Regulation in the United States before 1882," *International Review of Social History* 3 (1958): 269–95, 274. See also Neuman, *Strangers to the Constitution.*

11. Friedrich Kapp, quoted in Daniel J. Tichenor and Alexandra Filindra, "Raising *Arizona v. United States*: Historical Patterns in Immigration Federalism," *Lewis and Clark Law Review* 16:4 (2012): 1225.

12. Monica W. Varsanyi, "The Rise and Fall (and Rise?) of Noncitizen Voting: Immigration and the Shifting Scales of Citizenship and Suffrage in the United States," *Space and Polity* 9:2 (2005): 113–34; and Ron Hayduk, *Democracy for All: Restoring Immigrant Voting Rights in the U.S.* (New York: Routledge. 2006).

13. Law, "Lunatics, Idiots, Paupers."

14. Passenger Cases, 48 U.S. 283 (1849).

15. Ibid., 47.

16. Neuman, *Strangers to the Constitution*, 34.

17. Kate Hooper and Jeanne Batalova, "Chinese Immigrants in the United States," Migration Policy Institute, January 28, 2015, http://www.migrationpolicy .org/article/chinese-immigrants-united-states.

18. Henderson v. Mayor of New York, 92 U.S. 259 (1875): 273.

19. Daniel J. Tichenor, *Dividing Lines: The Politics of Immigration Control in America* (Princeton: Princeton University Press, 2002), 88.

20. Ibid.

21. There is a voluminous literature on the Chinese Exclusion Acts. See, e.g., Tichenor, *Dividing Lines*, chap. 4; Bill Ong Hing, *Defining America Through Immigration Policy* (Philadelphia: Temple University Press, 2004), chap. 2; Hiroshi Motomura, *Americans in Waiting: The Lost Story of Immigration and Citizenship in the United States* (New York: Oxford University Press, 2006); and Erika Lee, *At America's Gates: Chinese Immigration during the Exclusion Era, 1882–1943* (Chapel Hill: University of North Carolina Press, 2003).

22. See Tichenor, *Dividing Lines*, for a detailed and dramatic description of this political process.

23. See David A. Martin and Peter H. Schuck, eds., *Immigration Stories* (New York: Foundation Press, 2005), particularly chap. 1, 7–30. See also John S. W. Park, *Elusive Citizenship: Immigration, Asian Americans, and the Paradox of Civil Rights* (New York: New York University Press, 2004).

24. Chae Chan Ping v. United States, 130 U.S. 581 (1889).

25. Ibid., 606.

26. Fong Yue Ting v. United States, 149 U.S. 698 (1893). The Court also upheld the 1892 Geary Act, which required Chinese residents of the United States to carry a resident permit at all times, denied these residents bail in habeas corpus proceedings, and disqualified their testimony in court.

27. US Const. art. I, § 8, cl. 4.

28. US Cons. art. I, § 8. Regarding the historical "fix," see Anonymous, "The

Constitutionality of Immigration Federalism," *Harvard Law Review* 118:1 (2005): 12; and see also James H. Kettner, *The Development of American Citizenship, 1608–1870* (Chapel Hill: University of North Carolina Press, 1978).

29. Tichenor, *Dividing Lines,* 110. See also Lucy Salyer, *Laws Harsh as Tigers: Chinese Immigrants and the Shaping of Modern Immigration Law* (Chapel Hill: University of North Carolina Press, 1995); and Andrew Gyory, *Closing the Gate: Race, Politics, and the Chinese Exclusion Act* (Chapel Hill: University of North Carolina Press, 1998).

30. Gilbert King, "Where the Buffalo No Longer Roamed," Smithsonian.com, July 17, 2012, http://www.smithsonianmag.com/history/where-the-buffalo-no-longer -roamed-3067904/?no-ist.

31. Ibid.

32. Stephen A. Jones and Eric Freedman, *Presidents and Black America,* (Washington, DC: Congressional Quarterly Press, 2011), 218.

33. Desmond S. King and Rogers M. Smith, "Racial Orders in American Political Development," *American Political Science Review* 99:1 (February 2005): 75–92, 75. For a compelling discussion of the legal construction of race in the early decades of the twentieth century, see Ian Haney López, *White by Law: The Legal Construction of Race* (New York: New York University Press, 2006).

34. David Scott FitzGerald and David Cook-Martin, *Culling the Masses: The Democratic Origins of Racist Immigration Policy in the Americas* (Cambridge: Harvard University Press, 2014).

35. Stephen Skowronek, *Building a New American State* (New York: Cambridge University Press, 1982).

36. Soon to follow were the Mann Act prohibiting interstate transport for prostitution (1910), the Harrison Act (1914) strictly regulating narcotics, and the Volstead Act (1919) establishing Prohibition.

37. Kelly Lytle Hernández, *Migra! A History of the U.S. Border Patrol* (Berkeley: University of California Press, 2010); and Joseph Nevins, *Operation Gatekeeper: The Rise of the "Illegal Alien" and the Making of the U.S.-Mexico Boundary* (New York: Routledge, 2002).

38. See, e.g., Ngai, *Impossible Subjects.*

39. William F. McDonald, *The Changing Boundaries of Law Enforcement: State and Local Law Enforcement, Illegal Immigration, and Transnational Crime Control* (final report) (Washington, DC: National Institute of Justice, 1999).

40. See James D. McBride, "Gaining a Foothold in the Paradise of Capitalism: The Western Federation of Miners and the Unionization of Bisbee," *Journal of Arizona History* 23:3 (1982): 299–316; and Katherine Benton-Warren, *Borderline Americans: Racial Divisions and the Labor War in the Arizona Borderlands* (Cambridge: Harvard University Press, 2009).

41. Yick Wo v. Hopkins, 118 U.S. 356 (1886).

42. Graham v. Richardson, 403 U.S. 365 (1971).

43. David Fellman, "Consequences of Increased Federal Activity in Law Enforcement," *Journal of Criminal Law and Criminology* 35 (1944): 16–33. See also Ngai, *Impossible Subjects*, 74; McDonald, *Changing Boundaries of Law Enforcement*, 169; and William A. Geller and Norval Morris, "Federal and Local Police," *Crime and Justice* 15 (1991): 231–349.

44. Hiroshi Motomura, *Immigration Outside the Law* (New York: Oxford University Press, 2014), 31.

45. Daniel Kanstroom, *Deportation Nation: Outsiders in American History* (Cambridge: Harvard University Press, 2007), 158.

46. See Kitty Calavita, *Inside the State: The Bracero Program, Immigration, and the INS* (New York: Routledge, 1992), 53–61.

47. See Ngai, *Impossible Subjects*, 143; and Kelly Lytle Hernandez, "The Crimes and Consequences of Illegal Immigration: A Cross Border Examination of Operation Wetback," *Western Historical Quarterly* 37:4 (2006): 421–44. See also McDonald, *Changing Boundaries of Law Enforcement*, 177–78.

48. See Peter Schuck and John Williams, "Removing Criminal Aliens: The Pitfalls and Promises of Federalism," *Harvard Journal of Law and Public Policy* 22 (1999): 398.

49. In 2002, however, Attorney General John Ashcroft issued a memo that was for a time held secret. His memo claims that local police and sheriffs *do* have immigration enforcement power, a position that appeared to have been put to rest a decade later by the Court's decision in Arizona v. United States, 132 S. Ct. 2492 (2012). See Barbara E. Armacost, "Immigration Policing: Federalizing the Local," *Social Science Research Network*, September 1, 2014, http://papers.ssrn.com/s013/papers.cfm?abstract_id=2504042.

50. Schuck and Williams, "Removing Criminal Aliens," 408, 444.

51. Truax v. Raich, 239 U.S. 33 (1915): 34.

52. Plyer v. Doe, 457 U.S. 202 (1982). See also Michael Olivas, *No Undocumented Child Left Behind: Plyler v. Doe and the Education of Undocumented Schoolchildren* (New York: New York University Press, 2012).

53. Justice Anthony Kennedy, *Arizona v. United States*, 567 U.S. ___ (2012): 3 The Court determined that three key sections of SB 1070 unconstitutionally infringed on federal enforcement authority. It let stand the fourth section (2(b)), which permits officers to inquire about immigration status in the course of a stop or arrest undertaken for regular law-enforcement purposes, with the caveat that the stop may be no more prolonged than in a nonimmigration-related situation.

54. United States Commission on Civil Rights, *The Tarnished Golden Door: Civil Rights Issues in Immigration* (Washington, DC: US Commission on Civil Rights, September 1980), 93.

55. Ibid., 95.

56. Miriam J. Wells, "The Grassroots Reconfiguration of U.S. Immigration Policy," *International Migration Review*, 38 (2004): 1308–47; and Susan Coutín, *The*

Culture of Protest: Religious Activism and the U.S. Sanctuary Movement (Boulder: Westview Press, 1993).

57. Wells, "Grassroots Reconfiguration," 1319.

58. An example from Arizona is the policy of the Southside Presbyterian Church in Tucson. See Mariana Dale, "Church Sanctuary Movement of 1980s Revived in Tucson," *Arizona Republic*, August 22, 2014, http://www.azcentral.com/story/news/local/arizona/2014/08/22/church-sanctuary-movement-s-revived-tucson/14471415/.

59. Nicolas DeGenova "The Legal Production of Mexican/Migrant 'Illegality,'" *Latino Studies* 2:2 (2004): 160–85. See also Douglas S. Massey, Jorge Durand, and Nolan J. Malone, *Beyond Smoke and Mirrors: Mexican Immigration in an Era of Economic Integration* (New York: Russell Sage Foundation, 2002), esp. chaps. 1–4.

60. Gregorio T. v. Wilson, 908 F. Supp. 755 (C.D. Cal. 1995), upheld by the 9th Circuit Court of Appeals at 59 F3d 1002 (1995).

61. Monica W. Varsanyi, "Introduction: Immigration Policy Activism in U.S. States and Cities: Interdisciplinary Perspectives," in Monica W. Varsanyi, ed., *Taking Local Control: Immigration Policy Activism in U.S. Cities and States* (Stanford: Stanford University Press, 2010); 1–27; and Robin Dale Jacobson, *The New Nativism: Proposition 187 and the Debate over Immigration* (Minneapolis: University of Minnesota Press, 2008).

62. Kristen McCabe and Doris Meissner, "Immigration and the United States: Recession Affects Flows, Prospects for Reform," *Migration Information Source* (January 20, 2010), Migration Policy Institute, http://www.migrationpolicy.org/article/immigration-and-united-states-recession-affects-flows-prospects-reform. See also Varsanyi, "Introduction: Immigration Policy Activism."

63. Mathew Coleman, "The 'Local' Migration State: The Site-Specific Devolution of Immigration Enforcement in the U.S. South," *Law & Policy* 34:2 (2012): 159–90; and Heather M. Creek and Stephen Yoder, "With a Little Help from Our Feds: Understanding Immigration Enforcement Policy Adoption in American Federalism," *Policy Studies Journal* 40:4 (2012): 674–97.

64. See, e.g., Michael J. Wishnie, "Introduction: Immigration and Federalism," *NYU Annual Survey of American Law* 58 (2002): 283–94, esp. 286–88.

65. The US Supreme Court had ruled twice during the 1990s—in New York v. United States, 505 U.S. 144 (1992), and in Printz v. United States, 521 U.S. 898 (1997)—that the national government may not "commandeer" subnational governments by requiring them to perform a national function. The New York case related to a federal effort to require states to assume liability for radioactive waste generated within their boundaries, whereas *Printz* dealt with Congress' attempt to require local police to perform background checks on handgun purchasers.

66. Brian A. Reaves, "Census of State and Local Law Enforcement Agencies, 2008," Bulletin NCJ 233982 (Washington, DC: US Department of Justice, Office of Justice Programs, Bureau of Justice Statistics, July 2011), 2, http://www.bjs.gov/content/pub/pdf/csllea08.pdf.

67. Brian A. Reaves, "Federal Law Enforcement Officers, 2008," Bulletin NCJ

238250 (Washington, DC: US Department of Justice, Bureau of Justice Statistics, June 2012), http://www.bjs.gov/content/pub/pdf/fle008.pdf.

68. Matthew Lysakowski, Albert Antony Pearsall III, and Jill Pope, "Policing in New Immigrant Communities" (Washington, DC: US Department of Justice, Office of Community Oriented Policing Services, June 2009), http://www.vera.org/sites/default/files/resources/downloads/e060924209-NewImmigrantCommunites.pdf bjs.gov/content/pub/pdf/csllea08.pdf.

69. Major Cities Chiefs Association, "Major Cities Chiefs Statement on Immigration," June 8, 2006, website of Houston Police Department, City of Houston, http://www.houstontx.gov/police/nr/2006/june/nr060806-1.htm.

70. Criticism came from inside the federal government as well as outside. See the report by the Department of Homeland Security's Office of Inspector General, "The Performance of 287(g) Agreements" (2010), http://www.oig.dhs.gov/assets/Mgmt/OIG_10-63_Mar10.pdf.

71. Letter from Assistant Attorney General Thomas E. Perez to Maricopa County Attorney Bill Montgomery (December 15, 2011), 2, http://www.justice.gov/sites/default/files/crt/legacy/2011/12/15/mcso_findletter_12-15-11.pdf.

72. Ibid.

73. US Department of Homeland Security, "Budget in Brief, Fiscal Year 2013," 16, www.dhs.gov/xlibrary/assets/mgmt/dhs-budget-in-brief-fy2013.pdf.

74. US Immigration and Customs Enforcement, "Secure Communities," http://www.ice.gov/secure_communities/.

75. US Department of Homeland Security, "Budget in Brief, Fiscal Year 2013," 101; and Adam B. Cox and Thomas J. Miles, "Policing Immigration," *University of Chicago Law Review* 80:1 (2013): 87–136.

76. Migration Policy Institute, "U.S. Spends More on Immigration Enforcement than on FBI, DEA, Secret Service and All Other Federal Criminal Law Enforcement Agencies Combined," press release, January 7, 2013, http://www.migrationpolicy.org/news/us-spends-more-immigration-enforcement-fbi-dea-secret-service-all-other-federal-criminal-law. See also Ian Urbina and Catherine Rentz, "Immigrant Detainees and the Right to Counsel," *New York Times*, March 30, 2013, http://www.nytimes.com/2013/03/31/sunday-review/immigrant-detainees-and-the-right-to-counsel.html?pagewanted=all.

77. Transactional Records Access Clearinghouse, "At Nearly 100,000, Immigration Prosecutions Reach an All-Time High in FY 2013," TRAC Immigration, http://trac.syr.edu/immigration/reports/336/.

78. Urbana and Rentz, "Immigrant Detainees and the Right to Counsel."

79. Doris Marie Provine and Roxanne D. Doty, "The Criminalization of Immigrants as a Racial Project," *Journal of Contemporary Criminal Justice* 27:3 (2011): 261–77.

80. See, e.g., Judge John J. McConnell's decision in Ada Morales v. Bruce Chadbourne, US District Court for the District of Rhode Island, C.A. No. 12-301-M, http://www.riaclu.org/documents/Ruling_Morales_v_Chadbourne__021214.pdf.

81. Editorial board, "Mr. Obama's Wise Immigration Plan" *New York Times*, November 21, 2014.

82. For more than a decade, Congress has considered an exception for residents brought into the country as children, but in the meantime, thirteen states have taken action on their own, providing in-state tuition benefits to their undocumented students. This illustrates the increased role of states in immigration policy in the face of federal inaction.

83. Jeanne Batalova, Sarah Hooker, and Randy Capps, "DACA at the Two-Year Mark: A National and State Profile of Youth Eligible and Applying for Deferred Action," August 2014, *Migration Policy Institute,* http://www.migrationpolicy.org /research/daca-two-year-mark-national-and-state-profile-youth-eligible-and-applying -deferred-action.

84. National Immigration Law Center, "DAPA and Expanded DACA" (last updated March 2, 2015), http://www.nilc.org/dapa&daca.html.

85. See Marjorie S. Zatz and Nancy Rodriguez, *Dreams and Nightmares: Immigration Policy, Youth and Families* (Oakland: University of California Press, 2015).

86. Stephen Dinan, "Illegal Immigration Up, Deportations Down in 2014: DHS," *Washington Times,* December 18, 2014, http://www.washingtontimes.com/news/2014 /dec/19/illegal-immigration-deportations-down-2014-homelan/.

87. Mark Noferi, "DH Funding Controversy Over, But Enforcement-First Approach Remains," *American Immigration Council: Immigration Impact,* March 6, 2015, http://immigrationimpact.com/2015/03/06/dhs-funding-controversy-enforcement -first-approach-remains/.

88. Juliet Stumpf, "The Crimmigration Crisis: Immigrants, Crime, and Sovereign Power," *American University Law Review* 56 (2006): 367–419.

89. Ingrid V. Eagly, "Criminal Justice for Noncitizens: An Analysis of Variation in Local Enforcement," *New York University Law Review* 88 (2013): 1126–223.

90. TRAC, "In Two out of Three Pending Cases, Unaccompanied Children Have No Representation in Immigration Court," November 25, 2014, http://trac.syr .edu/whatsnew/email.141125.html.

91. See Immigration Policy Center, "Aggregated Felonies: An Overview," March 16, 2012, http://www.immigrationpolicy.org/just-facts/aggravated-felonies -overview.

92. See David DeConcini, Isabel Garcia, David Wolf, Leslie Carlson, and John Fife, "Injustice for Migrants: A Drain on Taxpayers," *Arizona Republic,* October 20, 2014, F5.

93. Stephen Legomsky, "The New Path of Immigration Law: Asymmetric Incorporation of Criminal Justice Norms," *Washington & Lee Law Review* 64 (2007): 469. See also Eagly, "Criminal Justice for Noncitizens."

94. Legomsky, "New Path of Immigration Law," 469.

95. Stumpf, "Crimmigration Crisis."

96. See, e.g., Katherine Beckett and Angelina Godoy, "Power, Politics, and Penality: Punitiveness as Backlash in American Democracies," *Studies in Law, Politics*

and Society 45 (2008): 139–74; and David Garland, *The Culture of Control* (Chicago: University of Chicago Press, 2001).

97. Marie Gottschalk, "Hiding in Plain Sight: American Politics and the Carceral State," *Annual Review of Political Science* 11 (2008): 235–60; and Joe Sim, *Punishment and Prisons: Power and the Carceral State* (London: Sage, 2009).

98. See Monica W. Varsanyi, ed., *Taking Local Control: Immigration Policy Activism in U.S. Cities and States* (Stanford: Stanford University Press, 2010).

99. See, e.g., National Conference of State Legislatures, "State Laws Related to Immigration and Immigrants," January 7, 2015, http://www.ncsl.org/research /immigration/state-laws-related-to-immigration-and-immigrants.aspx.

100. Peter L. Markowitz, "Undocumented No More: The Power of State Citizenship," *Stanford Law Review* 67 (2015): 869–915.

101. This is not surprising in light of federal legislation that explicitly provides room for state laws regarding business licenses. Courts, most recently in Chamber of Commerce v. Whiting (2011), have interpreted this power broadly to allow state laws punishing employers for hiring unauthorized immigrants. The power of states to take regulatory action regarding hiring of persons without legal status was established even earlier, in De Canas v. Bica (1976). Not all laws in this area, however, are unfavorable to immigrants. Employment is one of the areas in which some states have protected unauthorized immigrants, for example, by ensuring their access to workman's compensation, or by prohibiting municipalities from requiring employers to use E-Verify, the federal employment verification program.

102. Lina Newton, "Policy Innovation or Vertical Integration? A View of Immigration Federalism from the States," *Law & Policy* 34:2 (2012): 113–37.

103. Lina Newton, *Illegal, Alien, or Immigrant: The Politics of Immigration Reform* (New York: New York University Press, 2008).

104. National Conference of State Legislatures, "2012 Immigration-Related Laws and Resolutions in the States (Jan. 1–Dec. 31, 2012)," http://www.ncsl.org /issues-research/immig/2012-immigration-related-laws-jan-december-2012.aspx.

105. National Conference of State Legislatures, "State Laws Related to Immigration and Immigrants," http://www.ncsl.org/research/immigration/state-laws -related-to-immigration-and-immigrants.aspx.

106. Monica W. Varsanyi "Neoliberalism and Nativism: Local Anti-immigrant Policy Activism and an Emerging Politics of Scale," *International Journal of Urban and Regional Research* 35:2 (2013): 295–311; and Benjamin Fleury-Steiner and Jamie G. Longazel, "Neoliberalism, Community Development, and Anti-Immigrant Backlash in Hazleton, Pennsylvania," in Monica W. Varsanyi, ed., *Taking Local Control: Immigration Policy Activism in U.S. Cities and States* (Stanford: Stanford University Press, 2010).

107. Lozano v. Hazleton, 496 F. Supp. 2d 477 (2007) and 620 F. 3d 170 (2010); and Villas at Parkside Partners v. City of Farmers Branch, 726 F.3d 524 (5th Cir. 2013)

108. Though see Jennifer Chacon ("The Transformation of Immigration Federalism," *William and Mary Bill of Rights Journal* 21 [2012]: 577–618) for a discussion

of how, despite court attempts to uphold the federal government's plenary power, shifting enforcement priorities at the local level and the convergence of criminal and immigration law have fundamentally changed the immigration enforcement landscape. She writes, "State and local law enforcement had become the primary point of contact for many noncitizens coming into contact with the removal system and the federal executive branch has been the main architect of this new order" (598)

109. Law, "Lunatics, Idiots, Paupers."

110. See, e.g., Joseph H. Carens, *Immigrants and the Right to Stay* (Cambridge: MIT Press, 2010); and Doris Marie Provine, Monica W. Varsanyi, Paul G. Lewis, and Scott H. Decker, "Growing Tensions between Civic Membership and Enforcement," in Charis Kubrin, Marjorie Zatz, and Ramiro Martinez, eds., *Punishing Immigrants: Policy, Politics, and Injustice* (New York: New York University Press, 2012), 42–61.

Chapter Three

1. California state TRUST Act (AB 4), effective January 1, 2014. For analogous state and county policies, see http://www.catrustact.org/text-of-trust-acts.html.

2. Given the state's constitutional powers over policing, the federal government's Secure Communities program could only *request*, but not *require*, that local law enforcement hold individuals.

3. Donny Youngblood as quoted in José Gaspar, "Sheriff to Continue Immigration Holds Despite New Law," *Bakersfield Now*, January 10, 2014, http://www.bakersfieldnow.com/news/local/Sheriff-to-continue-with-immigration-holds-despite-new-state-law-239703661.html.

4. *US Immigration and Customs Enforcement*, "Secure Communities" (2013), http://www.ice.gov/secure_communities.

5. *US Immigration and Customs Enforcement*, "Secure Communities" (2013); and Antonio Olivo, "Cook County Bucks Immigration Officials," *Chicago Tribune*, September 8, 2011, http://articles.chicagotribune.com/2011–09–08/news/ct-met-county-immigration-policy-2–20110908_1_illegal-immigrants-detainers-sanctuary-ordinances.

6. James Queally, "Newark Police first in N.J. to refuse to detain undocumented immigrants accused of minor crimes," *NJ.com*, August 15, 2013, http://www.nj.com/essex/index.ssf/2013/08/newark_police_first_in_nj_to_refuse_to_detain_illegal_immigrants_accused_of_minor_crimes.html.

7. Daniel M. Kowalski, *LexisNexis Legal Newsroom Immigration Law*, December 2, 2013, http://www.lexisnexis.com/legalnewsroom/immigration/b/newsheadlines/rsscomments.aspx?WeblogPostID=429533.

8. For example, Eagly describes how Arizona, prior to SB 1070, used its state-level lawmaking and policing powers to pass and enforce a law regarding "alien

smuggling." The law empowered the prosecution not only of migrant smugglers but also of migrants themselves. See Ingrid V. Eagly, "Local Immigration Prosecution: A Study of Arizona before SB1070," *UCLA Law Review* 58 (2011): 1749–817.

9. US Department of Justice, "Complaint Filed against Arizona SB 1070," July 6, 2010, http://www.justice.gov/opa/pr/citing-conflict-federal-law-department-justice-challenges-arizona-immigration-law.

10. As an example, see the differential grant rates of asylum offices across the United States, a reality that Andrew I. Schoenholtz, Philip G. Schrag, and Jaya Ramji-Nogales call "Refugee Roulette" (*Lives in the Balance: Asylum Adjudication by the Department of Homeland Security* [New York: New York University Press, 2014]): between 1999 and 2005, the New York Regional Asylum Office granted 31 percent of cases, compared with 60 percent of cases in the San Francisco office (144). Even when looking at the grant rates for the same nationality across regional offices, the differences are striking, with the Chicago office granting 34 percent of Somali cases versus the San Francisco office granting 89 percent of Somali cases (149), and the Houston office granting 36 percent of Colombian cases versus the Miami office granting 56 percent of Colombian cases (149).

11. See, e.g., Harvard Law Review, "The Constitutionality of Immigration Federalism," *Developments in the Law: Jobs and Borders* 118 (2005): 1–24.

12. Peter J. Spiro, "The States and Immigration in an Era of Demi-Sovereignties," *Virginia Journal of International Law* 35 (1994): 121–78, and "Learning to Live with Immigration Federalism," *Connecticut Law Review* 29 (1997): 1627–46.

13. Spiro, "Learning to Live," 1627–8.

14. Ibid.

15. Peter H. Schuck, "Taking Immigration Federalism Seriously," *University of Chicago Legal Forum* (2007): 57–92.

16. Michael Hethmon, "The Chimera and the Cop: Local Enforcement of Federal Immigration Law," *University of the District of Columbia Law Review* 8 (2004): 83–140; and Kris W. Kobach, "The Quintessential Force Multiplier: The Inherent Authority of Local Police to Make Immigration Arrests." *Albany Law Review* 69 (2005): 179–235.

17. Cristina Rodríguez, "The Significance of the Local in Immigration Regulation," *Michigan Law Review* 106 (2008): 567–642; and Clare Huntington, "The Constitutional Dimension of Immigration Federalism." *Vanderbilt Law Review* 61 (2008): 787–853.

18. Rodríguez, *Significance of the Local*, 571.

19. Rick Su, "The Promise and Peril of Cities and Immigration Policy," *Harvard Law and Policy Review* 7 (2013): 299–319; Bill Ong Hing, "Immigration Sanctuary Policies: Constitutional and Representative of Good Policing and Good Public Policy," *UC Irvine Law Review* 2 (2012): 247–311; and Pablo A. Mitnik and Jessica Halpern-Finnerty, "Immigration and Local Governments: Inclusionary Local Policies in the Era of State Rescaling," in Monica W. Varsanyi, ed., *Taking Local*

Control: Immigration Policy Activism in U.S. States and Cities (Stanford: Stanford University Press, 2010), 51–72.

20. Pratheepan Gulasekaram and Karthick Ramakrishnan, "Immigration Federalism: A Reappraisal," *New York University Law Review* 88 (2013): 2112.

21. Linda S. Bosniak, "Immigrants, Preemption, and Equality," *Virginia Journal of International Law* 35 (1994): 179–99. See also Muzaffar A. Chishti, "The Role of States in U.S. Immigration Policy," *New York University Annual Survey of American Law* 58 (2002): 371–76; Hiroshi Motomura, "Immigration and Alienage, Federalism and Proposition 187," *Virginia Journal of International Law* 35 (1994): 201–16; Michael A. Olivas, "Preempting Preemption: Foreign Affairs, State Rights, and Alienage Classifications," *Virginia Journal of International Law* 35 (1994): 217–36, and "Immigration-Related State and Local Ordinances: Preemption, Prejudice, and the Proper Role for Enforcement," *University of Chicago Legal Forum* 2007 (2007): 27–57; and Huyen Pham, "The Inherent Flaws in the Inherent Authority Position: Why Inviting Local Enforcement of Immigration Laws Violates the Constitution," *Florida State University Law Review* 31 (2004): 965–1003.

22. Michael J. Wishnie, "Laboratories of Bigotry? Devolution of the Immigration Power, Equal Protection, and Federalism." *New York University Law Review* 76 (2001): 493–569.

23. Chishti, *"Role of States,"* 371–76; and Pham, "Inherent Flaws," 965–1003.

24. Cynthia J. Bowling and J. M. Pickerill, "Fragmented Federalism: The State of American Federalism 2012–13," *Publius: The Journal of Federalism* 43:3 (2013): 315–46.

25. David Brotherton and Luis Barrios, *Banished to the Homeland: Dominican Deportees and their Stories of Exile* (Columbia University Press, 2011); see also Daniel Kanstroom, *Aftermath: Deportation Law and the New American Diaspora* (New York: Oxford University Press, 2012).

26. Kyle E. Walker and Helga Leitner, "The Variegated Landscape of Local Immigration Policies in the United States," *Urban Geography* 32:2 (2011): 156–78; see also Mathew Coleman, "Immigration Geopolitics beyond the Mexico-U.S. Border," *Antipode* 39 (2007): 54–76; Mathew Coleman and Austin Kocher, "Detention, Deportation, Devolution and Immigrant Incapacitation in the US, Post 9/11," *Geographical Journal* 177:3 (2011): 228–37; and Mathew Coleman, "The 'Local' Migration State: The Site-Specific Devolution of Immigration Enforcement in the U.S. South," *Law & Policy* 34:2 (2012): 159–90.

27. See National Conference of State Legislatures, "2009 State Laws Related to Immigrants and Immigration January 1–December 31, 2009," http://www.ncsl.org/default.aspx?tabid=19232, and "2012 Immigration Related Laws and Resolutions in the States, January 1–December 31, 2012," http://www.ncsl.org/issues-research/immig/2012-immigration-related-laws-jan-december-2012.aspx.

28. For more on crimmigration, see chap. 2.

29. See also Angela Stuesse and Mathew Coleman, "Automobility, Immobility, Altermobility: Surviving and Resisting the Intensification of Immigrant Policing, *City & Society* 26:1 (2014): 51–72.

30. See, e.g., Leo R. Chavez, *The Latino Threat: Constructing Immigrants, Citizens, and the Nation* (Stanford: Stanford University Press, 2008).

31. Gabriella Sanchez and Doris Marie Provine, "Suspecting Immigrants: Exploring Links between Racialized Anxieties and Expanded Police Powers in Arizona," *Policing and Society* 21:4 (2011): 468–79.

32. See, e.g., Doris Marie Provine and Roxanne D. Doty, "The Criminalization of Immigrants as a Racial Project," *Journal of Contemporary Criminal Justice* 27:3 (2011): 261–77.

33. D. L. Turner and Catherine H. Ellis, *Images of America: Latter-Day Saints in Mesa* (Charleston: Arcadia, 2009).

34. George Gascón, "Crime and Immigration," *Arizona Republic*, October 14, 2007. After leaving Mesa, Gascón served as the police chief in San Francisco for two years and was elected in 2011 to be the first Latino district attorney of the city.

35. The case, as noted elsewhere in this volume, proceeded all the way to the Supreme Court, which found in the federal government's favor in Arizona v. United States, 567 U.S. ___ (2012).

36. Melendres, et al. v. Arpaio, et al., 598 F. Supp. 2d 1025 (D. Ariz. 2009). Supplemental permanent injunction/judgment order signed by Judge G. Murray Snow on October 2, 2013, http://www.gpo.gov/fdsys/granule/USCOURTS-azd-2_07 -cv-02513/USCOURTS-azd-2_07-cv-02513–19.

37. Puente Arizona v. Arpaio, No. CV-14-01356-PHX-DGC; see American Civil Liberties Union, "Plaintiffs Ask Court for a Preliminary Injunction of Enforcement of State Laws on which Raids are Based, August 7, 2014, https://www .aclu.org/immigrants-rights/workers-request-immediate-halt-arpaios-workplace -raids-pending-outcome-court-case.

38. Cristina Rodríguez, Muzaffar Chishti, Randy Capps, and Laura St. John, "A Program in Flux: New Priorities and Implementation Challenges for 287(g)" (Washington, DC: Migration Policy Institute, March 2010), http://www.migration policy.org/pubs/287g-March2010.pdf.

39. Diaz-Bernal v. Dept. of Homeland Sec., No. 3:09-CV-01734.

40. Chap. 5 addresses the issue of office discretion at greater depth.

41. See, e.g., Spiro, "Learning to Live," 1627–8.

42. In the influential "public choice" theory of metropolitan political economy, each local jurisdiction offers its own "package" of services and taxes, and residents "shop" for the tax/service package that best matches their preferences, thus generating more efficiency in the local government sector. See, e.g., Vincent Ostrom, Robert Bish, and Elinor Ostrom, *Local Government in the United States* (San Francisco: Institute for Contemporary Studies Press, 1988).

43. Bowling and Pickerill, "Fragmented Federalism."

44. Bayless Manning, "The Congress, the Executive and Intermestic Affair," *Foreign Affairs* 55 (1977): 306–24.

45. Doris Marie Provine, Monica W. Varsanyi, Paul G. Lewis, and Scott H. Decker, "Growing Tensions between Civic Membership and Enforcement in the Devolution of Immigration Control," in Charis E. Kurbrin, Marjorie S. Zatz, and Ramiro Martinez Jr., eds., *Punishing Immigrants: Policy, Politics, and Injustice* (New York: New York University Press, 2012), 42–61.

46. See, e.g., Kobach, "The Quintessential Force Multiplier"; Cristina Rodrí-guez, Muzaffar Chishti, and Kimberly Nortman, *Testing the Limits: A Framework for Assessing the Legality of State and Local Immigration Measures* (Washington: Migration Policy Institute, 2007); and Michael J. Wishnie, "Civil Liberties in a New America: State and Local Police Enforcement of Immigration Laws," *University of Pennsylvania Journal of Constitutional Law* 6 (2004): 1084–115.

47. Rick Su, "The Promise and Peril of Cities and Immigration Policy," *Harvard Law and Policy Review* 7 (2013): 299–319.

48. Chiefs and sheriffs were asked "how influential" various groups or individuals were in formulating their agency's practices and procedures regarding immigrants and immigration. Only 12–17 percent of respondents in the three surveys said that the practices of another city or county in the area were influential or very influential to their own approach. By contrast, the chief or sheriff themselves, command personnel from within the agency, and agency legal advisors were each viewed as much more influential.

49. Chap. 4 takes up the question of the contextual factors that motivate different styles of local immigration policing.

50. Michele Waslin, "Immigration Enforcement by Local and State Police: The Impact on Latinos," *Law Enforcement Executive Forum* 7 (2007): 15–32.

51. See United States v. Brignoni-Ponce, 422 U.S. 873 (1975), in which the Supreme Court held that Mexican appearance could be one relevant factor, but not the only factor, in determining whether a Border Patrol agent was reasonable in suspecting a person is in the country illegally. Whether this decision applies to interior enforcement decisions remains unclear.

52. Pew Hispanic Center, *2007 National Survey of Latinos: As Illegal Immigration Issue Heats Up, Hispanics Feel A Chill* (Washington, DC: Pew Hispanic Center, December 13, 2007; revised December 19, 2007), http://www.pewhispanic.org/files/reports/84.pdf.

53. See also Maureen Sweeney, "Shadow Immigration Enforcement and Its Constitutional Dangers," *Journal of Criminal Law and Criminology* 104:2 (2014): 227–82.

Chapter Four

1. See, esp., Rufus P. Browning, Dale Rogers Marshall, and David H. Tabb, *Protest is Not Enough: The Struggle of Blacks and Hispanics for Equality in Urban*

Politics (Berkeley: University of California Press, 1984); and Rufus P. Browning, Dale Rogers Marshall, and David H. Tabb, eds. *Racial Politics in American Cities* (White Plains: Longman, 1990). See also Zoltan L. Hajnal, *America's Uneven Democracy: Race, Turnout, and Representation in City Politics* (New York: Cambridge University Press, 2009); and Peter F. Burns, *Electoral Politics Is Not Enough: Racial and Ethnic Minorities and Urban Politics* (Albany: SUNY Press, 2006).

2. Timothy Marquez and Scot Schraufnagel, "Hispanic Population Growth and State Immigration Policy: An Analysis of Restriction (2008–12)," *Publius: The Journal of Federalism* 43 (2013): 347–67; Kyle E. Walker and Helga Leitner, "The Variegated Landscape of Local Immigration Policies in the United States," *Urban Geography* 32:2 (2011): 156–78; and Daniel J. Hopkins, "Politicized Places: Explaining Where and When Immigrants Provoke Local Opposition," *American Political Science Review* 104 (2010): 40–60.

3. Jorge M. Chavez and Doris Marie Provine, "Race and the Response of State Legislatures to Unauthorized Immigrants," *Annals of the American Academy of Political and Social Sciences* 623 (2009): 78–92; S. Karthick Ramakrishnan and Tom Wong, "Partisanship, Not Spanish: Explaining Municipal Ordinances Affecting Undocumented Immigrants," in Monica W. Varsanyi, ed., *Taking Local Control: Immigration Policy Activism in U.S. Cities and States* (Stanford: Stanford University Press, 2010), 73–93; and Pratheepan Gulasekaram and S. Karthick Ramakrishnan, "Immigration Federalism: A Reappraisal," *New York University Law Review* 88 (2013): 2074–319.

4. Heather M. Creek and Stephen Yoder, "With a Little Help from Our Feds: Understanding State Immigration Enforcement Policy Adoption in American Federalism," *Policy Studies Journal* 40 (2012): 674–97.

5. Alexandra Filindra and Melinda Kovacs, "Analyzing US State Legislative Resolutions on Immigrants and Immigration," *International Migration* 50:4 (2011): 33–50; Mathew Coleman, "The 'Local' Migration State: The Site Specific Devolution of Immigration Enforcement in the US South," *Law & Policy* 34: 2 (2012): 159–90; Adam B. Cox and Thomas J. Miles, "Policing Immigration," *University of Chicago Law Review* 80 (2013): 87–136; and Ingrid V. Eagly, "Criminal Justice for Noncitizens: An Analysis of Variation in Local Enforcement," *New York University Law Review* 88 (2013): 1126–223.

6. See, e.g., Vincent Ostrom, Robert Bish, and Elinor Ostrom, *Local Government in the United States* (San Francisco: Institute for Contemporary Studies Press, 1988); Paul G. Lewis, *Shaping Suburbia: How Political Institutions Organize Urban Development* (Pittsburgh: University of Pittsburgh Press, 1996); J. Eric Oliver, *Democracy in Suburbia* (Princeton: Princeton University Press, 2001); and Richard C. Feiock, ed. *Metropolitan Governance: Conflict, Competition, and Cooperation* (Washington, DC: Georgetown University Press, 2004).

7. David R. Berman, *Local Government and the States: Autonomy, Politics, and Policy* (Armonk: M. E. Sharpe, 2003); and Stephen Elkin, *City and Regime in the American Republic* (Chicago: University of Chicago Press, 1987), chap. 2.

8. Moreover, local immigrant policies may reverberate *upward* to influence state policy. Creek and Yoder ("With a Little Help from Our Feds," 686) find that where localities within a state adopt 287(g) enforcement agreements with the federal government, the state government is *less* likely to do so, controlling for a bevy of other political characteristics. Creek and Yoder interpret this finding as an instance of possible "steam-valve federalism," in which local anti-immigrant policies absorb the pressure that might otherwise be imposed on the state government.

9. In an earlier publication, we attempted to untangle some of the potential causal relationships among our sample of large cities; see Paul G. Lewis, Doris Marie Provine, Monica W. Varsanyi, and Scott H. Decker, "Why Do (Some) Local Police Departments Enforce Federal Immigration Law?," *Journal of Public Administration Research and Theory* 23 (2013): 1–25.

10. When investigating the *Enforcement Count*, we will only include sheriff offices that have some responsibility for street patrols in local communities *as well as* responsibility for county jails. An overwhelming share of the sheriff offices responding to our survey (91 percent) have at least some patrol responsibilities, whether in unincorporated areas of the county only (21 percent), or more commonly, in a combination of unincorporated areas and municipalities (where the sheriff often patrols under a contract with the municipal government). Likewise, the vast majority of sheriff offices (83 percent) administer at least one jail facility. Overall, 78 percent of the sheriff offices in our sample of respondents (197 of 254) are full-service agencies that provide both the patrol and corrections functions. These are the focus in this chapter when we discuss results for sheriff offices.

11. Jerome H. Skolnick, and David H. Bayley, *The New Blue Line: Police Innovation in Six American Cities* (New York: Free Press, 1986); and James Fyfe, Jack R. Greene, William Walsh, O. W. Wilson, and Roy C. McLaren, *Police Administration* (New York: McGraw-Hill, 1996).

12. It is possible that departments in some very small cities and counties might reply "yes" simply because of a lack of prior experiences with immigration cases. Later in the chapter we will consider whether local population size predicts responses on this question.

13. For sheriff offices, the wording was changed slightly to "Gaining the trust of unauthorized immigrants is a priority among sheriff's deputies/officers."

14. For simplicity, in this book we use the term *sheriff office* when referring to the organization that sheriffs manage, and we interchangeably use the terms *sheriff's officers* or *deputies* in referring to the sworn officers who work for the sheriff. The actual terminology in use varies from county to county.

15. For details on Bloomberg's executive orders, see New York City Mayor's Office of Immigrant Affairs, "Executive Orders 34 & 41," September 17, 2003, http://www.nyc.gov/html/imm/html/eoll/e041.shtml.

16. This is true regardless of whether the locality's policy orientation is specified along the five-point scale, or whether one instead uses dichotomous variables indicating the presence of a "pro-enforcement" or "anti-enforcement" policy.

17. Berman, *Local Governments and the States*; and Elkin, *City and Regime in the American Republic*.

18. Given the different dates of our three surveys, we used 2005–7 as the relevant time period in our analysis of large cities (which we surveyed in 2007–8), 2005–10 for small cities (surveyed in 2010), and 2005–9 for county sheriffs (surveyed in 2009–10).

19. Kenneth Scheve and Matthew Slaughter, "Labor Market Competition and Individual Preferences over Immigration Policy," *Review of Economics and Statistics* 83:1 (2001): 133–45; Anna Maria Mayda, "Who Is against Immigration? A Cross-Country Investigation of Individual Attitudes toward Immigrants," *Review of Economics and Statistics* 88:3 (2006): 510–30; Peter Burns and James G. Gimpel, "Economic Insecurity, Prejudicial Stereotypes, and Public Opinion on Immigration Policy," *Political Science Quarterly* 115:2 (2000): 201–25); and Jack Citrin, Donald P. Green, Christopher Muste, and Cara Wong, "Public Opinion toward Immigration Reform: The Role of Economic Motivations," *Journal of Politics* 59:3 (1997): 858–81.

20. Ramiro Martinez Jr. and Matthew T. Lee, "On Immigration and Crime," in *The Nature of Crime: Continuity and Change* (Washington, DC: US Department of Justice, 2000), 501–4; Matthew T. Lee and Ramiro Martinez Jr., "Immigration Reduces Crime: An Emerging Scholarly Consensus," *Sociology of Crime, Law, and Deviance* 13 (2009): 3–16; and John Hagan and Alberto Palloni, "Sociological Criminality and the Mythology of Hispanic Immigration and Crime," *Social Problems* 46:4 (1999): 617–32.

21. Ramakrishnan and Wong ("Partisanship, Not Spanish," 84–86) found that the percentage of local jobs that are in agriculture helped predict the passage (but not proposal) of municipal policies that are restrictive toward immigrants. Another relevant study, which examined *state-* rather than local-level policy climates toward immigrants for the period 2005–7, found that the importance of immigrants to key state industries moderated the relationship between immigrant demographic change ("threat") and anti-immigrant policies. See Jill Nicholson-Crotty and Sean Nicholson-Crotty, "Industry Strength and Immigrant Policy in the American States," *Political Research Quarterly* 64:3 (2011): 612–24. The Nicholson-Crottys examined the proportion of employment in the contract agriculture, food processing, construction, and janitorial-service industries, as well as the proportion of campaign donations to state legislative races originating from the first three of those sectors.

22. See, among many others, Floyd Hunter, *Community Power Structure: A Study of Decision Makers* (Chapel Hill: University of North Carolina Press, 1953); Matthew A. Crenson, *The Un-Politics of Air Pollution: A Study of Non-Decisionmaking in the Cities* (Baltimore: Johns Hopkins University Press, 1971); John R. Logan and Harvey L. Molotch, *Urban Fortunes: The Political Economy of Place* (Berkeley: University of California Press, 1987); and Clarence N. Stone, *Regime Politics: Governing Atlanta* (Lawrence: University Press of Kansas, 1989).

23. For European evidence relevant to this point, see Rafaela M. Dancygier and Michael J. Donnelly, "Sectoral Economies, Economic Contexts, and Attitudes toward Immigration," *Journal of Politics* 75:1 (2013): 17–35.

24. Audrey Singer, *Immigrant Workers in the US Labor Force* (Washington: Brookings Institution and Partnership for a New American Economy, 2012).

25. This is not to say that immigrant employment as domestic household workers never affects community attitudes. Maher's ethnographic research suggests that the growing number of Latino domestic workers in one part of Southern California made native-born residents of an upper-middle income neighborhood more anxious about their personal security and interested in gating their subdivision. See Kristen Hill Maher, "Workers and Strangers: The Household Service Economy and the Landscape of Suburban Fear," *Urban Affairs Review* 38:6 (2003): 751–86.

26. The American Community Survey's data on employment at the municipal and county levels is aggregated to a handful of broad industrial sectors due to fears about releasing proprietary data that might identify particular firms. Note that these data do not show the percentage of foreign-born or native-born workers in particular industries in specific communities, but rather the *percentage of all local jobs that are in these immigrant-heavy industries*.

27. The pairwise correlation is .13 ($p < .06$).

28. Correlation of $-.16$ ($p < .02$).

29. Correlation of .20 ($p < .01$).

30. It is possible that industrial structure is more relevant at broader geographic levels, such as the metropolitan area or the state (as in Nicholson-Crotty and Nicholson-Crotty, "Industrial Strength and Immigrant Policy") than it is at smaller geographic levels. In that case one would anticipate that the correlations we have noted here would be strongest for sheriff offices, since the county level is more inclusive of territory and population than the municipal level. However, this is not the case.

31. For instance, large cities tend to have more pro-growth postures toward land use and economic development than smaller municipalities, controlling for a bevy of other local characteristics. See Paul G. Lewis, and Max Neiman, *Custodians of Place: Governing the Growth and Development of Cities* (Washington, DC: Georgetown University Press, 2009).

32. To ascertain the size of each city or county in our samples, as with the other demographic variables discussed in this chapter, we rely on the American Community Survey (ACS). Given the different dates our surveys were administered, we used the 2005 ACS for the sample of large cities and the 2006–8 (three-year average) ACS for the small cities and the counties. For some very small cities and counties that did not meet the minimum size threshold for inclusion in the three-year ACS, we were forced to rely on the 2005–9 (five year) ACS. To ascertain the size of the police agency, we asked a question on our surveys of chiefs and sheriffs regarding the number of sworn officers in the police department or sheriff office.

33. Supporting this assumption, among all three of our samples, the population size of the jurisdiction is a highly significant predictor of whether the chief or sheriff holds a graduate degree. (We asked the responding law-enforcement executives to report their educational attainment.)

34. An exception is that there is no significant relationship between population size and *No ICE Participation* for any of our three samples.

35. This same result, however, does not hold for the sheriff offices.

36. For relevant perspectives, see Pamela Irving Jackson, *Minority Group Threat, Crime, and Policing: Social Context and Social Control* (Westport: Greenwood, 1989); Ryan D. King and Darren Wheelock, "Group Threat and Social Control: Race, Perceptions of Minorities and the Desire to Punish," *Social Forces* 85:3 (2007): 1255–80; Rene R. Rocha and Rodolfo Espino, "Racial Threat, Residential Segregation, and the Policy Attitudes of Anglos," *Political Research Quarterly* 62:2 (2009): 415–26; and Daniel J. Hopkins, "Politicized Places: Explaining Where and When Immigrants Provoke Local Opposition," *American Political Science Review* 104 (2010): 40–60.

37. In the sheriff sample, although the relationship between Latino population growth in the county and the *Enforcement Count* is also negative, it is not significantly different from zero.

38. On the bureaucratic incorporation of immigrants by police departments, see the study of California departments in Paul G. Lewis and S. Karthick Ramakrishnan, "Police Practices in Immigrant-Destination Cities: Political Control or Bureaucratic Professionalism?," *Urban Affairs Review* 42:6 (2007): 874–900.

39. Among others, see Citrin et al., "Public Opinion toward Immigration Reform"; Charles Chandler and Yung-Mei Tsai, "Social Factors Influencing Immigration Attitudes: An Analysis of Data from the General Social Survey," *Social Science Journal* 38:2 (2001): 177–88; Scheve and Slaughter, "Labor Market Competition"; Max Neiman, Martin Johnson, and Shaun Bowler, "Partisanship and Views about Immigration in Southern California: Just How Partisan is the Issue of Immigration?" *International Migration* 44:2 (2006): 35–56; and Johana Dunaway, Regina P. Branton, and Marisa A. Abrajano, "Agenda Setting, Public Opinion, and the Issue of Immigration Reform," *Social Science Quarterly* 91:2 (2010): 359–78.

40. For example, Ramakrishnan and Wong ("Partisanship, Not Spanish") find Republican partisanship predictive of local ordinances related to immigration. O'Neil describes a similar relationship (Kevin O'Neil, "Hazleton and Beyond: Why Communities Try to Restrict Immigration," *Migration Information Source* [2010], http://www.migrationinformation.org/Feature/print.cfm?ID=805). Chavez and Provine ("Race and the Response of State Legislatures") come to an analogous finding at the state level. By contrast, Hopkins ("Politicized Places") finds that county-level partisanship measures are not significant in explaining differences in anti-immigrant policy. And Nicholson-Crotty and Nicholson-Crotty

("Industry Strength and Immigrant Policy)" find no statistical relationship between state-level immigrant policy and measures of citizen ideology in the state, nor with the percentage of Republicans in the state legislature.

41. Indeed, we used the county-level voting measure in our own earlier study of large cities [Lewis et al., "Why Do (Some) Local Police Departments Enforce Federal Immigration Law?"]. The county-level measure of presidential voting and the preferred, city-level measure of ideology we use below are highly, but by no means perfectly, correlated (at $r = .68$ for our large cities and $r = .51$ for our small cities).

42. Chris Tausanovitch and Christopher Warshaw, "Measuring Constituent Policy Preferences in Congress, State Legislatures, and Cities," *Journal of Politics* 75:2 (2013): 333. Tausanovitch and Warshaw pooled about 275,000 respondents from recent Cooperative Congressional Election Study (CCES) surveys, and then administered an additional national survey in 2010 to 1,300 individuals, which contained numerous questions about policy issues that were worded identically to the earlier CCES surveys, as well as other detailed policy-preference measures. This "supersurvey" allowed for placement of all 275,000-plus respondents onto a common scale in "policy space." Tausanovitch and Warshaw then employed multilevel regression and poststratification, using information about each survey respondent's demographic characteristics and geographic context, in order to estimate city-level public opinion. Given how recent and challenging this data exercise was, the ideological estimates are not available longitudinally, and instead "should be interpreted as an average of the positions of the geographic areas in question between 2000 and 2011" (333). Fortunately, this places the ideology estimates in the same time period as our surveys of law-enforcement leaders.

43. The ideology measure is correlated with *Enforcement Count* at .25 for large cities and .32 for small cities, although our sample size is limited to 104 in the latter case due to missing values on the ideology measure for communities below the size threshold analyzed by Tausanovitch and Warshaw, "Measuring Constituent Policy Preferences." Among counties, the correlation between Republican presidential voting and the sheriff office *Enforcement Count* is .20. Each of these relationships are statistically significant at better than the 1 percent probability level.

If we substitute the county-level Republican voting measure for the municipal ideology measure among the small cities in order to retain the full sample size of 237, the correlation with *Enforcement Count* is a weaker .13 (still significant at the 5 percent level). We would argue, however, that the ideology variable is greatly preferred because it is measured at the correct geographic scale.

44. Google Earth was used to calculate the straight-line distance from the border to each city or county responding to our survey. Because of the very limited number of jurisdictions in our dataset that fall within the Border Patrol's one hundred–mile radius of the border, and the fact that borderland controversies have not been limited to that strip of land, we expanded the definition of border region to a two hundred–mile radius.

45. In addition to borderland location, we examined one other regional breakdown. Given the distinctive history of law enforcement in the US South and its longtime association with the racial hierarchy of that region, we assessed whether police and sheriff agencies in the South have distinctive approaches to immigration policing. Perhaps surprisingly, however, there were no significant bivariate correlations between location in the South and any of our three measures of policing practices, for any of the three samples of police agencies. It should be mentioned that, given the criteria for inclusion in our survey samples, an outsized percentage of the Southern respondents hail from two states, Texas and Florida. The latter state is arguably not very representative of the "deep South" and its racial attitudes. In any event, the lack of distinctiveness of our Southern respondents helps make the case that the roots of the immigration policing patchwork are derived more from local factors than from statewide or regional political cultures.

46. Given the differences in the nature of these three dependent variables, the analyses use ordinary least-squares, ordered logit, and probit regression, respectively. Please see the appendix for details.

47. Among counties, we estimate the *Enforcement Count* only for sheriff agencies that have full service responsibilities (i.e., both running a jail and engaging in street patrols). For the other two measures of policing practices, which are less focused on patrol, we broaden the sample to all sheriffs who responded to our survey. We considered including a control for the level of responsibility of each sheriff office (i.e., an indicator for "jail only" sheriff offices), but it never came close to being statistically significant in these models, so we have omitted it. Coefficients for the other variables remain approximately the same whether or not the indicator for jail-only sheriffs is included.

48. For a discussion of the factors that shape municipal governments' varied attempts to use public policy to secure local advantage, see Lewis and Neiman, *Custodians of Place*.

49. Structural equation modeling in our earlier study of the large cities [Lewis et al., "Why Do (Some) Local Police Departments Enforce Federal Immigration Law?"] suggests that the causal arrow between local government policy and police practices runs both ways.

50. For example, Hopkins ("Politicized Places") argues that periods of intense salience in the national political debate over immigration are key to understanding episodes of local political action on that topic.

Chapter Five

1. Jack R Greene, "Community Policing in America: Changing the Nature, Structure, and Function of the Police," *Policies, Processes, and Decisions of the Criminal Justice System* 3 (2000): 299–370; and M. D. Reisig, "Community and

Problem-Oriented Policing," *Crime and Justice: A Review of Research* 39 (2010): 2–53.

2. Michael S. Scott, in a review of the literature, describes community policing as "the watchword of policing strategy" by the 2000s: "Progress in American Policing? Reviewing the National Reviews," *Law & Social Inquiry* 34:1 (2009): 171–85, 176.

3. Greene, "Community Policing," and Jack R. Greene, "New Directions in Policing: Balancing Predictions and Meaning in Police Research," *Justice Quarterly* 31:2 (2013), http://dx.doi.org/10.1080/07418825.2013.840389; and Reisig, "Community and Problem-Oriented Policing."

4. See, e.g., Robert C. Davis, Edna Erez, and Nancy Avitabile, "Access to Justice for Immigrants Who Are Victimized: The Perspectives of Police and Prosecutors," *Criminal Justice Policy Review* 1:3 (2001): 183–96.

5. Debra A. Hoffmaster, Gerard Murphy, Shannon McFadden, and Molly Griswold, "Police and Immigration: How Chiefs are Leading Their Communities through the Challenges," Washington DC: *Police Executive Research Forum* (2010), http://www.policeforum.org/assets/docs/Free_Online_Documents/Immigration/police%20and%20immigration%20-%how%20chiefs%20are%20leading%20their%20communities%20through%20the%20challenges%202010.pdf. The problem of language barriers is particularly serious in cases of domestic abuse—see Leslye E. Orloff, Mary Ann Dutton, Giselle Aguilar Hass, and Nawal Ammar, "Battered Immigrant Women's Willingness to Call for Help and Police Response," *UCLA Women's Law Journal* 13 (2003): 43–100.

6. In the words of the International Association of Chiefs of Police (*Police Chiefs Guide to Immigration Issues* (2007): "One area identified as the strongest obstacle in building cohesive relationships with the immigrant community has been a lack of understanding because of different language barriers" (22), http://www.theiacp.org/Portals/0/pdfs/Publications/PoliceChiefsGuidetoImmigration.pdf.

7. Paul Lewis and S. Karthick Ramakrishnan, "Police Practices in Immigrant-Destination Cities: Political Control or Bureaucratic Professionalism?," *Urban Affairs Review* 42:6 (2007): 874–900.

8. The share of respondents saying that having bilingual officers or deputies was very or moderately effective as a policing technique was 91 percent among large-city chiefs, 70 percent among small-city chiefs, and 76 percent among sheriffs. The share of respondents saying that bilingualism counts in favor of applicants for law-enforcement jobs or for promotions within the agency was 68 percent in the large cities, 44 percent for small cities, and 46 percent for sheriffs.

9. Lorie Fridell and Mary Ann Wycoff, eds., *Community Policing: The Past, The Present, The Future* (Washington, DC: Police Executive Research Forum, 2004); and Greene, "New Directions."

10. Wesley Skogan, "Community Policing: Common Impediments to Success," in Fridell and Wycoff, *Community Policing*, 159–68.

11. Quoted in Peggy Fikac, "Officers Denounce Plans for Texas Immigration Enforcement" *Houston Chronicle*, February 18, 2011, http://www.chron.com/news /houston-texas/article/Officers-denounce-plans-for-Texas-immigration-1689120 .php.

12. Skogan, "Community Policing: Common Impediments to Success," 159–68; and see Gary W. Cordner, *Community Policing: Principles and Elements* (Washington, DC: Office of Community Oriented Policing Services, 1996).

13. See Bureau of Justice Assistance, *Resource Guide for Enhancing Community Relationships and Protecting Privacy and Constitutional Rights* (Washington, DC: US Department of Justice, November 2014), https://www.bja.gov/Publications /CommRelGuide.pdf.

14. Robert C. Davis and Edna Erez, *Immigrant Populations as Victims: Toward a Multicultural Criminal Justice System. Research in Brief* (Washington, DC: US Department of Justice, May 1998), https://www.ncjrs.gov/pdffiles/167571.pdf; and Glen A. Kercher and Connie Kuo, "Victimization of Immigrants," Crime Victims' Institute, Criminal Justice Center, Sam Houston State University (2008), http:// www.crimevictimsinstitute.org/documents/ImmigrantVictimizationfinalcorrected .pdf.

15. Richard S. Biehl, "Communities Are Safer When Law Enforcement Roles Are Clear," *The Hill*, July 15, 2015, http://thehill.com/blogs/congress-blog/home land-security/247880-communites-are-safe-when-law-enforcement-roles-are.

16. Cecilia Menjívar, "Liminal Legality: Salvadoran and Guatemalan Immigrants' Lives in the United States," *American Journal of Sociology* 111:4 (2006): 999–1037; and see Agnieszka Kubal, "Conceptualizing Semi-Legality in Migration Research," *Law & Society Review* 47:3 (2013): 555–87.

17. Kercher and Kuo, "Victimization of Immigrants," 4.

18. Nik Theodore, *Insecure Communities: Latino Perceptions of Police Involvement in Immigration Enforcement* (Chicago: University of Illinois, 2013), http:// www.policylink.org/sites/default/files/INSECURE_COMMUNITIES_REPORT _FINAL.PDF. Perceptions that the police act unfairly tend to reduce willingness to cooperate with police and help them control crime, according to survey evidence. See David S. Kirk, Andrew Papachristos, Jeffrey Fagan, and Tom R. Tyler, "The Paradox of Law Enforcement in Immigrant Communities: Does Tough Immigration Enforcement Undermine Public Safety?," *Annals of the American Academy of Political and Social Science* 641 (May 2012): 79–96.

19. Angela S. Garcia and David G. Keyes, *Life as an Undocumented Immigrant: How Restrictive Local Immigration Policies Affect Daily Life* (Washington, DC: Center for American Progress, 2012). See also Guadalupe Vidales, Kristen M. Day, and Michael Power, "Police and Immigration Enforcement: Impacts on Latino(a) Residents' Perceptions of Police," *Policing: An International Journal of Police Strategies & Management* 32:4 (2009): 631–53.

20. Alison Siskin, Andorra Bruno, Blas Nunez-Neto, Lisa M. Seghetti, Ruth Ellen Wasem, Immigration Enforcement within the United States," Congressional

Research Service Report for Congress, April 6, 2006, http://trac.syr.edu/immigration/library/P459.pdf.

21. Testimony of Muzaffar A. Chishti, director, Migration Policy Institute, before Committee on Homeland Security (US House of Representatives, Washington, DC, March 4, 2009), 4.

22. Quoted in Megan Cassidy, "Arpaio Contempt Hearing This Week: Intent is Key," *Arizona Republic*, April 21, 2015, 1, http://www.azcentral.com/story/news/local/phoenix/2015/04/19/arpaio-contempt-hearing-intent-key/26050811/.

23. Hiroshi Motomura, "The Discretion That Matters: Federal and the Civil-Criminal Line, *UCLA Law Review* (2011): 1819–58. Anna Pratt develops this theme in *Securing Borders: Detention and Deportation in Canada,* (Vancouver: University of British Columbia Press, 2005); she argues for considering discretion in enforcement of the law to be an aspect of sovereign power, a perspective that informs this discussion (215).

24. Aarti Kohli, Peter Markowitz, and Lisa Chavez, "Secure Communities by the Numbers" (Berkeley: Chief Justice Earl Warren Institute on Law and Social Policy, 2011).

25. American Immigration Lawyers Association, "AILA Urges Timeout on the Secure Communities Program," press release, May 3, 2011, http://www.aila.org/advo-media/press-releases/2011/aila-urges-timeout-on-secure-communities-program.

26. TRAC (Transactional Records Access Clearinghouse), "Immigration Prosecutions Reached All-Time High in FY 2013," http://trac.syr.edu/whatsnew/email.131125.html.

27. TRAC, "Secure Communities and ICE Deportation: A Failed Program?," April 8, 2014, http://trac.syr.edu/immigration/reports/349/.

28. Ironically, despite its high level of noncriminal deportations, Maryland's legislators have embraced several pro-immigrant policies, including allowing drivers' licenses and in-state tuition to unauthorized immigrants. This "schizophrenic" approach to immigration further muddies the water for the police officers who must enforce the law on a daily basis. See John Fritze, "Immigration Program Aimed at Criminals Deports Many with No Record," *Baltimoresun.com*, February 8, 2014, http://articles.baltimoresun.com/2014–02–08/news/bs-md-secure-communities-20140208_1_secure-communities-immigration-program-maryland.

29. See, e.g., Andrew Kennis, "Latinos Continue to be (Illegally) Told 'Show Me Your Papers,'" *Alternet*, September 27, 2011, http://www.alternet.org/story/152400/latinos_continue_to_be_%28illegally%29_told,_%27show_me_your_papers!%27.

30. Alan Gomez, "Feds Delay Review of Obama Immigration Program, *USA Today*, November 5, 2012, http://www.usatoday.com/story/news/nation/2012/11/05/feds-delay-review-of-obama-immigration-program/1684885/.

31. Department of Justice, "Justice Department Releases Investigative Findings on the Alamance County, N.C., Sheriff's Office," September 8, 2012, http://www.justice.gov/opa/pr/2012/September/12-crt-1125.html.

32. Immigration Policy Center, "More Problems with ICE's Secure Communities Program," October 1, 2010, http://arnolaw.blogspot.com/2010/10/more-problems -with-ices-secure.html.

33. Wesley Skogan, *Police and Community in Chicago: A Tale of Three Cities* (New York: Oxford University Press, 2006).

34. Amada Armenta, "From Sheriff's Deputies to Immigration Officers: Screening Immigrant Status in a Tennessee Jail," *Law & Policy* 34:2 (2012): 191–210.

35. Mathew Coleman, "The 'Local' Migration State: The Site-Specific Devolution of Immigration Enforcement in the US South," *Law & Policy* 34:2 (2012): 159–90.

36. Ibid.

37. Thomas S. Winkowski, memorandum, Department of Homeland Security, November 20, 2014, http://www.dhs.gov/sites/default/files/publications/14_1120 _memo_secure_communities.pdf.

38. Office of Enforcement and Removal Operations, US Immigration and Customs Enforcement, "Priority Enforcement Program," https://www.ice.gov/pep.

39. Juliet Stumpf, "D(E)volving Discretion: Lessons from the Life and Times of Secure Communities," *American University Law Review* 64 (2015): 1259–84.

40. Training about how to interact with unauthorized immigrants was offered by 45 percent of large-city departments, 32 percent of small-city departments, and 35 percent of sheriff offices. Analysis of our survey data helps identify some of the predictors of which departments and sheriff offices tend to offer such training. The agencies that provide training also tend to be the ones that have written, internal policies on how to handle interactions with immigrants. City governments that have a policy regarding unauthorized immigrants, particularly an enforcement-oriented policy, are also more likely to have police departments that provide officer training. (This latter pattern is not the case for sheriff offices. As noted in chap. 4, sheriffs have much greater political independence from their county governing boards than do city police chiefs.) Additionally, we found that the law-enforcement agency's commitment to community policing is a strong predictor of the presence of officer training for encounters with immigrants. This is true for all three samples of police agencies.

41. Charles R. Epp, *Making Rights Real: Activists, Bureaucrats, and the Creation of the Legalistic State* (Chicago: University of Chicago Press, 2009), 51.

42. See, e.g., the racial-profiling charges against the police in Durham, North Carolina, http://www.wncn.com/story/24823428/durham-police-on-defense-against -racial-profiling-charges. Similar charges have been levied in Miami Gardens, Florida (http://www.usatoday.com/story/news/nation/2013/11/22/miami-gardens-police -racial-profiling/3672119/) and Boston (http://www.bostonglobe.com/metro/2014/10 /08/aclu-charges-boston-police-engaged-racially-biased-tactics-police-call-report -inaccurate/Zev3p7jvRVQ210KSWncu2H/story.html). More generally, see Charles R. Epp, Steven Maynard-Moody, and Donald P. Haider-Markel, *Pulled Over: How Police Stops Define Race and Citizenship* (Chicago: University of Chicago Press, 2014).

43. Presentation by Amada Armenta, "Policing Immigrants: The Local Dilemmas of Immigration Enforcement," Annual Meeting of the Law and Society Association, May 31, 2009, Denver.

44. See, e.g., Steven Maynard-Moody and Michael Musheno, *Cops, Teachers, Counselors: Stories from the Front Lines of Public Service* (Ann Arbor: University of Michigan Press, 2003).

45. Michael Lipsky, *Street Level Bureaucracy: Dilemmas of the Individual in Public Services* (New York: Russell Sage Foundation, 2010), 13.

46. Ibid., xiii.

47. James Q. Wilson, *Varieties of Police Behavior: The Management of Law and Order in Eight Communities* (New York: Atheneum, 1976), 49; and see Alexandra Natapoff, "Underenforcement," *Fordham Law Review* 75 (2006): 1715–76.

48. Kenneth Culp Davis, *Police Discretion* (Minneapolis: West Publishing Company, 1975).

49. See, e.g., Egon Bittner, *The Functions of Police in Modern Society* (Cambridge: Oegeschlager, Gunn and Hain, 1980).

50. Michael K. Brown, *Working the Street: Police Discretion and the Dilemmas of Reform* (New York: Russell Sage Foundation, 1988), 62, 66–67.

51. Cf. Motomura, "Discretion that Matters."

52. Steven K. Herbert, "Police Subculture Reconsidered," *Criminology* 36:2 (1998): 343–69, 349; William K. Muir Jr., *Police: Streetcorner Politicians* (Chicago: University of Chicago Press, 1977); and Jerome H. Skolnick, *Justice Without Trial: Law Enforcement in Democratic Society* (New York: John Wiley and Sons, 1966).

53. Maynard-Moody and Musheno, *Cops, Teachers Counselors.*

54. Herbert, "Police Subculture Reconsidered," 349.

55. Armenta, "From Sheriff's Deputies to Immigration Officers."

56. Daniel Gonzalez, "Why Some Immigrants Are Let Go," *Arizona Republic,* June 14, 2009, http://www.azcentral.com/news/articles/2009/06/14/20090614phoeniximmig-ridealong0614.html

57. Arizona v. United States, 567 U.S. ___ (2012).

58. Maureen A. Sweeney, "Shadow Immigration Enforcement and its Constitutional Dangers," *Journal of Criminal Law and Criminology* 104:2 (2014): 227–82.

59. Ortega Melendres, et al. v. Arpaio, et al., Findings of Fact and Conclusions of Law, http://www.gpo.gov/fdsys/pkg/USCOURTS-azd-2_07-cv-02513/pdf/USCOURTS-azd-2_07-cv-02513–18.pdf; see also Puente Arizona v. Arpaio, M Complaint for Declaratory and Injunctive Relief, http://www.law.uci.edu/academics/real-life-learning/clinics/Puente-v-Arpaio-Complaint-061814.pdf.

60. Mary Romero, "Racial Profiling and Immigration Law Enforcement: Rounding Up of Usual Suspects in the Latino Community," *Critical Sociology* 32:2–3 (2006): 447–74.

61. Michael J. Wishnie, "State and Local Police Enforcement of Immigration Law," *University of Pennsylvania Journal of Constitutional Law* 6 (2004): 1084–115.

62. Susan M. Akram and Kevin R. Johnson, "Race, Civil Rights, and Immigration Law after September, 11, 2001: The Targeting of Arabs and Muslims," *NYU Annual Survey of American Law* 58 (2002): 295–699.

63. Wishnie, "State and Local."

64. See US Department of Justice, "Guidance for Federal Law Enforcement Agencies Regarding the Use of Race, Ethnicity, Gender, National Origin, Religion, Sexual Orientation, or Gender Identity," December 2014, http://www.justice.gov/sites/default/files/ag/pages/attachments/2014/12/08/use-of-race-policy.pdf.

65. Department of Justice Office of Public Affairs, "Attorney General Holder Announces Federal Law Enforcement Agencies to Adopt Stricter Policies to Curb Profiling," press release, December 8, 2014, http://www.justice.gov/opa/pr/attorney-general-holder-announces-federal-law-enforcement-agencies-adopt-stricter-policies-0.

66. American Civil Liberties Union, "U.S. Border Patrol's Interior Enforcement Operations," n.d., https://www.aclusandiego.org/wp-content/uploads/2014/11/100-Mile-Zone.pdf.

67. Mark Hugo Lopez, Ana Gonzalez-Barrera, and Seth Motel, "Recent Trends in U.S. Immigration Enforcement," Pew Hispanic Trust, December 28, 2011, http://www.pewhispanic.org/2011/12/28/ii-recent-trends-in-u-s-immigration-enforcement/.

68. Ronald John Weitzer and Steven A. Tuch, "Racially Biased Policing: Determinants of Citizen Perceptions," *Social Forces* 83 (2005): 1009–30.

69. Guadalupe Vidales, Kristin M. Day, and Michael Powe, "Police and Immigration Enforcement: Impacts on Latino(a) Residents' Perceptions of Police," *Policing: An International Journal of Police Strategies and Management* 32:4 (2009): 631–54.

70. Cecilia Menjívar and Cynthia Bejarano, "Latino Immigrants' Perceptions of Crime and Police Authorities in the United States: A Case Study from the Phoenix Metropolitan Area," *Ethnic and Racial Studies* 27:1 (2004): 120–48.

71. From its inception through December 31, 2014, DACA filed 727,164 requests for deferred action, of which 638,897 were approved. Among the 970,735 employment authorization applications, 825,640 were approved. Texas v. United States, no. 15-40238 in the Court of Appeals for the Fifth Circuit, "Attachments to Appellants' Emergency Motion for Stay Pending Appeal, p. 10, http://www.justice.gov/sites/default/files/opa/press-releases/attachments/2015/03/12/stay_attachments_filed_0.pdf.

72. Criteria for a Waiver of Grounds of Inadmissibility, informally known as a 601 waiver, can be found at http://www.uscis.gov/sites/default/files/files/form/i-601.pdf.

73. See Richard M. Stana, *Better Controls Needed over Program Authorizing State and Local Enforcement of Federal Immigration Laws* (Washington, DC: US Government Accountability Office, March 4, 2009), http://www.gao.gov/products/GAO-09-109.

74. Ibid.

75. Alexsa Alonzo, Kristin Macleod-Ball, Greg Chen, and Su Kim, "Immigration Enforcement Off Target: Minor Offenses with Major Consequences," American Immigration Lawyers Association, Doc. No. 11081609, August 2011, http://www.aila.org/File/Related/11081609.pdf.

76. Adam B. Cox and Thomas J. Miles, "Policing Immigration," *University of Chicago Law Review* 80 (2014): 87–136.

77. E. Treyger, A. Chalfin, and C. Loeffler, "Estimating the Effects of Immigration Enforcement on Local Policing and Crime: Evidence from the Secure Communities," *George Mason University Law and Economics Research Paper Series* (2014).

78. Among large-city chiefs, 20 percent said that useful information flowed primarily from their department to ICE, while only 2 percent said that useful information flowed mainly from ICE to their department; 43 percent said that such information flowed about equally in both directions, with the rest saying either that they had little or no interaction with ICE or that they didn't know. The analogous figures (useful information flowing up vs. flowing down) were 19 percent vs. 3 percent for small-city chiefs, and 24 percent vs. 2 percent for sheriffs.

79. Romero, "Racial Profiling."

80. Anna Gorman, "Cities and Counties Rely on U.S. Immigrant Detention Fees," *Los Angeles Times*, March 17, 2009, http://articles.latimes.com/2009/mar/17/local/me-immigjai117.

81. Such rules, defended in the name of public safety, do not necessarily prevent cooperative relations with ICE. See Lynn Tramonte, *Debunking the Myth of "Sanctuary Cities: Community Policing Policies Protect American Communities"* (Washington, DC: Immigration Policy Center, March 2009), http://www.immigrationpolicy.org/special-reports/debunking-myth-sanctuary-cities.

82. Elise Foley, "Why Some Cities Don't Rush to Turn Over Undocumented Immigrants to the Feds," *Huffington Post*, July 11, 2015, http://www.huffingtonpost.com/2015/07/09/sanctuary-cities-law-enforcement_n_7765058.html.

83. Charles R. Epp, *Making Rights Real.*

84. *Interim Report of the President's Task Force on 21st Century Policing* (Washington DC: Office of Community Oriented Policing Services, March 2015), http://www.cops.usdoj.gov/pdf/taskforce/Interim_TF_Report.pdf.

85. Valerie Jenness and Ryken Grattet, "The Law-in-Between: The Effects of Organizational Perviousness on the Policing of Hate Crime," *Social Problems* 52:3 (2005): 337–59.

86. Ibid., 355.

87. Coleman, "The 'Local' Migration State," 159; see also Armenta, "From Sheriff's Deputies."

88. Ingrid V. Eagly, "Criminal Justice for Noncitizens: An Analysis of Variation in Local Enforcement," *New York University Law Review* 88 (2013): 1126–223.

89. Antje Ellerman, *States Against Migrants: Deportation in Germany and the United States* (New York: Cambridge University Press, 2009); Joanne van der

Leun, "Excluding Illegal Migrants in the Netherlands: Between National Policies and Local Implementation," *West European Politics* 29:2 (2006): 310–26; and Arjen Leerkes, Monica Varsanyi, and Godfried Engbersen. "Local Limits to Migration Control: Practices of Selective Migration Policing in a Restrictive National Context," *Police Quarterly* 15:4 (2012): 446–75.

90. See, e.g., Kris Kobach, "The Quintessential Force Multiplier: The Inherent Authority of Local Police To Make Immigration Arrests," *Albany Law Review* 69 (2005–6): 179–235.

91. See, e.g., Major Cities Chiefs, "M.C.C. Immigration Committee Recommendations: For Enforcement of Immigration Laws by Local Police Agencies," adopted by Major Cities Chiefs, June 2006.

92. Julia Preston, "Republicans Resist Obama's Move to Dismantle Apparatus of Deportation," *New York Times*, January 15, 2015, http://www.nytimes.com/2015/01/16/us/secure-communities-immigration-program-battle.html?_r=0.

93. Bob Ortega, "27 Police Chiefs, Sheriffs Support Obama Immigration Action," *Arizona Republic*, January 13, 2015, http://www.azcentral.com/story/news/politics/immigration/2015/01/13/police-chiefs-sheriffs-amicus-brief-executive-action/21693485/.

94. Lomi Kriel, "Qualified Immigrants Still Face Threat of Deportation," *Houston Chronicle*, March 8, 2015, http://www.houstonchronicle.com/news/houston-texas/houston/article/Qualified-immigrants-still-face-threat-of-6122712.php. See also Matthew Kolken, "ICE Not Honoring Prosecutorial Discretion," *ImmigrationProf Blog*, February 26, 2015, http://lawprofessors.typepad.com/immigration/2015/02/matthew-kolken-reports-ice-not-honoring-prosecutorial-discretion.html

95. Pratt, *Securing Borders*, 215.

96. Jennifer Chacón, "Managing Migration Through Crime," *Columbia Law Review Sidebar* 109 (2009): 135–48; and Julie A. Dowling and Jonathan Xavier Indi, eds., *Governing Immigration through Crime: A Reader* (Stanford: Stanford University Press, 2013).

97. Kevin Johnson, "How Racial Profiling in America Became the Law of the Land: *United States v. Brignoni-Ponce* and *Whren v. United States* and the Need for Truly Rebellious Lawyering," *Georgetown Law Journal* 98 (2010): 1005–77.

98. Angela Stuesse and Mathew Coleman, "Automobility, Immobility, Alter-mobility: Surviving and Resisting the Intensification of Immigrant Policing," *City and Society* 26:1 (2014): 51–72, 51.

Chapter Six

1. Ronald Weitzer, "The Puzzling Neglect of Hispanic Americans in Research on Police-Citizen Relations," *Ethnic and Racial Studies* 36 (2013): 1–19.

2. Ibid., 14.

3. Gary Cordner, *Community Policing: Principles and Elements* (Washington,

DC: Office of Community Oriented Policing Services, 1996); and Michael D. Reisig, "Community and Problem-Oriented Policing," *Crime and Justice: A Review of Research* 39 (2010): 2–53.

4. Jacob Bucher, Michelle Manasse, and Beth Tarasawa, "Undocumented Victims: An Examination of Crimes against Undocumented Male Migrant Workers," *Southwest Journal of Criminal Justice* 7:2 (2010): 159–79; and David L. Carter, "Hispanic Perception of Police Performance: An Empirical Assessment," *Journal of Criminal Justice* 13:66 (1985): 487–500.

5. Robert C. Davis, Edna Erez, and Nancy Avitabile, "Access to Justice for Immigrants Who Are Victimized: The Perspectives of Police and Prosecutors," *Criminal Justice Policy Review* 12:3 (2001): 183–96; and Edna Erez, "Migration/Immigration, Domestic Violence and the Justice System," *International Journal of Comparative and Applied Criminal Justice* 26:2 (2002): 277–99.

6. Jacqueline Hagan, Brianna Castro, and Nestor Rodriguez, "The Effects of US Deportation Policies on Immigrant Families and Communities: Cross-Border Perspectives," *North Carolina Law Review* 88 (2009): 1799–824.

7. Ibid., 1815.

8. Ibid., 1810.

9. Kalina Brabeck and Qingwen Xu, "The Impact of Detention and Deportation on Latino Immigrant Children and Families: A Quantitative Exploration," *Hispanic Journal of Behavioral Sciences* 32:3 (2010): 341–61.

10. Jessica Vaughan, *Deportation Numbers Unwrapped: Raw Statistics Reveal the Real Story of ICE in Decline* (Washington, DC: Center for Immigration Studies, 2013), 1–16.

11. Hagan, Castro, and Rodriguez, "Effects of US Deportation Policies," 1815; and Jacqueline Hagan, Karl Eschbach, and Nestor Rodriguez, "US Deportation Policy, Family Separation, and Circular Migration," *International Migration Review* 42:1 (2008): 64–88; see also Nancy Hiemstra, "Geopolitical Reverberations of U.S. Migrant Detention and Deportation: The View from Ecuador," *Geopolitics* 17:2 (2012): 293–311.

12. Wayne A. Cornelius and Idean Salehyan, "Does Border Enforcement Deter Unauthorized Immigration? The Case of Mexican Migration to the United States of America," *Regulation and Governance* 1 (2007): 139–153.

13. El Paso played a central role in the massive expansion and shifting strategies of the federal Border Patrol that started in the mid-1990s. See Timothy Dunn, *Blockading the Border and Human Rights: The El Paso Operation that Remade Immigration Enforcement* (Austin: University of Texas Press, 2009).

14. Sheriff Richard Wiles, interview by authors, February 8, 2011.

15. Ibid.

16. Louie Gilot, interview by authors, February 8, 2011.

17. Tom A. Peter, "In El Paso, Residents Aren't Waiting for Congress to Fix Immigration," *Al Jazeera America*, February 20, 2014.

18. As cited in Ted Mellin, "Tropiano Plans To Ask Reversal on Sanctuary. City Should Encourage Respect, Obedience of Law, She Says," *Morning Call*, December 16, 1986.

19. As cited in Gerald Shields, "3 Allentown Residents Argue for Keeping Sanctuary Status," *Morning Call*, May 9, 1991.

20. Editorial board, "Boycott Tropiano Hearing," *Morning Call*, July 7, 1991.

21. Ibid.

22. Monica W. Varsanyi, ed., *Taking Local Control: Immigration Policy Activism in U.S. Cities and States* (Stanford: Stanford University Press, 2010).

23. Monica W. Varsanyi, "Neoliberalism and Nativism: Local Anti-Immigrant Policy Activism and an Emerging Politics of Scale," *International Journal of Urban and Regional Research* 35:2 (2011): 295–311.

24. Lou Hershman, interview by authors, July 22, 2009.

25. Joe Hanna, interview by authors, July 23, 2009. Hanna later became Allentown's chief of police.

26. Roger Maclean, interview by authors, August 27, 2009.

27. A community leader, interview by authors, July 22, 2009.

28. www.allentownpa.gov.

29. Els de Graauw, personal communication, 2013.

30. As quoted in Randy Kraft, "Allentown City Council Takes a Stand for U.S. Immigration Reform," *WFMZ-TV News*, March 20, 2014, http://www.wfmz.com/news/news-regional-lehighvalley/allentown-city-council-takes-a-stand-for-us-immigration-reform/25069284.

31. Alan Jennings, interview by authors, July 8, 2009

32. Chief Robin James, interview by authors, November 1, 2010.

33. Sheriff Dean Bush, interview by authors, November 2, 2010.

34. Sister Angela, interview by authors, November 2, 2010.

35. Monica Mersinger, "Salem Online History–Brief History," *Salem Online History* (Salem Public Library, 2005), http://www.salemhistory.net/brief_history/brief_history.htm.

36. Local resident quoted in Virginia Green and Katherine Wallig, "African Americans in Salem," *Salem Online History* (Salem Public Library, 2005–6), http://www.salemhistory.net/people/african_americans.htm.

37. Tim King, "Oregon Racism: A Deeply Rooted Problem," *Salem-News.com*, January 20, 2014.

38. ORS181.850, *Enforcement of Federal Immigration Laws*, http://www.oregonlaws.org/ors/181.850.

39. City Council Policy No. A-9, *Role of City of Salem Relating to the Immigration and Naturalization Services (INS)*, December 15, 1997, http://www.cityofsalem.net/Departments/Legal?Council%20Policy%20Manual/Role%20of%20City%20of%20Salem%20Relating%20to%20Immigration%20and%20Naturalization%20Service%20(INS).pdf; and Marion County Policy 208, *Role of Marion County*

in Relation to Immigration Customs Enforcement (ICE), June 1997, http://apps.co
.marion.or.us/APAP/policy.aspx?p=policy&pid=208.

40. Gosia Wozniacka and Steven Dubois, "Oregonians To Vote on Immigrant Driver's Licenses," *HeraldNet*, October 18, 2013, http://www.heraldnet.com/article /20131018/NEWS03/710189814.

41. National Conference of State Legislatures, "States Offering Driver's Licenses to Immigrants," November 5, 2014, http://www.ncsl.org/research/immigration /states-offering-driver-s-licenses-to-immigrants.aspx.

Chapter Seven

1. Reynolds Farley, *The Kerner Commission Report Plus Four Decades: What Has Changed? What Has Not?*, National Poverty Center Working Paper Series No. 08–15 (Ann Arbor: National Poverty Center, 2008), 27.

2. Ibid., 28.

3. Editorial board, "A Brighter Line on Immigration Policing," *New York Times*, August 17, 2013, http://www.nytimes.com/2013/08/18/opinion/sunday/a-brighter-line -on-immigration-policing.html.

4. Final Report of the President's Taskforce on 21st Century Policing, Recommendation 1.9 and Action item 1.9.1, May 2015, http://www.cops.usdoj.gov/pdf /taskforce/TaskForce_FinalReport.pdf.

5. Ibid.

6. On bureaucratic incorporation, see Helen B. Marrow, "Immigrant Bureaucratic Incorporation: The Dual Roles of Professional Missions and Government Policies," *American Sociological Review* 74 (2009): 756–76. On the welcome accorded immigrants, see Linda M. Williams, "Beyond Enforcement: Welcomeness, Local Law Enforcement, and Immigrants," *Public Administration Review* 75:3 (2015): 433–42.

7. Ming Hsu Chen, "Where You Stand Depends on Where You Sit: Bureaucratic Incorporation of Immigrants in Federal Workplace Agencies," *Berkeley Journal of Employment and Labor Law* 33:2 (2012): 227–98.

8. Department of Homeland Security Secretary Jeh Johnson admitted as much in his memo dated November 20, 2014, announcing the termination of the Secure Communities program. See also Melanie A. Taylor, Scott H. Decker, Doris M. Provine, Paul G. Lewis, and Monica W. Varsanyi, "Illegal Immigration and Local Policing," in Michael D. Reisig and Robert J. Kane, eds., *The Oxford Handbook of Police and Policing* (New York: Oxford University Press, 2014), 409–29.

9. Jack R. Greene, "New Directions in Policing: Balancing Predictions and Meaning in Police Research," *Justice Quarterly* 31:2 (2014): 193–228.

10. S. Karthick Ramakrishnan and Paul G. Lewis, *Immigrants and Local Governance: The View from City Hall* (San Francisco: Public Policy Institute of California, 2005).

11. Angela Stuesse and Mathew Coleman, "Automobility, Immobility, Alter-mobility: Surviving and Resisting the Intensification of Immigrant Policing," *City and Society* 26:1 (2014): 51–72.

12. Rene R. Rocha, Daniel P. Hawes, Alisa Hacklin Fryar, and Robert D. Wrinkle, "Policy Climates: Enforcement Rates, and Migrant Behavior: Is Self-Deportation a Viable Immigration Policy?" *Policy Studies Journal* 42:1 (2014): 79–100.

13. For an argument asserting the possibility of forward-looking action at the state level, a new states' rights approach, see Peter L. Marcowitz, "Undocumented No More: The Power of State Citizenship," *Stanford Law Review* 67 (2015): 869–916.

Appendix

1. The other two possible responses are as follows: (1) "Our local government supports a policy . . . of 'don't ask, don't tell' regarding unauthorized immigrants living in or traveling through our jurisdiction unless they are involved in serious crime" (score of 2); or (2) "Our local government has developed, or is developing, policies designed to encourage local law enforcement to participate with federal authorities in controlling certain kinds of crime associated with unauthorized immigration" (score of 4).

Index

The letter *f* following a number denote a figure; the letter *t* denotes a table.

The Chicago Series in Law and Society

EDITED BY JOHN M. CONLEY AND LYNN MATHER

Series titles, continued from frontmatter: